Authority and Dissent
in Jewish Life

Studies in Jewish Civilization
Volume 31

Proceedings of the Thirty-First Annual Symposium of
the Klutznick Chair in Jewish Civilization, the Harris
Center for Judaic Studies, and the Schwalb Center for
Israel and Jewish Studies, October 28–29, 2018

Other volumes in the
Studies in Jewish Civilization Series
Published by Purdue University Press

2010 – Rites of Passage:
How Today's Jews Celebrate, Commemorate, and Commiserate

2011 – Jews and Humor

2012 – Jews in the Gym:
Judaism, Sports, and Athletics

2013 – Fashioning Jews:
Clothing, Culture, and Commerce

2014 – Who Is a Jew?
Reflections on History, Religion, and Culture

2015 – Wealth and Poverty in Jewish Tradition

2016 – Mishpachah:
The Jewish Family in Tradition and in Transition

2017 – *olam ha-zeh v'olam ha-ba*:
This World and the World to Come in Jewish Belief and Practice

2018 – Is Judaism Democratic?
Reflections from Theory and Practice Throughout the Ages

2019 – Next Year in Jerusalem:
Exile and Return in Jewish History

Authority and Dissent in Jewish Life

Studies in Jewish Civilization
Volume 31

Editor:

Leonard J. Greenspoon

The Klutznick Chair in Jewish Civilization

Purdue University Press
West Lafayette, Indiana

Cataloging-in-Publication Data is on file with the Library of Congress.
Print: 978-1-61249-627-6
Epub: 978-1-61249-628-3
Epdf: 978-1-61249-629-0

CONTENTS

ACKNOWLEDGMENTS

T HE 31ST ANNUAL Symposium on Jewish Civilization took place on Sunday, October 28, and Monday, October 29, 2018, in Omaha, Nebraska. The title of the symposium, from which this volume also takes its name, was "Authority and Dissent in Jewish Life." All of the papers collected here are based on presentations at the symposium itself.

The academic sponsors of this symposium represent three major institutions of higher learning in Nebraska: Creighton University (the Klutznick Chair in Jewish Civilization, the Kripke Center for the Study of Religion and Society), the University of Nebraska–Lincoln (the Harris Center for Judaic Studies), and the University of Nebraska Omaha (the Schwalb Center for Israel and Jewish Studies).

In large measure, the symposium owes its success to two groups of dedicated and talented individuals. First are my academic colleagues: Dr. Ronald Simkins (Creighton University), Dr. Jean Cahan (University of Nebraska–Lincoln), and Dr. Curtis Hutt (University of Nebraska Omaha). To use language drawn from this volume's title: we exercise our collective authority collaboratively and creatively; dissent ensures that we consistently maintain individual and institutional integrity.

The second group consists of people who really know how to get things done. From Creighton, there is Colleen Hastings; from UNO, Kasey De Goey; and from the Omaha Jewish Federation, Jennie Gates Beckman. Their unexcelled excellence adds luster to every symposium-related activity.

The publication schedule we devised with Purdue University Press results in a period of two years between each symposium and its volume. My friends outside the world of education are always asking, What takes so long? My academic colleagues know well that our publications are exemplary in both the speed with which they appear and the quality of their contents. This is possible only because of the high level of dedication and professionalism displayed by the staff at Purdue University Press, with whom we have had an excellent relationship for more than a decade.

In addition to the organizations mentioned above, this symposium is also generously supported by

The Ike and Roz Friedman Foundation
The Riekes Family
The Henry Monsky Lodge of B'nai B'rith
Drs. Bernard H. and Bruce S. Bloom Memorial Endowment
Karen and Gary Javitch
Donald Gerber
Creighton University Lectures, Films, and Concerts
Creighton University College of Arts and Sciences
And others

Leonard J. Greenspoon
Omaha, Nebraska
March 2020
ljgrn@creighton.edu

EDITOR'S INTRODUCTION

R ELIGIOUS LEADERS. POLITICAL leaders. Military leaders. They have been among the most prominent members of the establishment, Jewish and non-Jewish, for millennia. From their positions (elected, appointed, or stolen) they have exercised authority, which has on occasion been met with dissent.

As I reflected one last time on the essays in this volume and the symposium where presenters made their presentations, I was once again struck by how universal and yet distinctively Jewish so many phenomena are at one and the same time. As has been the case before, so here too it seems like a swatch of autobiography most efficiently makes the point.

Many years ago, sometime in the 1980s, I was president of the Conservative synagogue in Greenville, South Carolina. Because the membership numbers were relatively modest, I was able to pass through the various stages of the cursus honorum, from member at large to president, while I was still a pretty young guy. But because of the time—1950s and '60s—and the place—Richmond, Virginia—of my upbringing, I was especially attuned to the nuances of deference I was expected to pay to those older than myself.

Giving senior members of the congregation essentially carte blanche to discourse on any topic for almost any amount of time led not surprisingly to very long meetings. (Come to think of it, why did they ever reelect me?!) Very quickly I observed that the older males (rarely females) on the board could talk with seemingly great authority on just about any theme, secular or religious, I could imagine. And, of course, some topics I would never have thought of. Their authority as promoters of a given set of beliefs was invariably matched by others who held out in dissent.

How, I wondered, could everyone know just about everything, pro and con, on any and every topic? Of course, I was young and naïve then. But the question still intrigues me. Is there a special type of authority and expression of dissent that Jews characteristically voice? The answer I got then, which fit its context pretty well, went something like this: "Each of us board members started and grew a small business. We could figure it out in the office or store. And we could figure it out in shul or synagogue. No one could tell us anything we didn't already know. Although we were blessed, if you will, with a unique knack for lighting the way of our otherwise unenlightened colleagues."

It seemed about right to me then—each individual developed a unique quality of authority based largely on his own unique experience. And when, as inevitably occurred, there was a clash of authority derived from a righteous sense of dissent, how was resolution achieved? As I remember it, the clamor of thunderous rhetoric on often the most seemingly picayune point was resolved only by the infinitive patience of our ever-nimble young hero—I mean me.

If, as I do, you sometimes appreciate the ad hoc (if not ad hominem) nature of such vignettes, we can agree that this mid-1980s account from Upstate South Carolina is an at least adequate reflection of a given set of circumstances as experienced and recalled by one individual.

I make no excuses for that. But I also offer sincerest personal and professional gratitude to the more than a dozen of my colleagues who bring the range of their scholarship as well as their storytelling to instances of authority and dissent in over two millennia of Jewish life. That is what this book is all about.

The first four essays look back to historical accounts from rabbinic through the Byzantine period. First is "Figurative Language of Authority and Rebellion in the Story of the Death of Rabbi Judah ben Bava" by Chen Marx, The Max Stern Yezreel Valley College. In his essay Marx examines the martyrological tale of Rabbi Judah ben Bava, who was brutally murdered by the Romans after the Bar Kokhba Revolt (136 CE) as punishment for ordaining five of his disciples as rabbis, an action that preserved the Jewish faith. The tales of ben Bava deal with how his memory should be preserved. Marx enumerates the ways rabbinic figurative language represents ideological struggles and how the Jewish religion has faced and interpreted rebellion, failure, and victory.

Azzan Yadin-Israel, Rutgers University, offers the second study, on "Midrash, Oral Law, and the Question of Rabbinic Authority." As Yadin-Israel explicates, the early rabbis are characterized in two ways: they are masters of midrash and they are adherents of the Oral Law, a tradition handed down from master to disciple that stretches back to Moses himself. What is generally overlooked is the potential incommensurability of these claims: each implies a different model of religious authority. As a result, there can be disputes between them. Yadin-Israel traces the contours of this foundational struggle in the rabbinic sources and the ultimate triumph of midrash and decline of Oral Law as a source of authority.

In "Dissenting Literature and Social Formation in the Antique Mediterranean," Zachary B. Smith, Creighton University, expands the basis of our analysis through his exploration of some of the issues of written dissent in texts from the classical and late antique periods. Persuasive literature was the primary vehicle in the process of elite social formation. While not a genre per se, dissent literature was a subset of persuasive literature that attempted to mitigate the effects of authoritative literature. Dissent literature employed a variety of tactics, from ad hominem attacks to intellectual disputes. In Smith's analysis, the kinds of persuasion used in dissent literature tell us something about the conditions, positions, and dispositions of the authoritative and dissenting parties.

Joel Gereboff, Arizona State University, then asks us to consider the nature of King David in "When the Memory of David Is Not Enough to Authenticate the Temple in Jerusalem." Gereboff first shows how King David's connection to the building of the Temple in Jerusalem is described somewhat differently in biblical texts. Rabbinic sources assigned a greater role to David. Some midrashim specifically asserted that in Solomon's time the Temple gates opened only when David was actually present either by bringing in his coffin or through his revival. Thus, the invoking of David's memory alone was not seen as sufficient. Gereboff then correlates these Jewish traditions with developments in the Byzantine era, when they were written.

The next two essays, by Ori Z. Soltes, Georgetown University, and Gil Graff, Builders of Jewish Education, are far-reaching in their chronological and methodological range. Soltes titles his essay "From Acosta and Spinoza to Arendt to Laurence and Aylon: Verbiage and Visual Art as Instruments of Dissent in Modern Jewish Thought." Through discussion, disagreement, and dissent, rabbinic literature offered multiple perspectives on every issue. As Soltes shows, one consequence of this was that the concept of "heresy" did not functionally exist within Judaism. The first notable instances of accusations of heresy were against Uriel Acosta and Baruch Spinoza in seventeenth century Amsterdam. Centuries later, Hannah Arendt and Geoff Laurence embodied Spinoza-like modes of dissent from accepted understandings of Holocaust trauma. Later, Helène Aylon addressed the very concept of dissent against traditionally conceived rabbinic authority.

The title of Graff's study, which was the symposium's keynote presentation, was "Jewish Law and the Law of the State: A Study in Authority and Dissent." Graff observes that from Talmudic times the principle "the law of the kingdom is the law" framed the relationship of Jews and Judaism to the ruling power. With the onset of modernity, state jurisdiction extended to matters long left to religious authorities.

Napoleon brought the issue of defining church-state relationships to a head. In the modern era, "the law of the kingdom is the law" was variously invoked, as Jews charted divergent paths. Echoes of nineteenth and twentieth century debates reverberate today.

The next four essays cover distinctive developments from the mid-nineteenth to the mid-twentieth centuries in Europe and the United States. Motti Zalkin, Ben-Gurion University of the Negev, explores "'The Terrible Animal Known as the Masses': The Status and Authority of the Community Rabbi in Nineteenth Century Eastern Europe." The status of the community rabbi and his relations, both tension and cooperation, with local elites in his community has been discussed extensively in historical research. This situation changed dramatically with the rise of "the politics of the masses" in the second half of nineteenth century Europe. Traditional elites rapidly lost their exclusive status; the voice of the middle and sometimes lower classes was heard. In his essay Zalkin focuses attention on the impact of this process on the public status of the community rabbi.

Theodore Albrecht, Kent State University, follows with a musically themed study titled "Thumbing Mendelssohn's Nose at the Nazis: Hans Pfitzner's Symphony in C, Op. 46 (1940)." Paul Cossmann (1869–1942) and Hans Pfitzner (1869–1949) grew up as friends in Frankfurt, Germany. When the Nazis came to power in 1933, they arrested Cossmann, who was Jewish, for his writings. Pfitzner interceded on Cossmann's behalf. When the Nazis asked Pfitzner for new music to Shakespeare's popular "Midsummer Night's Dream," he replied that he could never improve upon that written by the Jewish Mendelssohn. In 1940, Pfitzner wrote a Symphony in C, using a disguised theme from Mendelssohn's beloved Italian Symphony as a defiant gesture against the Nazi regime.

Victoria Khiterer, Millersville University, takes a close look at "Not So Silent: Jewish Religious and Cultural Life in Kiev, 1945–1970s." In the second half of the 1930s–1940s, Soviet authorities sought to close Jewish scholarly, educational, and cultural organizations. In this essay, Khiterer examines official Soviet reports showing that, in spite of these efforts, a significant percentage of Kievan Jews continued to attend synagogue or clandestine minyanim after the Second World War and celebrated Jewish religious holidays. The authorities deprived accreditations of several Kiev rabbis, but religious life continued even without a rabbi in Kiev. The Kiev synagogue became the place of dissent and spiritual resistance against Soviet state antisemitism and assimilation policy.

In "When Authority Was a Form of Dissent: Postwar Guides to Reform Practice," Joan S. Friedman, College of Wooster, looks at a phenomenon of post–World War II America. In Friedman's analysis, Reform Judaism's perpetual paradox is that a Jewish movement rooted in rejection of halachic authority nevertheless requires modes of communal religious behavior and agreed-upon methods of determining what those behaviors should be. The quarter century after World War II brought the publication of the first books on Reform practice. Each of their rabbinic authors sought to offer ritual guidance to Reform Jews as well as to establish the theoretical basis for offering such guidance and the extent to which it could be "authoritative" within the Reform context.

The final four essays of this collection bring us up to the first decades of the twenty-first century. Eitan Abramovitch, The Institution for the Advancement of Rav Shagar's Writings, provides a close reading of a key element in the writing of Rav Shagar in "'Dispute for the Sake of Heaven': Dissent and Multiplicity in Rav Shagar's Thought." Rav Shagar (Shimon Gershon Rosenberg, 1949–2007) was one of the most original thinkers in Modern Orthodoxy. The central place that he gives to concepts like dissent, dispute, and multiplicity is one of the innovative elements of his thought. Instead of striving for harmony, he prefers multiplicity and even dissent. He connects this attitude to the central place of multiplicity in postmodern philosophy. His influence can be demonstrated, for example, in the claim that the ability to live with multiplicity can open new ways for the coexistence of Jews and Palestinians.

Shlomo Abramovich, Ariel University, introduces another Israeli development in "Limiting the Authority of the Country: Disobedience in the IDF." The history of Israel is full of examples of disobedience and refusal of soldiers motivated morally and ideologically. On the right, it is most often refusal to participate in the evacuation of Jewish settlements. Abramovich's essay focuses on the withdrawal from Gaza in 2005, when discussions about refusal, especially among Religious Zionists, raised fundamental questions like these: What is the importance of the State of Israel and what are the limitations of its authority? What happens when there is a contradiction between the country and its institutions (like the army) and Jewish values?

Mark Trencher, Nishma Research, provides the results of quantitative research is his essay, "Leaving the Fold: Dissent from Communal Authority in the Orthodox World?" The objective of the quantitative research Trencher conducted was to understand why people are leaving Orthodoxy and to explore the extent to which such leaving represents dissent from community authority figures and/or normative behaviors versus their being lured out by the external world. Trencher's research showed that for every ten responses citing outside societal attractions as a "luring factor," there were seventeen citing a communal element from which the departed were dissenting as a "repelling factor." For the American Orthodox population, departure is ultimately how they often manifest dissent.

In the volume's last essay, Lindsey Jackson, Concordia University, introduces readers to "Brit without Milah: Adapting and Remixing the Dominant Ritual System." The debate about male circumcision has garnered increased attention, permeating the Jewish community and propelling some Jews to action. Focusing on Jews in Canada and the United States, Jackson's research consists of an ethnographic study of Jewish parents and their engagement with, adaptation of, or rejection of brit milah. Using non-circumcision Jews as the focus of this analysis, she argues that they are challenging authority, reclaiming power, and demanding change by opting out of brit milah and creating alternative rituals that are better suited to their ethical concerns about circumcision and unique understandings of Judaism.

Leonard J. Greenspoon

CONTRIBUTORS

Shlomo Abramovich   6, Te'ena Street
Aley Zahav, 7194900
ISRAEL
shlomo23@gmail.com

Eitan Abramovitch   POB594
Tekoa 9090800
ISRAEL
eynatan@gmail.com

Theodore Albrecht   1635 Chadwick Drive
Kent, OH 44240
talbrech@kent.edu

Joan S. Friedman   1643 Gasche Street
Wooster, OH 44691
JFriedman@wooster.edu

Joel Gereboff   930 Lido Lane
Foster City, CA 94404
Joel.Gereboff@asu.edu

Gil Graff   9628 Lockford Street
Los Angeles, CA 90035
GGraff@bjela.org

Lindsey Jackson   150 Strathearn North
                         Montreal, Quebec
                         CANADA H4X 1X9
                         lindsey.hall.jackson@gmail.com

Victoria Khiterer   130 Springdale Lane
                         Millersville, PA 17551
                         Victoria.Khiterer@millersville.edu

Chen Marx   164, Ibn Gabirol Street
                         Tel-Aviv
                         ISRAEL
                         chen.marx@mail.huji.ac.il

Zachary B. Smith   Department of Theology
                         Creighton University
                         2500 California Plaza
                         Omaha, NE 68178
                         ZacharyBSmith@creighton.edu

Ori Z. Soltes   5114 Westridge Road
                         Bethesda, MD 20816
                         solteso@georgetown.edu

Mark Trencher   Nishma Research
                         50 Miamis Road
                         West Hartford, CT 06117
                         mark@nishmaresearch.com

Azzan Yadin-Israel   Jewish Studies and Classics
                         Rutgers University
                         12 College Avenue
                         New Brunswick, NJ 08901
                         ayadin@jewishstudies.rutgers.edu

Motti Zalkin   Department of Jewish History
                         Ben-Gurion University of the Negev
                         Beer Sheva
                         ISRAEL
                         mottizalkin@gmail.com

FIGURATIVE LANGUAGE OF AUTHORITY AND REBELLION IN THE STORY OF THE DEATH OF RABBI JUDAH BEN BAVA

CHEN MARX

INTRODUCTION

The words of the wise are like goads, and like nails well planted are the words of masters of assemblies, they were given by one shepherd. (Eccl 12:11)

SOLOMON, THE PRESUMED author of Ecclesiastes, refers here to the words of wise men, likening them to a whip used to drive a plowing ox and to nails well planted, both used by one master, viz. God.[1]

In the Talmudic period, the sages interpreted this metaphor from Ecclesiastes as follows:

[You might think that] just as the nail only diminishes [as it is driven into a material] and does not increase, so, too, the words of the Torah only diminish and do not increase—therefore the text says: "well planted." Just as a plant grows and increases, so the words of Torah grow and increase. (*b. Hag.* 3a)

This is a perplexing midrash. How is the Torah comparable to a nail? And what does the body that the nail penetrates represent?[2]

These questions illustrate the difficulty we face when we encounter figurative language. It is figurative language that will be at the center of this essay.[3]

This essay discusses the Bar Kokhba Revolt and its repercussions. It focuses on the way in which the sages described the harsh reality of their time in similes and how, at the end of this process, these similes became reality itself.[4] The essay also examines how the sages dealt with a crisis that reality put in their way and how literature and figurative language played a significant role in the process of reconstruction and rehabilitation. Lastly, it considers a possible answer to the question What is the significance of the nails to which the Torah was likened in the midrash that we have read?

THE DESTRUCTION OF THE SECOND TEMPLE

The historical background of the stories we will deal with is the destruction of the Second Temple, which occurred in 70 CE, and the subsequent Bar Kokhba Revolt, which occurred in the years 132–136 CE.

The Jews' Great Revolt against Rome took place in 70 CE. It was not a planned revolt. No clear leadership directed it. No preparations were made for it. It broke out almost spontaneously. Ultimately, four years after it had begun, the Romans laid siege to Jerusalem, conquered the city, and burned the Temple.[5]

It is hard for us today to comprehend the full impact of the destruction of the Temple. Fundamentally, the very existence of the Temple validates the covenant between God and Israel.[6] The Temple renews the covenant on a daily basis through the sacrificial worship. Moreover, the sacrifices purify the Temple and allow God to reside in it. Each and every day sacrifices were made in the Temple to cleanse the people of Israel of their sins, making them a holy people with whom God himself could have a covenant, a people within whom he can reside.

This is how it is described in the Book of Exodus: "And let them make me a sanctuary; that I may dwell among them" (Exod 25:8). The Temple was the nexus around which the people of Israel came together socially, politically, and religiously. Its existence should have been as eternal as the covenant between God and Israel itself. The physical structure of the Temple was a tangible representation of that covenant.

One can only imagine their shock when the people of Israel learned that the Temple had been destroyed. They must have struggled to understand what such an event could signify.

On the face of it, the destruction of the Temple meant that the covenant itself had been invalidated. However, the people of Israel could rely on a historical precedent for the destruction of the Second Temple: the destruction of the First Temple by Nebuchadnezzar, King of Babylon. More importantly, they could rely on its reconstruction seventy years later, the result of the seemingly miraculous decree by Cyrus the Great, king of Persia.

The people of Israel knew that the Temple had been destroyed and rebuilt once before. This fact proved to be fateful. To understand its significance, we must first present the notion of cyclical history and its relation to the Bible.

CYCLICAL HISTORY

Rabbinic thought considered the Torah to be as eternal as God. This implied that reading the Bible could teach a person not only what has happened in the past, but also what is happening in the present and what will happen in the future.[7]

This means that if the First Temple was destroyed and then rebuilt seventy years later, it was reasonable to assume that a Third Temple would be built seventy years after the destruction of the Second. Put simply, the Third Temple would be built in 140 CE.

It is no surprise, then, that sixty-two years after the destruction of the Second Temple, the Jews launched a new revolt—the Bar Kokhba Revolt—hoping that the Third Temple would be rebuilt in due time.

THE BAR KOKHBA REVOLT

The Bar Kokhba Revolt was based on the assumption that a new Temple would be built seventy years after the destruction of the last, just as happened after the first destruction in the sixth century BCE.

Unlike the revolt that led to the destruction of the Second Temple, the Bar Kokhba Revolt was well organized, and it was led by a man whom the sages believed to be the Messiah: "When Rabbi Akiva would see Bar Kuzeva [the name by which the Talmud refers to Bar Kokhba, often understood to mean Son of Falsehood] he would say—'This is the King Messiah.'" (*J. Ta'an.* 4). Yet, though the revolt was well planned and organized, and despite the messianic hopes placed on it, and despite all the Jewish victories and the many Roman casualties, the Jews lost.

The Romans were hardly gracious victors. The Roman historian Cassius Dio claims that 580,000 Jews died during the suppression of the Bar Kokhba Revolt (a rough estimate puts this as 40 percent of the Jews living in the Land of Israel at the time). Five hundred Jewish forts were taken, and a thousand Jewish villages were razed to the ground.[8] Rabbinic literature describes the killings as creating rivers of blood:

And they [the Romans] would kill them [the Jews] and continue until the horse would sink in blood to its muzzle. And the blood would roll rocks the size of forty seah [a unit of volume, approximately eight liters], until the blood flowed four miles into the sea; and lest you say it is near the sea, it is forty miles from the sea. (*J. Ta'an.* 24b)

But the failure of the Bar Kokhba Revolt must be measured by more than its casualty statistics. The real tragedy of the Bar Kokhba Revolt was the loss of Torah.

To properly understand this phrase, "loss of Torah," we must first say a few words about the concept of the Oral Torah. Today, if we were to go to the library and ask librarians for the Jews' Oral Torah, they would lead us to shelves of rabbinic literature and show us such collections as the Mishnah, the Talmud, or the Midrash. In effect, they would be taking us to books written after 220 CE.

Today, the Oral Torah is not oral. It is written. But before 220 CE it was, quite literally, oral. Writing it down was forbidden. In other words, unlike the Bible (the written Torah), the innovations of the sages (the Oral Torah) were not allowed to be written.[9]

After the destruction of the Second Temple there was a tremendous blossoming of literature created by the sages.[10] The sages led the people with their words, but their words could not be written down. The sages' actions, which were basically verbal, remained intangible, and the only way to preserve them was through memory. And so, each sage embodied the Torah itself. He embodied, produced, and memorized the Torah. He replaced the written book—he was the written book.[11]

By the time the Bar Kokhba Revolt was over, some 40 percent of the Jewish people in Judea had died at the hands of the Romans. This statistic encompasses every part of the population: 40 percent of the sages, who produced and memorized the Torah, were among the dead. In other words, the Romans quite literally destroyed 40 percent of the Oral Torah, the very Torah that the sages had created up until that time.

It should be noted that the Torah—both Written and Oral—was believed to be eternal. The Torah was supposed to protect its bearers and could not be destroyed—it must be everlasting. And yet, following the Bar Kokhba Revolt, the survivors discovered that the Torah could be destroyed, quite easily, and that it did not protect the sages.[12]

THE DEATH OF R. BEN BAVA

Rabbi Judah ben Bava lived after the Bar Kokhba Revolt had been suppressed. He experienced the decrees enacted by the Romans following the Revolt.[13] One of these was a prohibition on the ordination or appointment of new sages. The punishment for violating this prohibition was death. Despite this decree, R. ben Bava ordained five disciples:

Rab Judah said [the following] in the name of Rab: "Verily that man, R. Judah ben Bava by name, be remembered for good, for were it not for him the laws of fines would have been forgotten in Israel." [The Talmud then asks:] 'Forgotten'? Surely, they could be studied? [And so, the Talmud corrects itself:] Nay, they would have been abolished. (*b. 'Abod. Zar.* 8b).

What the Talmud meant is that there would no longer be any dayanim [judges] ordained to rule in such cases. This is how it happened:

For the wicked Government of Rome issued a decree that he who ordains a Rabbi shall be slain, likewise he who is ordained shall be put to death, the town in which an ordination takes place shall be destroyed and the tehum [region, municipality] in which the ordination is held shall be laid waste.

What did R. Judah ben Bava do? He went and sat between two mountains and between two large towns, between two tehums [municipalities], namely, between [the towns of] Usha and Shefar'am, and there he ordained five elders: R. Meir, R. Judah [b. Il'ai], R. Jose, R. Simeon and R. Eleazar b. Shammua. R. Awia adds: also R. Nehemiah.

On seeing that they were detected by the enemies, he [R. ben Bava] said to them, "Flee, my children!" But they said to him, "And you, O Rabbi, what about you?" "I," he replied, "will lie still before them as a stone that cannot be moved." It was stated that the Romans did not move from there until they drove three hundred iron spears into his body and made his corpse like a sieve! (*b. 'Abod. Zar.* 8b)[14]

The story presents the protagonist R. ben Bava as concerned with the general welfare of the people. Although he is aware of the persecution and the threat of death, he is able to find creative solutions to the problems that circumstances put in his way. This is why he does not ordain his disciples within the limits of any specific city. This way, the Romans would have no grounds to punish the residents of any specific city. Despite the Roman threat, R. ben Bava ensures the continuity of Torah, at the price of his own continuity, by this act of ordaining his disciples.

Figurative language plays an important role in the story:

On seeing that they were detected by the enemies, he [R. ben Bava] said to them, "Flee, my children!" But they said to him, "And you, O Rabbi, what about you?" "I," he replied, "will lie still before them as a stone that cannot be moved." It was stated that the Romans did not move from there until they drove three hundred iron spears into his body and made his corpse like a sieve! (*b. 'Abod. Zar.* 8b)

This dialogue between the disciples and R. ben Bava is full of difficulties. For one, the disciples' question, "What about you," is ambiguous. Are they asking "What will become of you" or perhaps "What will you do"? The fact that R. ben Bava chose to answer in figurative language, "I will lie still before them . . . as a stone that cannot be moved," only intensifies this difficulty. It is unclear what the disciples meant by their question and what R. ben Bava meant by his answer.[15]

This is because his answer is a simile. R. ben Bava depicted himself as a large, heavy stone, immovable and impenetrable. And this simile can be contrasted with another simile, one created by the Romans through their actions in the world. Put differently, while R. ben Bava presented himself as solid, stable, and immobile, the simile presented to the reader by the Romans is that of a sieve: a mobile, pierced, and penetrated object.

This creates two frames of reality: the first is the immediate reality in the world of action—R. ben Bava's body, pierced like a sieve. In contrast to this simile stands the one R. ben Bava uses for himself—an unturned stone. This simile represents the other frame of reality—the future one, which will come to be long after the Romans disappear and their persecution will cease. It is a frame of reality we are exposed to in light of the entire segment.

R. ben Bava's simile was triumphant. In the reader's reality, laws concerning fines ultimately survived thanks to R. ben Bava's sacrifice. Thus, his teaching and actions were as eternal as an immovable rock.

While it is true that in this clash of similes the one created by the Romans was triumphant for a brief time, it was the simile proposed by R. ben Bava that achieved a permanent victory. R. ben Bava's pierced and bleeding body disappears and is replaced by the simile of an immovable and impenetrable rock. Furthermore, it offers insight into the true status of the Torah. If originally we thought that it met its demise with the death of this righteous man, this story consoles us by saying that the Torah lives on. Not only does it survive, but it also spreads and gains followers, thanks to the actions of this righteous man just prior to his death.

CALCULATING THE LEAP YEAR
IN BIQ'AT RIMON

I would now like to turn to another story, this one from the Jerusalem Talmud. It features most of the disciples ordained by R. ben Bava:[16]

> R. Yona [said] in the name of R. Hiyya bar Ba: It so happened that seven elders came to calculate the leap year in Biq'at Rimon. And who were they? R. Meir, and R. Yehuda, and R. Yossi, and R. Shim'on, R. Nehemia, and R. Eliezar ben Ya'akov, and R. Yochanan the Shoemaker. (*j. Hag.* 3a)

Note that four sages from this list were ordained by R. ben Bava, excluding R. Nehemiah, who some claim was also ordained at the same time. In any case, this group includes four out of the five disciples whom R. ben Bava had ordained just before he was killed by the Romans.

The action they are performing here would determine the precise dates of the holidays. Just like ordination, it was forbidden in the persecution that followed the failed Bar Kokhba Revolt. By their very action, these disciples were returning national and religious authority to the Land of Israel.[17] Their action signified the end of the period of persecution.

> And they were calculating the leap year. . . . And left with a kiss, and whoever did not have cover—his friend would cut off some of his cover and give him. (*j. Hag.* 3a)

Note the relationship between the sages R. ben Bava ordained. They are not entangled in power struggles. Rather, they cooperate and share an interdependent relationship and kiss each other when they part ways. It seems that they coalesced as a group as a result of the adversities they faced immediately after the Bar Kokhba Revolt.

But just before they part, they do something else: "When they were about to go they said: 'Let us show what we have done'" (*j. Hag.* 3a). The sages say: we want to show our actions and achievements to the living, so that they may see what we have done. Torah, however, is abstract—it has no physical form in the world. Calculating the leap year has no tangible shape. The sages are trying to illustrate an abstract idea in the physical world.

> And this is what they do: And there was a rock of marble there, and each took one nail and fixed it in it, and it sunk in it, as in dough, and even today it is called the hobnailed rock. (*j. Hag.* 3a)

The sages ordained by R. ben Bava create a monument to represent their action. They take an abstract, shapeless action and present it in the tangible form of the material world. As a symbol, the disciples choose a marble rock, just like the immovable rock to which R. ben Bava had likened himself.

The sages approach this rock and drive iron nails into it, just as the Romans drove their spears into R. ben Bava's body. The Roman simile of the penetrated body and R. ben Bava's simile of himself as an unmovable rock are intertwined to relay an entirely new message.

In this system of similies, the marble rock represents R. ben Bava. But it would be wrong to think of him as an ordinary man. He is not just a man. In this context R. ben Bava is the very sages that he ordained. He is the embodiment of the Torah that he taught and created.

Ben Bava's disciples choose a marble rock as a symbol for him, a marble rock that had been penetrated not by enemies but by the very disciples that he himself had ordained. The sharp iron implements, which pierce and penetrate the rock, do not symbolize the Roman spears but rather the new Torah that the disciples ordained by R. ben Bava created. The action of driving the nails into the marble rock does not take Torah away from it. Instead, it adds a new dimension to it, which was not there before.

In that sense, it echoes the metaphor from Ecclesiastes, with which we opened the essay, and the midrash from the Babylonian Talmud, which expounded on it:

> [You might think that] just as the nail only diminishes [as it is driven into a material] and does not increase, so, too, the words of the Torah only diminish and do not increase—therefore the text says: "well planted," Just as a plant grows and increases, so the words of Torah grow and increase. (*b. Hag.* 3a)

When a person hammers a nail into the wall, the material removed from it forms a pile of dust on the floor below. The Torah is likened to a nail here, but it does not remove anything from the wall it penetrates. On the contrary, it adds to it. When R. ben Bava's disciples want to demonstrate their actions, they liken themselves to nails penetrating a marble rock. In so doing they reenact the scene in which they became sages, at the price of losing their Rabbi, the one who ordained them. Seemingly, the Torah had been lost then. Seemingly, it had died. However, even though at that moment it seemed as if the Torah was destroyed, it lived on. Not only it had not been diminished in the slightest, but the sages ordained by R. ben Bava had increased it. Just as they increased the rock by adding the nails to it, they had added new Torah to the existing one.

CONCLUSION

When a revolt such as the Bar Kokhba Revolt fails, the believers face several fundamental questions. How could a revolt that was both political and religious have failed? How could the Torah embodied in the sages suffer bitter defeat and be put to death? Who is truly in control of the world: those who use force to shape the material world, or those who live in a world of similes and shape reality through words?

From the stories we have read, we can conclude that when reality becomes too hard to bear, the world of similes blossoms. Reality is presented as more than what it first seems to be. There is an entirely different world behind it, an invisible world described through figurative language.

The stories we have just examined describe the path taken by a simile, from the world of reality to the world of figurative language and from the world of figurative language back to reality. Put differently, in the stories we have just read, the simile gains a body and a presence in reality.[18] In that process, the dead, pierced man really does become a stone, unharmed and undiminished by the iron spears. In fact, the iron nails do not diminish but increase the Torah that he embodied.

NOTES

1. This verse can also be interpreted to mean the barbs at the end of the whip.

2. In the following paragraph I take a similar approach to David Stern, *Midrash and Theory: Ancient Jewish Exegesis and Contemporary Literary Studies (Rethinking Theory)* (Evanston: Northwestern University Press, 1996), 19–21, in which Stern interprets the sages' commentary on Ecclesiastes.

   The traditional approach, however, satisfies itself with understanding the simile of a nail as a well-planted, immovable object. See, for example, the words of Azariah dei Rossi, "As are the commandments . . . as nails planted in our hearts," in Reuven Bonfil, ed., *The Writings of Azariah dei Rossi* (Jerusalem: Bialik Institution, 1991), 172, and the footnote there.

3. Literary scholarship has taken a number of approaches to figurative language, beginning with the distinction between a symbol and an allegory in Walter Benjamin, *The Origin of German Tragic Drama* (trans. J. Osborne; New York and London: Verso, 1977), 177–78. This was followed by Paul de Man, *Blindness and Insight, Theory and History of Literature* (Minneapolis: University of Minnesota Press, 1983), 187–228. Later extensive research was conducted in George Lakoff and Mark Johnson, *Metaphors We Live By* (Chicago and London: University of Chicago Press, 1980). See them for additional references.

4. In my Ph.D. thesis I expounded on the way sages considered figurative language, similes, and metaphors. See Chaim Natan Marx, "Bound Phrases: The Question of Similarity and Association in the Tales of the Sages in the Babylonian Talmud" (Ph.D. diss., The Hebrew University, 2011), 238–41. See also Alan Mintz, *Hurban: Responses to Catastrophe in Hebrew Literature* (New York: Columbia University Press, 1984), 34–38, 66; as well as David Stern, *Parables in Midrash: Narrative and Exegesis in Rabbinic Literature* (London: Harvard University Press, 1991); and Gail Labovitz, "The Language of the Bible and the Language of the Rabbis: A Linguistic Look at Kiddushin, Part 1," *Conservative Judaism* 63:1 (2011): 25–42, and additional references there.

5. Menahem Mor, who was kind enough to join us in the conference on the Bar Kokhba Revolt and its historic causes, writes on the subject in Menahem Mor, "The Second Jewish Revolt: The Bar Kokhba War, 132–136 CE," in *The Brill Reference Library of Judaism*, vol. 50 (ed. Alan Avery-Peck, et al.; Leiden-Boston: Brill, 2016, 51–145). See also additional references there. In recent years there has been a revival in the research on the Bar Kokhba Revolt. Scholars emphasize elements overlooked by their

predecessors and manipulations in scholarship itself, manipulations stemming from the national needs of past scholars. See the work done by Haim Weiss, e.g., Haim Weiss, "There Was a Man in Israel—Bar-Kosibah Was His Name!" *Jewish Studies Quarterly* 21:2 (2001): 99–115.

6. For the way the Temple embodies the convenant, see Guy G. Stroumsa, *The End of Sacrifice: Religious Transformations in Late Antiquity* (trans. S. Emanuel; Chicago: University of Chicago Press, 2009).

7. See also David Stern, *Midrash and Theory*, 14–38.

8. For more on Cassius Dio, see Fergus Millar, *A Study of Cassius Dio* (Oxford: Oxford University Press, 1971). For a full review of Dio's comments on the revolt and their historical reliability, see the second chapter in Menahem Mor, "The Second Jewish Revolt," in which an entire section is dedicated to the subject. See also Menahem Mor, "Are There Any New Factors Concerning the Bar-Kokhba Revolt?" *Studia Antiqua et Archaeologica* 18:1 (2012): 161–93.

9. See *b. Tem.* 14b for a discussion of this issue and of the reasons for the writing of the Oral Torah despite the prohibition.

10. In the absence of the religious center—the Temple—which was controlled by the priests, the sages became the leading religious authority. See Robert T. Herford, *The Effect of the Fall of Jerusalem upon the Character of the Pharisees* (London: Society of Hebraic Studies, 1917), 3–22. See also Shaye J. D. Cohen, "The Significance of Yavneh: Pharisees, Rabbis, and the End of Jewish Sectarianism," *Hebrew Union College Annual* 55 (1984): 27–53; and Israel L. Levin, *The Place of Sages in the Land of Israel in Talmudic Times* (Jerusalem: Yad Ben-Zvi, 1986), 8–9, 130–31.

11. See a discussion of a similar case in Devora Steinmetz, "Like Torah Scrolls That Are Rolled Up: The story of the Death of Rabbi Eliezer in Sanhedrin 68a," in *Tiferet Leyisrael: Jubilee Volume in Honor of Israel Francus* (ed. Joel Roth, et al.; New York: Jewish Theological Seminary of America, 2010), 153–79.

12. Many stories in rabbinic literature refer to this phenomenon of the death of Torah through the death of the sage. One feature is the recurring phrase "such Torah and such a reward." This phrase is repeated when a sage who was killed by the Romans is discussed. The word "such" is used deictically here. It refers to the actual dead body of the sage. The phrase "such Torah and such a reward" means "this is not a dead person, but a dead Torah." If it is Torah, how can this be the reward Torah itself receives? See Marx, *Bound Phrases*, 300–13, and references there.

13. The edicts of persecution issued in the days of Antoninus Pius (138–161 CE) were laws meant to eradicate the Jewish faith. See Yosef Dan, "Pirkey Hekhlot Rabbati and the Ten Martyrs," *Eshel Beer Sheva* 2 (1981): 63–80; and Solomon Zeitlin, "The Legend of The Ten Martyrs and Its Apocalyptic Origins," *The Jewish Quarterly Review* 36 (1945): 1–16.

14. The story is repeated in *b. Sanh.* 13b–14a. See comparisons and an examination of manuscripts in Marx, *Bound Phrases*. Briefly stated, there are no significant differences and none that meaningfully alter the story.

15. See additional discussion on the meaning of the dialogue in Marx, *Bound Phrases*, 240–41.

16. I compare here a story of a Babylonian origin and a story originating in the Land of Israel. This has two clear disadvantages. First, it violates Jonah Frankel's principle that the Aggadah is a closed text (Jonah Frankel, "Hermeneutic Questions in the Study of Aggadah," *Tarbiz* 47 [1978]: 139–72). This principle has attracted much opposition in recent years. See the literary review in Chaim Natan Marx, "How Biblical Verses Became an Enchantment against the Evil Eye (Gen 48:16; 49:22 in *Berakhot* 20a and Ibid., 55b)," in *Studies on Magic and Divination in the Biblical World* (ed. G. Philippe, et al.; Piscataway: Gorgias Press, 2013), 211–25. It is also problematic in terms of the material I put side by side. Comparing texts from the Land of Israel with Babylonian texts is unusual in scholarship. See an extensive discussion of the topic and how the two types can be compared in Marx, *Bound Phrases*, 307–15, 325–26.

17. The story of calculating the leap year in Biq'at Rimon can be understood as a part of the struggle between the sages in the Land of Israel and those outside it with the question of what is the religious center. See *b. Ber.* 63a; *y. Ned.* 40a. In this context, calculating the leap year in Biq'at Rimon symbolizes the moment in which the sages in the Land of Israel took authority back. See Aharon Oppenheimer, *Rabbi Judah ha-Nasi* [Hebrew] (Jerusalem: Zalman Shazar Center, 2007), 118–21. See also Moshe David Herr, *The History of Eretz Israel: The Roman Byzantine Period, The Mishnah and Talmud Period and the Byzantine Rule (70–640)* [Hebrew] (Jerusalem: Yad Yitzchak Ben Zvi and Keter Press, 1985), 87–88.

18. It can be argued that the Oral Torah, which developed from a Torah that could not be written and had no body or shape until being written and having form, is like the simile, which began as an abstract utterance and later gained physical manifestation.

MIDRASH, ORAL LAW, AND THE QUESTION OF RABBINIC AUTHORITY

AZZAN YADIN-ISRAEL

RABBI DAVID ZVI Hoffmann, a late-nineteenth century scholar who first taught at and then directed the Berlin Rabbinic Seminary, played a noteworthy role in the study of the legal midrashim—that is, the early rabbinic commentaries on the laws of the Hebrew Bible. His foundational study of legal midrash opens with a discussion of the two forms in which tannaitic legal arguments were transmitted: apodictically (without reference to Scripture) and midrashically. In terms of the tannaitic sources, apodictic arguments predominate in the Mishnah and its companion the Tosefta, though these also contain midrashic passages. The systematic interpretation of the Torah is found in the legal midrashim, which are divided into the school of Rabbi Aqiva and the school of Rabbi Ishmael. This division, first proposed by Hoffmann himself, is based on differences in legal terminology, the names of the sages that appear in each, and interpretive principles.[1] The *Mekhilta of Rabbi Ishmael* (to Exodus) and the *Sifre Numbers* make up one group, the *Sifra* (to Leviticus) and *Sifre Deuteronomy* make up the other; the former group is associated with Rabbi Ishmael, the latter with Rabbi Aqiva, whose circle also produced the Mishnah.[2]

The extent to which these works can be traced to a particular sage is a matter of controversy[3] and in any case not relevant to my argument. The different interpretive patterns, terminology, and traditions that Hoffmann identified in the legal midrashim are meaningful regardless of their precise provenance.[4] As far as the division between apodictic and midrashic legal statements is concerned, it is not surprising that Hoffmann first cites a ruling from the Mishnah, which is not linked to a biblical prooftext, then from the *Sifra*, the commentary to Leviticus:[5]

1. If a man slaughtered a quadruped and found therein an embryo, he whose appetite is robust may eat it ... if the embryo emerged only partially, it is forbidden as food. (*m. Ḥul.* 4.7)
2. "Any that has hoofs, with clefts, and that chews its cud from among the quadrupeds—it may you eat" (Lev 11:3): "[It] may you eat," to include the embryo. Might it be that this is the case even if it emerges only partially? Scripture teaches, saying "it." (*Sifra Shemini* pereq 3.1, Weiss 48b)[6]

The two sources clearly present the same legal position: a person is generally allowed to consume the embryo of a slain quadruped, except if the embryo had already begun to emerge from its mother's body at the time of the slaughter. Setting aside the (fairly disgusting, for most modern readers) content of the ruling, the juxtaposition of the two sources raises a thorny question: why is the same law presented both as a scripturally derived teaching and as an apodictic statement, divorced from Scripture? One possible answer is to assert the priority of midrash and explain the difference as a matter of genre: the Mishnah is merely distilling rabbinic insights culled from Scripture and presenting them in a more accessible manner. This is the position championed by the prominent Talmud scholar David Weiss Halivni:

> No law is really binding on the Jew unless it can be shown to have its origin in the Bible. Midrashic form continued to exist, therefore, even after the change to Mishnaic form. It existed in the laws that are found only in the Midreshei Halakhah (that is, those not found in the Mishnah), and it existed concomitantly in the laws that are found in both the Midreshei Halakhah and the Mishnah. For the latter, Midrash served as the ground, the justification, the life support. Indeed, one may legitimately wonder whether the Mishnah would have survived at all were it not for the parallel existence of Midreshei Halakhah.[7]

Though many readers may find this view quite plausible, it entails two critical difficulties. The first is that the Mishnah does present itself in these terms. To the contrary, the Mishnah enunciates a clear, non-scriptural model of authority, most famously in the opening of tractate *Avot*:

> Moshe received the Torah from Sinai and transmitted it to Yehoshua, and Yehoshua to the Elders, and the Elders to the Prophets, and the Prophets transmitted it to the Men of the Great Assembly. (*m. Avot* 1.1)

More important than any one ideological affirmation is the integration of extra-scriptural tradition into the discursive practices of the Mishnah. This is evident when, for example, *shama'nu* and *lo' shama'nu* ["we have heard" and "we have not heard"] refer to having received/not received a legal tradition from one's master, or in the use of the root *q-b-l* to refer regularly (but not exclusively[8]) to the reception of legal traditions, as in this example:

> Nahum the Scribe said: I have received a tradition [*mequbbal ʾani*] from Rabbi Measha, who received [*qibbel*] from his father, who received [*qibbel*] from the pairs, who received [*qibblu*] from the prophets as a *halakhah* given to Moses at Sinai, that if a man sowed his field with two kinds of wheat. (*m. Peah* 2.6)[9]

This then is one challenge to Halivni's position. If the Mishnah were merely an anthology of legal decisions culled from rabbinic midrash, it would not need to anchor its teachings in an extra-scriptural model of rabbinic authority. It would not, in other words, present the rabbis as heirs to what would later come to be known as the Oral Torah, often identified as constitutive of rabbinic Judaism itself.[10]

The second difficulty involves the *Sifra's* interpretation of the phrase "it may you eat" in Leviticus 11:3, which draws the permission to eat an embryo from the phrase "may you eat" and the prohibition on eating a partially emerged embryo from the pronoun "it." Let us begin with the plain sense of the verse—namely, the determination that animals with cleft hooves that chew their cud are edible: "Any that has hoofs, with clefts, and that chews its cud from among the quadrupeds—it may you eat." Though the *Sifra* does not make this claim explicitly, the starting point of its interpretation is the arguably marked syntax of the verse, which first describes the animal and then concludes with "it may you eat" [אתה תאכלו]. The *Sifra* does not state explicitly what it finds unusual about the phrase, only that it is a warrant to midrashically augment the verse. The interpretive logic of this move is familiar from early rabbinic midrash: an anomaly in the verse elicits a rabbinic response. What is puzzling is the legal content that the *Sifra* adduces: "'[It] may you eat,' to include the embryo"—that is, the phrase indicates that it is permitted to consume the embryo of the animal being slaughtered.

But the *Sifra* does not link the embryo to the language of Leviticus 11:3, or of any other verse for that matter, so there is no direct scriptural justification for this specific conclusion. Why does the phrase "it may you eat" sanction the inclusion of the embryo rather than any other element not specified in the verse? This is not clear. The disengagement from Scripture is more pronounced in the argument's next step, where the pronoun "it" [אתה] anchors the ruling that if the embryo has partially emerged from its mother's body, it is prohibited. Again, the *Sifra* does not provide guidance as to what it finds remarkable about the pronoun. Perhaps the issue is that the meaning of the verse remains intact without the pronoun, or maybe it is the fact that direct object pronouns can be expressed in Hebrew either as an independent word [אתה תאכלו] or as a pronominal suffix to the verb [תאכלוה]. Or perhaps it is another issue; the *Sifra* is silent on the question. Irrespective, the real difficulty is the legal decision the pronoun is made to bear regarding the partially birthed embryo. For on what grounds can the phrase "it may you eat" be divided into its constitutive elements, "it" on one side and "may you eat" on the other, each made the basis for a different type of legal argument: "may you eat" expands the scope of the biblical verse to include the embryo, while "it" qualifies the expansion by excluding the partially emerged embryo? Returning to Halivni's statement, it is not clear to what extent we can say that the law in question, even when the *Sifra* presents it as a midrash to Leviticus 11:3, is "shown to have its origin in the Bible."

Rather than clarify the question of the dual presentation of rabbinic law—midrashic and extra-scriptural—the discussion to this point has complicated it. If Mishnah states that it is permitted to consume an embryo except in the case that it is partially emerged, why does the *Sifra* anchor the same rulings in such a problematic and perplexing discussion of Leviticus 11:3? A possible clue involves the fierce debate within late antique Jewish sources regarding the relationship between scriptural interpretation and received tradition. I state at the outset that I know of no sources that reject the authority of the Torah. The dispute hinges on whether Scripture is the sole source of Jewish legal authority or whether an extra-scriptural chain of tradition represents a second, independent source of authority. In Book 13 of the *Antiquities of the Jews*, Josephus refers briefly to one of the differences between the Pharisees and the Sadducees:

> What I would now explain is this, that the Pharisees have delivered to the people a great many observances by succession from their fathers, which are not written in the laws of Moses; and for that reason it is that the Sadducees reject them, and say that we are to esteem those observances to be obligatory which are in the written word, but are not to observe what are derived from the tradition of our forefathers. And concerning these things it is that great disputes and differences have arisen among them. (*Ant.* 13.10.6 §297)[11]

One group unequivocally situated on the *sola scriptura* side is the Qumran community, whose writings reflect a single-minded commitment to scriptural authority. Part of this commitment is evident in the way Torah study is legislated into the very fabric of the community:

> And in the place in which the Ten assemble there should never be missing a man to interpret the *torah* day and night, always, one relieving another. And the Many shall be on watch together for a third of each night of the year in order to read the book, explain the regulation, and bless together. (1QS 6.6–8)

Beyond the communal engagement of Scripture, Torah study plays an important role in the Scrolls' historiographic writings, as when Israel's failure to uphold God's covenant is linked to the fact that "David had not read the sealed book of the *torah* which was in the ark, for it had not been opened in Israel since the day of the death of Eleazar and of Joshua" (CD 5.2–4). The betrayal of Torah attributed to David and the generations that followed was ongoing, as we see in the Rule of the Community's demand that new members of the Qumran community "revert to the Torah of Moses" (1QS 5.7–10), the implication being that Scripture had yet to regain its rightful place as the chief and indeed sole source of authority.[12] This implication becomes explicit in the Scrolls' repeated attacks on *dorshe ḥalaqot*, "those looking for easy interpretations" (see, e.g., Pesher Nahum 2.7 and the Damascus Document 1.18–19). Joseph Baumgarten was the first to suggest that *dorshe ḥalaqot* is a polemic play on *dorshe halakhot*, those who seek after (or: who interpret) extra-scriptural traditions, a position that has been widely accepted.[13] If so, the commitment to Torah in the Dead Sea Scrolls is framed in opposition to those who acknowledge the legitimacy of *halachot*, received traditions.

The last late antique Jewish source I will cite is the New Testament, where we find an interesting division between the synoptic gospels, on the one hand, and Paul's epistles, on the other. The former contains a number of explicit attacks on the authority of received tradition [*paradosis*]. For example, when the Pharisees and scribes criticize Jesus for allowing his disciples to contravene "the traditions of the elders" by eating with unwashed hands, he condemns them as hypocrites who "abandon the commandment of God and hold to [*krateō*] human tradition" (Mark 7:8; parallel at Matt 15:2).[14] Paul's epistles, in contrast, regularly employ the language of tradition and its transmission and regular recourse to the terminology of transmitted tradition: "For I *handed on to you* as of first importance what I in turn had received" (1 Cor 15:3), "For I received from the Lord what I also *handed on to you*" (1 Cor 11:23). Paul praises his followers for their fidelity to the traditions "because you have been mindful of me in everything and are *holding to the traditions*, just as I *passed them on to you*" (1 Cor 11:2). Elsewhere, he urges them to "stand firm and hold fast [*krateite*][15] to the *traditions* that you were taught by us, either by word of mouth or by our letter" (2 Thess 2:15).[16] Each of these sources merits, and has generated, separate analysis. In the present context, however, I put them forward in the service of a broad claim—namely, that the relationship between Scripture and received tradition was hotly debated in the first century CE, a debate that serves as a backdrop to the early rabbis.

TANNAITIC SOURCES

Modern scholarly attempts to come to grips with the presentation of early rabbinic law as both midrash and received tradition have generally gone one of two routes: categorical affirmation of one mode over the other or a diachronic survey that accords primacy first to one mode and then to the other. We have already encountered an example of the former in David Weiss Halivni's claim that "no law is really binding on the Jew" if it is not scriptural;[17] a diametrically opposed position is staked out by Isaac Halevy, who asserts that extra-scriptural tradition enjoyed absolute and unquestioned dominance in Second Temple and post-70 Judaism.[18] Though formulated in less extreme terms, other scholars also accord clear priority to one mode of authorization. Hanoch Albeck presents the Oral Law as merely an explication of the written Torah rather than an independent source of legal authority;[19] David Zvi Hoffmann, in contrast, claims that "the sages use interpretation only as a means for *ex post facto* support" for received traditions "or to provide a firmer foundation, or to preserve them lest they be forgotten,"[20] and this view is echoed by J. N. Epstein, who writes that "scriptural prooftexts are provided for *halakhah*, one does not derive or innovate legal traditions on the basis of Scripture."[21]

The second, diachronic route posits a shift within rabbinic culture, generally from a midrashic approach (considered to be the earlier) to extra-scriptural authority.[22] The important point for the present discussion is that all these scholars assume that rabbinic sources speak with a single voice. Though some accounts represent these sources as constant and others as varying over time, neither allows for internal dissent or debate. I consider this approach a fundamental error and argue that tannaitic sources are internally divided on this question. Further, these divisions correspond in the main to the distinction between the schools of Rabbi Ishmael and Rabbi Akiva.

The first point to make in this regard is that the two authorizing models do not lend themselves to easy harmonization—for one, because they are associated with different ideal types, in the Weberian sense of the word.[23] Authority anchored in midrash assumes literacy and a thorough familiarity with the biblical text; scholarly genealogy plays no role. The master of extra-scriptural tradition, in contrast, claims authority by virtue of his status as a disciple of a recognized master and therefore as an authorized recipient of extra-scriptural *halachot*. He is part of a scholarly genealogy that traces back to Moses (a counterpart to the priesthood's biological genealogy that reaches back to Aaron) but need not be a skilled interpreter of Scripture, or even for that matter literate.

The Rabbi Ishmael and Rabbi Akiva midrashim clearly differ in this regard. The Rabbi Ishmael sources, which champion a thoroughly midrashic or textualist position, never cite extra-scriptural dicta "in the name of" [משום] a sage, nor do they cite "testimonies" [עדויות], "decrees" [גזרות], "words of the scribes" [דברי סופרים], or "words of the sages" [דברי חכמים], all of which appear in both the Mishnah and in certain parts of the *Sifra*. Rabbi Ishmael, moreover, never recognizes another sage as his master—there is no tannaitic statement identifying his teacher, an impossible situation for a scholar whose authority derives from oral tradition. Indeed, a derashah cited in the name of Rabbi Ishmael radically delimits the scope and currency of extra-scriptural traditions [*halachot*]:

"You shall take an awl" (Deut 15:17): This was the source of Rabbi Ishmael's saying: In three places extra-scriptural tradition (*halakhah*) circumvents Scripture: the Torah says: "He shall pour out its blood and cover it with earth" (Lev 17:13) while the *halakhah* says: "With anything that grows plants"; the Torah says: "He writes her a document of divorce" (Deut 24:1) while the *halakhah* says: "[He may write] on anything that was separated from the ground"; the Torah says "With an awl." (*Sifre Deuteronomy* §122)[24]

As I have argued at length elsewhere, this derashah indicates that there are only three extra-scriptural traditions that circumvent Scripture, which is tantamount to asserting that there are only three traditions that stand as an independent source of legal authority.[25] By limiting the number of independent traditions to three, the derashah radically marginalizes the role of this source of authority, acknowledging its legitimacy in only a bare minimum of instances.

In the rabbinic sources associated with Rabbi Akiva, in contrast, we find numerous references to the priority of extra-scriptural traditions over scriptural interpretation. In one *Sifra* passage, the phrase "a bull of the flock" [literally: "a bull the son of the flock," פר בן בקר] in Leviticus 4:4 is explained as a three-year-old bull "in keeping with the words of the sages."[26] The implication is that the Torah is to be interpreted in light of rabbinic dicta. This principle is presented as a sine qua non for proper interpretation in the *Sifra's* discussion of the status of contaminating mold in Leviticus 13, specifically the instruction that when mold appears on a fabric, the material must be burned. Anonymous sages ask Rabbi Eliezer what is to be done if the affection appears on only one stripe of the fabric, and he replies: "I have heard no tradition about this." Since there is no received teaching on this matter, another rabbi, Judah ben Batirah, indicates he will examine the question, and Rabbi Eliezer cautions: "If in order to sustain the words of the sages—yes." After Rabbi Judah offers an argument, Rabbi Eliezer responds: "You are a great sage, for you sustained the words of the sages."[27] Agreement with received tradition is, then, the explicit criterion by which Rabbi Judah ben Batirah's argument is assessed.

Rabbi Judah ben Batirah's argument is not midrashic, but there are passages in which scriptural interpretation is presented as ancillary support for extra-scriptural traditions, as in this exchange between Rabbi Akiva and Rabbi Tarfon from Mishnah *Ohalot*:

Any movable object conveys impurity if it is as thick as an ox-goad. Rabbi Tarfon said: "May I lose my sons if this is not a perverted tradition which the hearer heard wrongly: when a husbandman passed by [a tomb] with the ox-goad over his shoulder and the one end of it overshadowed the tomb, they declare him impure by virtue of the law of the vessels which overshadow a corpse." Rabbi Akiva said: "I will amend [this oral tradition] so that the words of the Sages shall be sustained. Any movable

object conveys uncleanness to him that carries the object if it is as thick as an ox-goad;
and the object conveys the uncleanness to itself whatsoever its thickness, but to other
men and vessels only if it is one handbreadth wide." (*m. 'Ohalot* 16.1)

Rabbinic law recognizes a category known as "tent impurity" or "canopy impurity,"
which occurs when there is an overhang directly above an impure object that "captures"
the object's impurity and transmits it to anyone within the enclosure. The Mishnah
begins with an anonymous statement regarding the minimum size for a movable object
to convey such impurity. Rabbi Tarfon disputes the legitimacy of this tradition, arguing that it was perverted—misremembered or misunderstood—in the course of its
transmission. Rather, the correct ruling refers to the ox-goad, but only in assessing
its breadth, insofar as a herdsman who carries one over his shoulder creates a canopy
of sorts and is thus susceptible to the impurity of a tomb by which he passes. There
are, then, two competing oral traditions that refer to the ox-goad, and Rabbi Tarfon
believes his is correct, while the anonymous statement is a corruption ("the hearer
heard wrong"). Faced with this apparent deadlock, Rabbi Akiva seeks to "amend [this
halakhah] so that the words of the sages shall be sustained," by proposing a third
legal statement that incorporates elements of both the anonymous ruling and Rabbi
Tarfon's tradition—another indication of the status of received traditions in some
tannaitic sources.

Perhaps the most telling statement concerning the topic under discussion is from
Rabbi Yehoshua, one of Rabbi Akiva's rabbinic masters. Leviticus 11:33 states that
everything in an earthenware vessel becomes impure if a dead animal falls into it, but
Rabbi Akiva midrashically interprets "shall be impure" as "shall transmit impurity."
According to Leviticus, if a dead animal falls into a vessel, the vessel becomes impure
with first-level impurity, and a loaf in the vessel contracts second-level impurity. Rabbi
Akiva interprets Leviticus 11:33 as indicating that the second-level impure loaf then
transmits third-level impurity if it comes in contact with another loaf. Upon hearing
this interpretation, Rabbi Yehoshua said: "Who will uncover the dust from your eyes,
Rabbi Yohanan ben Zakkai, for you used to say that a future generation will declare
the third-level loaf pure since it is not scriptural [*she-lo' min ha-torah*]—but your disciple Rabbi Akiva adduced a scriptural prooftext for its impurity, as it is written 'everything inside it shall be impure.'"[28]

In other words, Rabbi Yehoshua invokes his deceased master, Rabbi Yohanan Ben
Zakkai, recalling his fear that the received tradition concerning the transmission of
third-level impurity would be forgotten since "it is not scriptural." But now, Rabbi
Yehoshua continues, Rabbi Akiva has anchored the ruling in Scripture, meaning it
will be maintained by future generations. Nota bene: third-level impurity was known
and accepted in Rabbi Yohanan ben Zakkai's time even though it is not scriptural;
Rabbi Yohanan ben Zakkai's concern was that future generations might not abide by

the ruling in light of its non-scriptural nature. In other words, the *Sifra* lauds Rabbi Akiva as a great interpreter insofar as he is able to support extra-scriptural traditions midrashically.

Taken together, these sources indicate that scholarship has failed to appreciate that tannaitic sources are fundamentally divided on the status of extra-scriptural traditions, though this division has been obscured by the ascendancy of midrashic authority, so much so that it has become axiomatic to think of the rabbis as interpreters of Scripture. This shift is already evident in, inter alia, Rabbi Yohanan ben Zakkai's fear lest "a future generation will declare the third level loaf pure since it is not scriptural." I want to emphasize that he is not concerned that the adherents of oral tradition will waver in their commitment to the ruling, only that "a future generation" will require a midrashic argument. Even to champions of extra-scriptural authority, it was clear that this approach was under threat from a shift toward scriptural interpretation as the dominant and perhaps exclusive religious authority.

That this shift did in fact take place is evident from the Babylonian Talmud's propensity for citing tannaitic legal traditions—then asking *mena hanei milei?* ["whence do we learn these matters?"] and identifying a biblical verse as the putative source for the tannaitic dictum. From a legal-traditional point of view, the Talmud's question is nonsensical. How can you cite the legal teaching of, say, Rabbi Meir, and then ask, "Whence do we know this?" For the Mishnah, the answer is self-evident—it is a legal teaching transmitted by Rabbi Meir. There may be conflicting traditions or questions regarding the fidelity of transmission, but the authority of the tradition as such does not require (nor does the Mishnah generally provide) biblical support.

To assume otherwise—to search for underlying scriptural justification—is to deny implicitly the independent authority of the received dictum and of the broader oral-traditional claims that undergird it. The casual self-evidence with which those Bavli passages set out to uncover the scriptural basis of tannaitic teachings bespeaks a fundamentally scripturalist assumption. Why such an assumption takes root and what effects it has on the internal dynamics of rabbinic law—these are both important questions. For the present, however, I have sought only to demonstrate that even the mechanisms buttressing rabbinic authority were in fact sites of dissent.

NOTES

This essay presents some of the questions that have guided my study of early rabbinic legal hermeneutics, as found in Azzan Yadin, *Scripture as Logos: Rabbi Ishmael and the Origins of Midrash* (Philadelphia: University of Pennsylvania Press, 2004), and *Scripture and Tradition: Rabbi Akiva and the Triumph of Midrash* (Philadelphia: University of Pennsylvania Press, 2015).

1. See H. L. Strack and Günter Stemberger, *Introduction to Talmud and Midrash* (trans. Markus Bockmuehl; Minneapolis: Fortress, 1996), 247–51. For a summary of the distinguishing criteria, see J. N. Epstein, *Prolegomena to Tannaitic Literature* [Hebrew] (Tel Aviv and Jerusalem: Dvir and Magnes Press, 1957), 495–746.

2. The editions used are *Sifre Numbers*, H. S. Horovitz, ed. (Jerusalem: Shalem, 1992; repr. of Leipzig 1917); *Mekhilta de-Rabbi Ishmael*, H. S. Horovitz and I. Rabin, eds. (Jerusalem: Bamberger and Wahrman, 1960; repr. of Frankfurt, 1931); H. Weiss, *Sifra: Commentar zu Leviticus* (Wien: Schlossberg, 1862). These are the fullest collections that have received the lion's share of scholarly attention. Additional legal midrashim are H. S. Horovitz, *Sifre Zutta*, bound with his edition of *Sifre Numbers* (Leipzig: Gustav Fock, 1917; repr. Jerusalem: Shalem, 1992); J. N. Epstein and E. Z. Melamed, *Mekhilta of Rabbi Shimon ben Yohai* (Jerusalem: Mekize Nirdamim, 1956); and, recently, Menahem I. Kahana, *Sifre Zuta on Deuteronomy: Citations from a New Tannaitic Midrash* [Hebrew] (Jerusalem: Magnes, 2002).

3. See the questions raised in Gary Porton, "The Artificial Dispute: Ishmael and 'Aqiva,'" in *Christianity, Judaism and other Greco-Roman Cults: Studies for Morton Smith at Sixty* (ed. Jacob Neusner; Leiden: E. J. Brill, 1975), 18–29; Jay Harris, *How Do We Know This: Midrash and the Fragmentation of Modern Judaism* (Albany: SUNY Press, 1995), 25–72.

4. The phrases, "Rabbi Ishmael midrashim" and "Rabbi Akiva midrashim," are shorthand for "the distinct and recognizable interpretive practices, assumptions, and terms that appear in the legal midrashim associated with these sages, respectively."

5. David Tzvi Hoffmann, *Le-ḥeqer Midreshei ha-Tanna'im* (trans. A. S. Rabinowitz, in *Mesilot le-Torat ha-Tannaim*; Tel Aviv: Carmiel, 1928), 1.

6. There is no full critical edition of the *Sifra*. I cite Isaac Hirsch Weiss, *Sifra: Commentar zu Leviticus* (Wien: Schlossberg, 1862), and MS Assemani 66 (also known as Vatican 66), a facsimile edition of which was published by Louis Finkelstein, *Sifra or Torat Kohanim* (New York: Jewish Theological Seminary, 1956).

7. David Weiss Halivni, *Midrash, Mishnah, and Gemara* (Cambridge: Harvard University Press, 2014), 47–48.

8. The substantive *qabbalah*, which by all accounts should refer to a received tradition, is instead a technical term for the hagiographa. On this, see my "Qabbalah, Deuterōsis, and Semantic Incommensurability: A Preliminary Study," in Ra'anan Boustan, et al., eds., *Envisioning Judaism: Studies in Honor of Peter Schäfer on the Occasion of His Seventieth Birthday* (Tübingen: Mohr Siebeck, 2013), 917–40.

9. Similar pronouncements are made, inter alia, in *m. Yevamot* 16.7; *m. Yadayim* 3.5, 4.2, and 4.3; *m. Gittin* 6.7; *m. Eduyot* 1.6 and 8.7; *m. Zevaḥim* 1.3. The phrase also appears a handful of times in the Tosefta and once in the *Sifra* (*Shemini* parashah 1.33, Weiss 45c [part of *Mekhilta de-Miluim* that is not associated with Rabbi Akiva]).

10. See Martin Jaffee, *Torah in the Mouth: Writing and Oral Tradition in Palestinian*

Judaism 200 BCE–400 CE (Oxford and New York: Oxford University Press, 2001).

11. Josephus Flavius, *Antiquities of the Jews* (trans. William Whiston; *The Works of Josephus*; Peabody: Hendrickson, 1987).

12. Adiel Schremer, "'[T]he[y] Did Not Read in the Sealed Book': Qumran Halakhic Revolution and the Emergence of Torah Study in Second Temple Judaism," in *Historical Perspectives: From the Hasmoneans to Bar Kokhba in Light of the Dead Sea Scrolls* (ed. David Goodblatt, et al.; Leiden: Brill, 2001), 105–26.

13. Joseph Baumgarten, *Studies in Qumran Law* (Leiden: Brill, 1977), 32, n. 78. See also A. Baumgarten, "The Name of the Pharisees," *Journal of Biblical Literature* 102 (1983): 420–22.

14. For a discussion of the Jewish theological context of this dispute, see Yair Furstenberg, "Defilement Penetrating the Body: A New Understanding of Contamination in Mark 7.15," *New Testament Studies* 54 (2008): 176–200.

15. Paul here casts *krateō*—the same verb appears in Mark's polemic against the Pharisee tendency to "hold fast" to the traditions of the elders—as a positive, normative action. See Earl J. Richard, *First and Second Thessalonians* (Sacra Pagina 11; Collegeville: Liturgical Press, 1995), 358.

16. It does not matter for the present discussion whether 2 Thessalonians was composed by Paul or by one of his associates, since it bears witness to the currency of tradition as a theological category regardless.

17. Halivni's position closely tracks that of Rabbi Meir Leibush ben Jehiel Michel Weiser, better known as Malbim (born in nineteenth century Poland). Malbim's works most directly relevant to the present analysis are *Ha-Torah ve-ha-Mitzvah*, a commentary on the Pentateuch, and his essay *Ayelet ha-Shaḥar*, which was published alongside the Leviticus volume of the commentary *Ha-Torah ve-ha-Mitzvah* (Bnei Brak: Mosdot Hasidei Alexander, 2000).

18. See Yitzhak Isaac Halevy Rabinowitz, *Dorot ha-Rishonim* (6 vols.; Frankfurt: M. Slobotzky, 1906).

19. Hanoch Albeck, *Introduction to the Mishnah* (Jerusalem: Mossad Bialik, 1967), 3.

20. David Zvi Hoffmann, *Commentary to Leviticus* (trans. Tzvi Har-Sheffer and Aharon Lieberman; Jerusalem: Mossad Harav Kook, 1966), 5.

21. J. N. Epstein, *Prolegomena to Tannaitic Literature* (Tel Aviv and Jerusalem: Dvir and Magnes, 1957), 511.

22. Thus, David Zvi Hoffmann held that extra-scriptural traditions were adopted in the days of Hillel and Shammai; Zechariah Frankel located the shift in the days of Rabbi Akiva; while A. H. Weiss argued that midrash was replaced by abstract *halachot*, but during the days of Hillel reasserted its priority. See the sources and analysis in Yekutiel Neubauer, "*Halakhah* and *Midrash Halakhah*," in his *Ha-Rambam 'al Divre Soferim* (Jerusalem: Mossad Harav Kook, 1957), 140.

23. See the discussion in Max Weber, *Economy and Society: An Outline of Interpretive*

Sociology (ed. Guenther Roth and Claus Wittich; trans. Ephraim Fischoff, et al.; 2 vols.; New York: Bedminster Press, 1968), 1.9–10.

24. Louis Finkelstein, ed., *Siphre ad Deuteronomium* (New York: Jewish Theological Seminary of America, 1993), 180.

25. Yadin, *Scripture as Logos*, 143–44.

26. *Sifra Ḥovah* pereq 3.1, Weiss 17b; TK 74.

27. *Sifra Tazri'a Nega'im* pereq 16.9, Weiss 69c–d; TK 286), (=*m. Nega'im* 11.7).

28. *Sifra Shemini* parashah 7.12, Weiss 54b; TK 226 (=*m. Soṭah* 5.2).

DISSENTING LITERATURE AND SOCIAL FORMATION IN THE ANTIQUE MEDITERRANEAN

ZACHARY B. SMITH

UTHORITY AND DISSENT are concepts that operate with reference to power—authority holds power, but dissent attempts to negate, neuter, or negotiate power. In this essay, I would like to explore the operation of authority and dissent with reference to power systems and social formation, seen through selected texts from Mediterranean antiquity—Paul of Tarsus's first letter to the Jesus Movement community in Corinth, Cicero's *De Officiis*, Plutarch's *Sayings of Kings and Commanders*, and late antique Christian monasticism. My essential approach to these texts is to read for the kind of persuasive activity in which the creators engaged, either authoritative persuasion or dissenting persuasion. Each category of persuasion functions in different ways to attempt to form readers and the social spaces that readers inhabit. Authoritative persuasion (such as in Paul's writing to the Corinthian followers of Jesus) dominates by imposing the author's ideas on the readers who view the author as an authority. Dissenting persuasive literature, however, is conservative and points to idealized, mythologized past as the model for contemporary social formation. This last point is the key argument of my essay—that dissenting persuasion in the antique Mediterranean is a conservative endeavor.

Seeing dissent as conservative is, to my mind, underappreciated. Shaped in a post-Enlightenment world, we often see dissent as a forward-looking, change-oriented enterprise. Nineteenth century ideas such as liberalism, socialism, or Zionism dissented from historical or contemporary social orders and looked to a future changed from the past. What I read in the antique Mediterranean, however, suggests that pre-Enlightenment dissent looked backward to an ideal society and encouraged the conservation of that social order. While I confine my exploration here to the region and time period of my expertise, the Mediterranean in antiquity, I think this principle applies to other times and places, and applies to other parts of the antique Mediterranean that I do not here explore (e.g., Second Temple or early rabbinical Judaism, as there are far better experts on Judaism in this volume). Thus, I do not mean to suggest that there is only one kind of dissent, but that the conservative dissent of antiquity is something that warrants consideration.

I look at the purpose and process of writing in the antique Mediterranean in my first section, demonstrating that this expensive activity required a compelling motivation. I then briefly examine persuasive literature and persuasion as an activity, adding to the discussion the approaches of power and social formation. My third section is a brief look at a piece of authoritative persuasive literature (Paul of Tarsus's first letter to the Jesus Movement in Corinth) to establish a point of comparison to dissenting persuasive literature. I spend the remainder of the essay demonstrating how dissenting persuasive literature in the antique Mediterranean was a conservative activity that pointed to the past as the model for present social construction.

"Authoritative literature," "dissent literature," and "persuasive literature" are not technical literary genres utilized by scholars for the antique periods of Mediterranean history, nor do I intend here to create new formalized textual categories. Instead, they provide a useful heuristic device for gathering texts that appear to engage in similar kinds of persuasive activity, hold similar relationships to power, and attempt to form social groups along similar lines. I suggest that a useful method for reading historical texts starts with the single question—what change does the author want to see as a result of this text being produced, read, and (if applicable) enacted? Most of what we would call "literature" in classical and late antiquity, regardless of its genre, seeks to persuade the reader or hearer about something. Most frequently, the author intends the reader to make some mental, emotional, or active change as a result of interacting with the text. Whether a biography or a religious/philosophical treatise or even a collection of stories and sayings, authors intended to make a point when they engaged in the expensive enterprise of textual production.

WHY WRITE?

Writing, in antiquity, was a costly activity. In addition to the materials,[1] there was a basic outlay either for education to learn to write for oneself or to hire someone who could write. While Roger Bagnall demonstrated that "there was no necessary link between wealth or officeholding on the one hand and literacy on the other" in late antique Egyptian villages,[2] wealthy, high-classed townspeople were more likely to be literate but also not infrequently hired others to write for them.[3] Learning to write was costly, so unless absolutely necessary (for one's job or because of social standing), most people did not learn it—and even those who did know how to write not infrequently relied on groups of writing professionals to ensure that the documents came out looking and sounding correct.[4]

Outside of writing exercises, receipts, or incidental documents, the production of a text took time, money, and consideration—thus the contents of the text were considered either important enough to preserve or important enough not to entrust to word-of-mouth delivery. The purpose of writing was to create a record—something verifiable, transferable, and persistent. A written product, though, was not simply an unbiased record of information. The decision to write consisted of micro decisions about what details to include, what details to leave out, how to frame the information, what kinds of rhetorical devices to deploy, how long or short the document ought to be, how much of the author's position or self to reveal, how much and what to say explicitly versus implicitly, and what to elide. In short, writing involved a series of considerations revolving around the author and the reader and around what the author intended for the reader to think, believe, feel, or desire after reading the text.

TO PERSUADE

I see persuasion as the primary purpose in producing most texts in antiquity. Authors intended their texts to impact the reader, to make a change in the reader's internal orientation. Not infrequently, such changes in internal orientation could lead to changes in social organization. I follow Blossom Stefaniw, who has made the case for partially abandoning the genre-classification approach to late antique texts. She argued that fruitful work could instead come from examining how texts approach the related topics of making knowledge and making human subjects.[5] By extension, I argue that reading texts from their persuasive perspective gives us insight into the kinds of social groups that the authors desired, sometimes as a function of the kinds of human subjects they wish to form and sometimes in their project of social formation writ large. Authors used texts not just to create new subjects in their desired images but also to form those subjects into social groups that followed certain norms and expectations. In other words, successful texts formed people, people formed groups, and those groups followed patterns outlined by the texts. When we read texts as persuasive literature, it allows us to uncover something of the social orders in which the texts arose and something of the author's desires for social reformation. Writing of letters in antiquity,

Stanley Stowers suggested that "it is more helpful to think of letters in terms of the actions that people performed by means of them" than it is to think about letters simply transmitting information.[6] Writing moves the reader; it is not just a neutral activity intended to spread data.[7]

In this way, I agree with Annemaré Kotzé's assertion that classifying according to genres has more to do with exploring a work's specific purpose than with assigning any technical features to a work. For her (and our) purposes, this lens is especially true of persuasive literature.[8] Where I depart from Kotzé is in adhering to technical ancient genres such as protreptic, and its related category of paraenetic, however modified modern definitions of those genres might be.[9] James Henderson Collins II's work on early Greek protreptics proves useful here, particularly his discussion of genre development.[10] Whereas he conceptualized protreptic as a more concretized genre in later literature, of early protreptic literature he developed a "fluid model of rhetorical genres" that means scholars "are not forced to draw firm lines between explicit and implicit protreptic, external and internal criteria—and then transgress them—because protreptic discourse in the fourth century [BCE] is not yet a genre in form or content; it is rooted in a speaker's objective and shift in attitude."[11] Instead of a technical genre, the speaker/author's goal and desired result, however they appear in the text, define the texts as a protreptic—Collins's view of early protreptics is a better approach for later protreptic literature as well. Abandoning technical classifications, we read instead for persuasion—what kind of people the author wanted to create, what knowledge the author utilized to make those people, and what social order (whether desired, idealized, or actual) those people so persuaded would create.

When reading for persuasion, we must also read for the power position of the speaker/author, either real or perceived (and whether self-perceived or externally perceived), and how that affects their persuasive discourse. I posit paired classifications of persuasive literature, authoritative and dissenting, according to the power capabilities and power positions of the authors. Authoritative literature functions persuasively from a position of actual or perceived power. If the author holds sway over the reader, then his[12] words carry the mark of being desirable for the reader, if only so that the reader will avoid possible sanction or the internalized feelings of fear that might come from the possibility of sanctions. Dissenting persuasion recognizes disparate power dynamics and seeks to make a case in the face of potential sanction, meaning sometimes the dissenting persuasion is covert. Dissenting literature functions persuasively either by trying to present the best possible argument or by appealing to the emotions of the reader. Each kind of persuasion utilizes different methods to make the case for social (or individual) formation based on the kind of power that the author holds in perception or reality.

PERSUADING AUTHORITATIVELY FROM POWER FOR SOCIAL FORMATION

As an example of persuasion from a position of power, I turn to Paul of Tarsus's mid-50s CE letter to the ethnically and religiously mixed Jesus Movement community in the Greek port city of Corinth. The Corinthian Jesus Movement at this time faced a number of fractures—mainly over allegiances to divergent teachers (1 Cor 1–4) and debates over who to include in the community (1 Cor 5–6)—apart from a series of issues that the community itself wrote about to Paul, asking for his guidance.[13] Jews and non-Jews seemed to have common places and options for leadership and liturgy, and this overlap caused problems as competing social and religious expectations mixed in a single community (for example, the dispute over eating meat dedicated to gods or goddesses in 1 Cor 8: 1–11.1).[14] Paul reminded the community early in the letter that he was one of their founders and that he was among the Movement's leaders who knew best the teachings of Jesus.[15] Part of the opening section on unity was Paul's reestablishing himself as an authority to the community and establishing that this letter was authoritative. He then legislated certain matters for the community, with punishment ranging from expulsion from the community (1 Cor 5) to the fracturing of individual relationships with the divine (1 Cor 11:27–32), and then announced that he was sending a series of people who would check up on the community (1 Cor 16:10–12), culminating in Paul himself (1 Cor 16:5–8).

The entire letter addressed problems within the community, most frequently problems of division. The social group was not coherent, and Paul desired close social cohesion. Since some of these fractures appeared along ethnic lines (or along other lines, such as dietary practices, that could closely map to certain ethnic groups), Paul proposed a novel solution—deemphasize the ethnic lines, remove the divisions. He wrote therefore to the Corinthians that entry into the community homogenized them and that "Jew and Greek" were now subordinated by the one community following Jesus of Nazareth, whom Paul and the Corinthian community following Jesus believed to be messiah.[16] He desired a unified social group that embraced a single identity, so he sublimated (in the archaic sense) their previous identities.[17] Paul's reordering the social group to deemphasize ethnic difference is an example of an authoritative text issuing a directive intended to change individual orientation for the purpose of forming a homogenous social group. Because he was (or viewed himself as) an authority to the community, Paul was able to repeatedly direct the readers toward particular behaviors and identities—his authoritative persuasion was direct; it was prescriptive and proscriptive to form the people and form the community.

Paul's letter to the Jesus Movement followers in Corinth also reveals an insidious element of social formation through authoritative persuasive literature. When he told the members of the Jesus Movement community in Corinth to reorient their former ethno-religious identities, it was not a benign act. Telling Greeks that their Greek identity was less important than their new identity as messiah followers while living in a Hellenized Roman city on the isthmus between Athens and Sparta, on the site of what had been a major Greek city—surrounded by Greco-Roman buildings, temples to the Romanized Greek deities, Hellenistic culture, and the Greek language—changed little. Everything around them reminded them of who they were—they were Greeks. For the Jewish members of the Jesus Movement, however, deemphasizing their Jewish identity—the identity of a minority religious and ethnic group in a Greek city—was destructive, taking away their history, culture, kinships, and self-conception.[18] Even if Paul were expanding the border of "Jewish" by incorporating non-Jews into the community of those acceptable to God,[19] the very expansion of the border eliminated the old identity encompassed by "Jewish."

Paul was able to accomplish this rhetorical move that functionally abolished Jewish identity, or at least the prior form of Jewish identity, because of his authority (perceived or actual) within the community. Throughout the letter to the Corinthians Paul sought to eliminate discohesive differences within the community, in some instances differences between the Jews and Greeks; so he called for the replacement of ethnic identities with a religious one centered on the person Jesus. Effectively, his persuasive authoritative discourse on the ground served to highlight the otherness of the Jews living in Corinth, to take the minority identity that was always at risk of deemphasis and move it closer to destruction in the new community.[20] That this reorientation was more than just deemphasizing, but functionally destructive, is supported by another letter Paul of Tarsus wrote to another Jesus Movement community, decisively declaring "there is neither Jew, nor Greek" in the new Jesus Movement identity.[21] The effect of Paul's words demonstrates that authoritative persuasive discourse can be destructive when forming a community.[22]

Authoritative persuasion depends on the author/speaker operating in a position of power to form people and social groups.[23] The individual's power (real or perceived) over others creates the "authority" of authoritative discourse and allows the speaker to attempt direct change. When authors or speakers lack power or are disenfranchised in a particular social context, however, they must rely on other discursive means to attempt to persuade people. Because they speak from a position without power, critiquing the power system (dissenting from the social order) required them to find a common ground from which they could persuade those against whom they dissent. This common ground, in many instances, appears to be an appeal to the past that calls for the conservation of older forms of being or social ordering. Power is the determining factor in whether a piece of persuasive literature is authoritative or dissenting—does the author have the power to tell people what to do?

DISSENTING PERSUASION AND CONSERVATIVE APPEAL TO THE PAST

Dissenting persuasive literature operates in opposition to power from a position of disenfranchisement. Because dissenting literature cannot rely on its own authority, it may appeal instead to an earlier, often idealized form of society in which the author stood (or had the opportunity to stand) in a position of power. A good example of this strategy comes from the death throes of the Roman Republic and the ensuing wars, especially in Marcus Tullius Cicero's last treatise, *De Officiis*, from late 44 BCE.[24] After the assassination of Julius Caesar and with Rome still fractured, Cicero outlined, in this work addressed to Cicero's son, how to work out apparent contradictions between one's moral duties and the things that appear necessary to preserve and enlighten one's life. Cicero focused especially on the conduct of public officials; he clearly disliked Julius Caesar and expressed that dislike openly.[25] For Cicero, Caesar was the improper public official.[26] However, Cicero's other opponent, Mark Antony, received very little open mention. Cicero lamented the collapse of Roman republican (though more an oligarchy than a true republic) political order[27] but did not disparage Mark Antony and the party of Caesar by name. He instead inveighed against "the miscreants with whom the world abounds,"[28] and perhaps he had Mark Antony's machinations in mind when he wrote, "Who fails to see that those promises are not binding which are extorted by intimidation or which we make when misled by false pretenses?"[29] In this treatise that denounces the misdeeds of Caesar and was written while Cicero was delivering the *Philippics* against Mark Antony, Cicero never mentioned Mark Antony by name in *De Officiis*. The *Philippics* praised Octavius, Caesar's heir, by name; *De Officiis* did not mention him. Cicero addressed the proper conduct of Roman public officials but did not name the major living official whom he saw as acting poorly—namely, his opponent Mark Antony.

It seems clear that Cicero wrote *De Officiis* in part as a piece of dissenting persuasive literature against Mark Antony and the collapse of the Republic, meant to appeal to the morality of the Caesarian partisans—Cicero's own opponents.[30] The *Philippics* appealed to Cicero's own senatorial party, attacking Mark Antony and persuading them to oppose him directly. *De Officiis* encouraged dissent among the Caesarians against Mark Antony, and possibly even hedged against a potential power grab by Caesar's newly adopted son, Octavius, by appealing to the Roman idea of duty.[31] To the Caesarian faction, Cicero was not in a position of authority—he was one of the most visible figures in the opposition. The normal levers of power, the ones Cicero had trained to use, were eroding or gone entirely. If he openly criticized Caesar's supporter Mark Antony in *De Officiis*, he would be less likely to persuade the opposing Caesarian faction. So, being in the dissenting position to the Caesarians, he criticized in vague generalities and wrote an entire treatise about weighing moral obligations and the desire to advance one's own position—a pointed, though tacit, indictment of those who no longer fulfilled their moral duties and instead sought only their own gain.

In writing *De Officiis*, Cicero sought to return the levers of power to their previous positions—the Senate, the consulship, the courts—reshaping and returning Roman society to an original (if idealized) republican form. In late 44, Cicero used both kinds of persuasive literature—authoritative and dissenting in the *Philippics* and *De Officiis*, respectively—to persuade people to reject the Caesarians' position (especially in the person of Mark Antony) and restore the social and political order of the Roman Republic. From *De Officiis*, though, we see a key component of dissenting persuasive literature—it appeals to idealizations of some past glory, of a time before the mess of the author's contemporary context. Cicero referenced past authorities as exemplars for contemporary people in ways that were more than just the standard appeals to the authority of antiquity. The past was good and provided a moral model; the present is bad and breaks with the moral model. Past leaders were best and (mostly) followed the best ways to act; present leaders are worst and have broken the norms of behavior. Ideas from the past should be normative, particularly ideas about civil governance and the qualities of leaders, while new ideas that reshape the political reality and the terms of political leadership should be shunned.[32] And, most importantly, past social forms should be preserved, while new social forms go to the dustbin of failed experimentation. This was Cicero's conservative, backward-looking, dissenting persuasion.

Some of Cicero's examples of good and bad moral and political behavior were comparatively recent—in his own lifetime—while other examples were from other periods or other regions. All the examples, though, served the double purpose of demonstrating to Marcus the proper conduct of a public official and how to train for public service, and demonstrating to other readers the reasons (and persons responsible) for the Republic's downfall. Because of his dissenting persuasive task, Cicero inserted certain asides about the collapse of old Rome, the recent civil war, and the future of Rome:

> Let me add, however, that as long as the empire of the Roman people maintained itself by acts of service, not of oppression, wars were waged in the interest of our allies or to safeguard our supremacy; the end of our wars was marked by acts of clemency or by only a necessary degree of severity; the senate was a haven of refuge for

kings, tribes, and nations; and the highest ambition of our magistrates and generals was to defend our provinces and allies with justice and honor. And so our government could be called more accurately a protectorate of the world than an empire.[33]

Marcus had fought under Pompey in the civil war[34] and so knew well, and agreed with, Cicero's position against the Caesarians and how they had led to the collapse of the Roman Republic. So his lament that "in Rome only the walls of her houses remain standing . . . but our republic we have lost forever"[35] appealed more to the sensibilities of others who may not have seen as clearly how Rome had fallen. Cicero continually appealed to the moral sensibilities of his readers, a sensibility shaped by an idealized and preferred past, to convince them of the precarious position of contemporary Rome—a persuasion from the dissenting position to those Caesarians who still might be moved to act (as Brutus once had been) for the good of Rome.

This appeal to the past, I submit, is as destructive (and potentially dangerous) as what we saw in Paul of Tarsus's authoritative discourse that functionally removed only the minority identity and retained the dominant one. Appeal to the past is dangerous because it can make dissent literature an essentially conservative enterprise.

Conservatism is a notoriously difficult concept to define, and I do not here want to wade into the century-long debates about the nature or origins of philosophical, political, or social conservatism. The essence of conservatism, though, lies in retention—retaining a political or social system, retaining a track record over innovation, retaining or conserving the object under consideration in its traditional form (especially in reference to power and authority). In the most common example, conservative politics seeks to retain the levers of power in the hands of people in the social order who have habitually wielded them. One of the mechanisms of conserving power is to retain a particular kind of society, perhaps an older and more homogenized form of the society, in order to limit the number or kind of people able to wield that power. Conservative religious groups seek to retain the religion in an earlier, older form that the practitioners view as more proper. Conservatism looks to the past for a model of how to create the present. Dissent literature, as a conservative enterprise, did the same thing in antiquity. It idolized the past to create an idealized future social form. Frequently we consider dissent as being in the realm of progressive ideations (dissenting to move forward thoughts or social systems), but I suggest that it may in fact be conservative.

We return to Cicero to see this conservative appeal to the past in action. While I contend that his primary antagonists in De Officiis were the Caesarians, Cicero even disagreed with some of his contemporary allies, such as Cato the Younger,[36] who was known for his deeply republican bent and his dedication to Stoic morality. Cicero sanctioned Cato, however briefly, in a discussion of what to do when what is apparently expedient for an individual appears to go against the accepted morality. For an example of how true expediency never violates morality, Cicero felt compelled to look back two hundred years to the First Punic War between Rome and Carthage and the conduct of the Roman general Marcus Atilius Regulus.[37] In brief, the Carthaginians captured Regulus, but then released him to return to Rome under one condition — either he secured the release of captured Carthaginian nobility, or he returned himself to Carthage to face punishment. Upon returning to Rome, he argued that Rome should not release the Carthaginian generals and, according to the story Cicero believed, Regulus returned to Carthage. Regulus argued that his disadvantage was not outweighed by the advantage to Rome of holding a number of upper-classed Carthaginian generals. Cicero compared this to the actions of a number of other people — later than Regulus — who decided to advocate what was to their advantage instead of what was to the advantage of the Republic. In some instances, Cicero praised Regulus for his devotion to the Republic; in others, Cicero praised Regulus for his devotion to the moral order. Cicero wrote of Regulus, "From the many splendid examples in history, therefore, we could not easily point to one either more praiseworthy or more heroic than the conduct of Regulus."[38]

Keeping with his consistent appeal to the past, Cicero's praise of Regulus extended beyond the person and to the nature of his environment, the Roman Republic in the mid-200s BCE. He wrote, "For the fact of his returning [to Carthage] may seem admirable to us nowadays, but in those times he could not have done otherwise. That merit, therefore, belongs to the age, not to the man."[39] Throughout *De Officiis*, Cicero condemned the wrongdoing of public figures and then near the very end praised the past actions of Regulus not as individual actions in themselves but as functions of the kind of social order that Regulus inhabited. The older social order. The better social order. The process of social formation was paramount to Cicero, as he indicated when he wrote a little earlier, "This, then, ought to be the chief end of all men, to make the interest of each individual and of the whole body politic identical. For if the individual appropriates to selfish ends what should be devoted to the common good, all human fellowship will be destroyed."[40]

Under the guise of a treatise to his son — and training his son was partly, but only partly, what Cicero intended — Cicero wrote his *De Officiis* as a piece of dissenting literature that attacked the bad conduct of his contemporary public figures by a conservative appeal to the past. That he did not mention Mark Antony, even though he wrote the treatise while delivering his *Philippics* against Mark Antony, suggests that Cicero's secondary audience was people in the Caesarian faction whom he considered persuadable. To openly attack Mark Antony would make them unlikely to listen. By appealing to the better order of the older age, Cicero invited the comparison and suggested to the reader that what they saw in the immediate aftermath of the Roman Civil War did not match the Roman ideals. This is the heart of the conservative enterprise of dissenting literature.

Two additional brief examples illustrate my argument that dissenting persuasion was conservative in antiquity. The first, from Greek literature, is Plutarch's *Sayings of Kings and Commanders*,[41] a collection of sayings written to the Roman emperor Trajan—if we take the introductory letter as genuine—who ruled between 98 and 117 CE.[42] Plutarch wrote to Trajan that the words of an individual, more than his actions, reveal best his nature.[43] And so Plutarch wrote a collection of sayings by great military and political leaders from the past—a collection in which Plutarch selectively omitted some sayings that he included in other sayings texts.[44] The act of omission suggests that Plutarch intended his *Sayings of Kings* to serve a purpose beyond simply offering a compendium of good ideas. Plutarch intended these sayings to form Trajan and his leadership by pointing him to the idealized leaders of the past whose words should shape the actions of Emperor Trajan, actions that would form societies. Hence Plutarch called these leaders people worth remembering.[45]

What Plutarch would have Trajan remember of these leaders was their moral character, prowess in administration, wisdom, and abilities leading armies—in short, the ways that leaders from the past formed their societies. While Plutarch spent the majority of the *Sayings* quoting from Greek and Persian leaders across the centuries, he ended with sayings from the Roman Republic and from Julius Caesar and Caesar Augustus, the transitional leaders into the Roman Empire. The very last saying that Plutarch included found Piso carefully building a sturdy house, leading Caesar Augustus to draw a comparison between a well-built house and the eternality of Rome—by building well, Piso suggested a belief in Rome's perpetuity and helped guarantee that perpetuity by building something to last.[46] This final apophthegm holds the key to interpreting how Plutarch wanted Trajan to remember the leaders he recorded in the *Sayings of Kings*—by emulating their wisdom, morality, and leadership, Trajan would ensure the perpetuity of the Roman Empire and the Roman social order by building an orderly house.

Plutarch did not appeal to any philosophical arguments for building the solid Roman house. Instead, he appealed to examples from the past, asking Trajan to repeat the past to ensure a good present and future. That Plutarch may have written from a position of dissent comes from reading the opening dedication, in which Plutarch wrote that biographies of leaders, such as his, required considerable time to extract the wise words of leaders from the morass of their actions and the activities surrounding them. Since extensive citations take too much time, Plutarch produced a summary of the words of leaders that could cut to the heart of what Plutarch desired Trajan to learn about leadership in the service of social formation or building the Roman house into perpetuity.[47] There was clearly something about Trajan's conduct that Plutarch desired his biographies of the Roman emperors and his *Sayings* to correct; Plutarch is thus in the dissenting position regarding Trajan's leadership. We cannot be entirely sure about the details of Plutarch's dissent, but his appeal to the past is the form that his dissenting persuasion took.

Perhaps Trajan's war against the Parthian Empire, expanding the Roman Empire to its farthest eastern point and attempting a point even further, was a point of contention for Plutarch. Plutarch opened his section of sayings by Alexander with an apophthegm that finds Alexander as a boy lamenting his father's many victories as leaving him nothing to conquer when he grows up: "What does it help . . . if I have much but achieve nothing?"[48] The point is that expansion and possession, for their own sakes, are not desirable. This saying, and perhaps the whole *Sayings*, could be read in Trajan's context as a pointed referendum on territorial overreach at the expense of management. Plutarch may have written his sayings text in part from a position of dissent, wishing Trajan to refocus his military and political attention and ambitions on the empire he had instead of expanding the borders north and east. Indeed, many of the sayings focus on political administration, highlighting one of the forms of leadership that Plutarch emphasized to Trajan.

My final, and briefest, example comes from fifth century monastic Christianity, during which the religion found itself fracturing under the weight of determining exact beliefs regarding the complicated nature of the Christian God.[49] One group of people within Christianity, the monks, seemed immune to these debates.[50] There was ample room in the deserts of Egypt, Judea, and Syria for varieties of opinion. Some monks believed strongly one way or another regarding doctrines, but the majority seemed to have taken a "live and let live" approach to the broader debates. This attitude worked until Christian leaders began deploying uneducated monks as brute force troops against their opponents and started to force the monks onto sides in the debates. An institution that had been largely immune to the fighting, unified in a collective desire to live apart from mainstream society, was now embroiled in the controversies. Monasteries split along ideological lines; monks exiled and excommunicated each other; monks used violent force against each other. The previous ideal of monastic unity broke.[51]

Enter an anonymous author in the late fifth century who wrote a text of collected sayings ostensibly to teach people how to be monks in this highly charged atmosphere—teaching that relied on an appeal to the past. I argue elsewhere that part of his purpose was to separate monks from the controversies of mainstream Christianity and return them to their unified state of common ascetic practice. The author makes this argument by appealing to the past forms of monasticism and by highlighting them as the better forms. Some sayings speak about the former virtue of monks, arguing that fifth century monks are vastly inferior by comparison. The text tacitly attacks bishops and priests, the authorities in mainstream Christianity, by suggesting that they hold no authority over monks or, even worse, are morally inferior to monks. Given the increasing power of bishops in a religion now married to Roman imperial might, the author could not directly attack the imperially backed Christian authorities. So he painted them as inferior by comparison and painted his contemporary monastic society as inferior to the previous iteration in which monks were more unified in practice and less troubled by bishops arguing about the nature of God.[52] The author took a conservative rhetorical turn, desiring to return monasticism to an idealized earlier form in which bishops did not interfere and pull apart the (perhaps fictious) unity and cohesion of the monastic life. He dissented from contemporary monastic disharmony and, blaming bishops, advocated a tacit return to earlier and seemingly superior social forms.

CONCLUSION

From these three examples of dissent literature (Cicero, Plutarch, and fifth century monks) from classical and late antiquity, spanning approximately 550 years, and the example of authoritative literature from the mid-first century CE (Paul's letter to Corinth), we see that persuasion was a major goal of literature in these periods. The purpose of this literature was not just to change people or minds but also to change how societies were formed. Moreover, the examination of select pieces of dissent literature suggests that dissent in the Roman and Byzantine world was a conservative enterprise intended to return society to a previous iteration or at least to the author's idealized previous iteration.[53]

So, what do we do with this understanding of authoritative and dissenting literature? Authoritative literature persuades from a position of actual or perceived power. Dissenting literature can persuade by appealing to a mythologized, idealized past.[54] I want to suggest that these two ways of looking at texts—any kind of text, not just written texts—helps us decode social situations and social formations, and the dispositions of the parties producing and using the texts, in all periods of history. What I hope this essay provides is a different framework for approaching texts to understand how the authors desired to form social groups and that these persuasive texts operate with differing toolsets depending on the author's position as authoritative or dissenting. Reading for persuasion helps decode discourse about social formation by looking at the kind of persuasion deployed. Finally, I offer an initial suggestion about dissent being, counterintuitively, a conservative enterprise. This approach to dissent can help us reframe how we understand dissenting desires for social formation, a formation that is the heart of textual creation in antiquity.

ACKNOWLEDGMENTS

I thank Leonard Greenspoon for this opportunity and for his patience; Ron Simkins (Creighton University), Sherri Brown (Creighton University), and Joel Gereboff (Arizona State University) for conversations that helped me work through my ideas; and Margaret Gurewitz Smith (Bellevue University) for her suggestions and comments and for reading an initial draft of this essay.

NOTES

1. There is some debate on exactly how much the materials cost. Taking papyrus as an example, see T. C. Skeate, "Was Papyrus Regarded as 'Cheap' or 'Expensive' in the Ancient World?" *Aegyptus* 75 (1995): 75–93. While it is unclear exactly how much a roll or sheet of papyrus cost in antiquity, Skeate's research suggests that it was not overly expensive. Costs grew considerably with parchment, but even papyrus was frequently wiped clean and reused (see Chrysi Kotsifou, "Books and Book Production in the Monastic Communities of Byzantine Egypt," in *The Early Christian Book* [ed. William E. Klingshirn and Linda Safran; Washington, DC: Catholic University of America Press, 2007], 48–66, at 60–63). In any case, Kotisfou claimed that "the prohibitive cost of books encouraged extensive borrowing among readers" (54)—this cost, in my opinion, likely had more to do with the hiring of scribal talent to produce the books than the cost of materials.

2. Roger S. Bagnall, *Egypt in Late Antiquity* (Princeton: Princeton University Press, 1993), 240–44, quotation on 243.

3. Ibid., 246–47, 255–56.

4. Ibid., 258–59.

5. Blossom Stefaniw, "Knowledge in Late Antiquity: What Is It Made of and What Does It Make?" *Studies in Late Antiquity* 2:3 (2018): 266–93.

6. Stanley K. Stowers, *Letter Writing in Greco-Roman Antiquity* (Library of Early Christianity 5; Philadelphia: Westminster Press, 1986), 15, see also 22–23.

7. Incidental texts, such as receipts or some writing exercises, may be an exception here.

8. Annemaré Kotzé, *Augustine's Confessions: Communicative Purpose and Audience* (Supplements to Vigiliae Christianae 71; Leiden: Brill, 2004), 45–51, esp. 49–51.

9. Ibid., 52–58.

10. James Henderson Collins II, *Exhortations to Philosophy: The Protreptics of Plato, Isocrates, and Aristotle* (New York: Oxford University Press, 2015), 1–42.

11. Ibid., 33. See also Mark D. Jordan, "Ancient Philosophic Protreptic and the Problem of Persuasive Genres," *Rhetorica: A Journal of the History of Rhetoric* 4 (1986): 309–33, esp.

330: "One defines in terms of a desired effect in a definite situation. Protreptics are just those works that aim to bring about the firm choice of a lived way to wisdom—however different the form of those works and their notions of wisdom might be."

12. Authors in antiquity were overwhelmingly men, so I use the gendered masculine as shorthand for ancient authors more broadly.

13. Paul explicitly references this request in 1 Corinthians 7:1.

14. See also L. L. Welborn's argument that, according to Paul, the Jesus Movement group in Corinth ought to represent an alternative political-social ordering to what was present in Corinth ("How 'Democratic' Was the Pauline *Ekklēsia*? An Assessment with Special Reference to the Christ Groups of Roman Corinth," *New Testament Studies* 65 [2019]: 289–309), though the occasion of Paul's writing was the community's failing to live up to that expectation in some instances.

15. See, e.g., 1 Corinthians 1:1, 1:14–17, 2:1–2, 3:5–11, 4:15–17, 11:1–2. Others have argued alternatively that Paul was not always writing from a position of authority but was instead seeking to establish that authority. See Antoinette Clark Wire, *The Corinthian Women Prophets: A Reconstruction through Paul's Rhetoric* (Minneapolis, Fortress Press, 1990), 1–11; and Elisabeth Schüssler Fiorenza, *Rhetoric and Ethics: The Politics of Biblical Studies* (Minneapolis: Fortress Press, 1999), 169–70. Whether Paul of Tarsus had actual power or just self-perceived power, he wrote from a position of authority—this is what defines his discourse as authoritative.

16. "For just as the body is one and has many members, and all the members of the body, though many, are one body, so it is with Christ. For in the one Spirit we were all baptized into one body—Jews or Greeks, slaves or free—and we were all made to drink of one Spirit. Indeed, the body does not consist of one member but of many" (1 Cor 12:12–14, NRSV). Καθάπερ γὰρ τὸ σῶμα ἕν ἐστιν καὶ μέλη πολλὰ ἔχει, πάντα δὲ τὰ μέλη τοῦ σώματος πολλὰ ὄντα ἕν ἐστιν σῶμα, οὕτως καὶ ὁ Χριστός· καὶ γὰρ ἐν ἑνὶ πνεύματι ἡμεῖς πάντες εἰς ἓν σῶμα ἐβαπτίσθημεν, εἴτε Ἰουδαῖοι εἴτε Ἕλληνες εἴτε δοῦλοι εἴτε ἐλεύθεροι, καὶ πάντες ἓν πνεῦμα ἐποτίσθημεν. Καὶ γὰρ τὸ σῶμα οὐκ ἔστιν ἓν μέλος ἀλλὰ πολλά (1 Cor 12:12–14, NA27).

17. As Denise Kimber Buell discussed in *Why This New Race*, racial and ethnic identities were somewhat fluid, but early Christians (her book primary explores the post-Pauline era) did define themselves more or less as a group that replaced other markers of distinction (*Why This New Race: Ethnic Reasoning in Early Christianity* [New York: Columbia University Press, 2005]). Much of what she argued may apply to Paul, especially in her summary: "Early Christian universalizing claims can be fruitfully understood in terms of local attempts to negotiate and construct collective identities in a complex socio-rhetorical landscape. In depicting Christianness as the universal ideal of humanity, early Christians often do so by speaking of Christians as a people distinct from other kinds of peoples" (Ibid., 164). While her exploration in this book

is post-Pauline, we may say similar things about Paul's attempts in 1 Corinthians to make Christianity a universal, and exclusivizing, identity.

18. On the perils of maintaining Jewishness in Hellenized regions, see Victor Tcherikover, *Hellenistic Civilization and the Jews* (Philadelphia: Jewish Publication Society of America, 1959; repr. Peabody: Hendrickson Publishers, 1999) 296–332, 344–77.

19. See John M. G. Barclay, *Jews in the Mediterranean Diaspora: From Alexander to Trajan (323 BCE–117 CE)* (Berkeley: University of California Press, 1999), 387–94; Denise Kimber Buell and Caroline Johnson Hodge, "The Politics of Interpretation: The Rhetoric of Race and Ethnicity in Paul," *Journal of Biblical Literature* 123 (2004): 235–51.

20. If Louis H. Feldman was correct about the success of Jews gaining converts or sympathizers (*Jew & Gentile in the Ancient World: Attitudes and Interactions from Alexander to Justinian* [Princeton: Princeton University Press, 1993], 288–382), this may have been one reason for Paul's deemphasis of ethnic or religious identity and his emphasizing the newer identity of Jesus-follower—he was competing against religion and cult for the bodies and minds of his people, including competing against other Jewish groups in the Diaspora (see also Barclay, *Jews in the Mediterranean*, 381–95, esp. 385–89).

21. "There is no longer Jew or Greek, there is no longer slave or free, there is no longer male and female; for all of you are one in Christ Jesus" (Gal 3:28, NRSV). οὐκ ἔνι Ἰουδαῖος οὐδὲ Ἕλλην, οὐκ ἔνι δοῦλος οὐδὲ ἐλεύθερος, οὐκ ἔνι ἄρσεν καὶ θῆλυ· πάντες γὰρ ὑμεῖς εἷς ἐστε ἐν Χριστῷ Ἰησοῦ (Gal 3:28, NA27). I disagree slightly with Denise Kimber Buell and Caroline Johnson Hodge's reading of Paul in Galatians 3 ("The Politics of Interpretation," 235–51). They argued that Paul reoriented "gentiles" or "Greeks" into an ethnic identity that preserved their previous distinctiveness while also creating new kinships in the community that tied them to Jewish (whom the authors retranslate as "Judean") community members. The result, according to Kimber Buell and Johnson Hodge, is that ethnic identities are not eliminated by Christian identity but that Christianity modifies that ethnicity (at least for the Greeks). Alain Badiou similarly argued that the universalizing impulse in Paul did not remove the reality of human particularities, nor did Paul intend it to (*Saint Paul: The Foundation of Universalism* [trans. Ray Brassier; Cultural Memory in the Present; Stanford: Stanford University Press, 2003], esp. 98–111). While they may be correct, all three seem not to recognize that the result was that the previous ethnic identity ceased to exist—in effect, the previous ethnic identity was destroyed in favor of the newly reoriented identity (Christian). Paul did use what Kimber Buell termed "ethnic reasoning" in order to define the Christian group, but I contend that that reasoning damaged the previous ethnic identities and that the most damaged in the Corinthian context was the minority identity. After modification, the old ethnic form was no more. This view

is part of the line taken by Daniel Boyarin (*A Radical Jew: Paul and the Politics of Identity* [Berkeley: University of California Press, 1994]).

22. Daniel Boyarin argued in his book *Border Lines* that the distinctions between "Judaism" and "Christianity" in the early centuries of the common era were imposed and that there was not a natural progression of Christianity away from Judaism (*Border Lines: The Partition of Judaeo-Christianity* [Divinations: Rereading Late Ancient Religion; Philadelphia: University of Pennsylvania Press, 2004]). Part of the dissolution involved defining who was and who was not considered authoritative in the diverging intellectual traditions, as well as which ideas were considered authentic to the expression of each religious movement, often in opposition to a constructed version of the "other" religious group (see, e.g., ibid., 37–86). Thus the formation of Christianity and Judaism as distinctive traditions may be considered double-destructive—destroying the actual in order to construct the counterpoint against which one would argue and in that argument outlining the borders so strongly that other possibilities could not exist in the newly defined territory.

23. Helpful here are Michel Foucault's 1978 lectures about the techniques deployed by systems (including political and religious) to ensure human subjects operated in specific ways within those systems, ways designed to protect and perpetuate the systems (Michel Foucault, *Security, Territory, Population: Lectures at the Collège de France, 1977–1978* [ed. Michel Senellart; trans. Graham Burchell; New York: Picador, 2007]). He discussed how "counter-conduct" arose as a way to work against the systems designed to direct human conduct (Ibid., 194–204). Systems for conducting human life depend on the deployment of power on the subjects being conducted—the power to tell people how to behave. Foucault explored this deployment of power to conduct human life in two realms, institutional Christianity and political governing, and in each there was an unequal power distribution that created authority to force the adherence of the majority by the minority. The authority of the minority forced the creation of subjects and societies comprised by the majority. Inherent in creating one system of behavior is the automatic negation of other behaviors, resulting in the creation of counter-conducts that encompass some part of those other possible behaviors. The people and community formed by operations of power to control conduct destroys the other forms of being a subject or subjects in community—power forces compliance, negating or making dangerous any forms of noncompliance. Counter-conduct, to use Foucault's term, is the dissent to the systems of power that engage authoritative discourse and actions and attempt to destroy other ways of conducting selves.

24. Marcus Tullius Cicero, *De Officiis* (C. Atzert, ed., *M. Tulli Ciceronis scripta quae manserunt omnia*, vol. 48 [Leipzig: Teubner, 1963]). Translations are composite

of my own edits to Walter Miller, *Cicero: De Officiis* (Loeb Classical Library; New York: Macmillan, 1921).

25. In this way, Cicero broke from his earlier friendliness with Caesar and his party, the relationship quickly souring as Caesar moved toward kingship after defeating Pompey and Cato; see Thomas N. Mitchell, *Cicero: The Senior Statesman* (New Haven: Yale University Press, 1991), 236–88.

26. E.g., *De Off.* 1.8.26, 1.14.43, 2.7.23.

27. Ibid., 3.1.2.

28. Ibid., 3.1.3 (*sceleratorum quibus omnia redundant*).

29. Ibid., 1.10.32 (*Iam illis promissis standum non esse quis non uidet quae coactus quis metu quae deceptus dolo promiserit.*)

30. Andrew R. Dyck argued that Cicero wrote for both his son and the Roman youth who would undertake public life (*A Commentary on Cicero,* De Officiis [Ann Arbor: University of Michigan Press, 1996], 10–16, 29–36). I add that Cicero seemed also to consider his political opponents a secondary audience, attempting to persuade them back to what he considered the correct social order.

31. Octavian eventually allied fully with Mark Antony and M. Lepidus, ending the Republic and forming an official, legal triumvirate of dictators in late 43 BCE (see Mitchell, *Cicero*, 317–24). The triumvirs ordered Cicero's execution, which took place on 7 December 43 BCE.

32. Even Cicero's condemnations of others from history followed a similar pattern—they were condemned because they broke with the old or ideal (moral) models.

33. *De Off.* 2.8.26–27 (*Verum tamen quam diu imperium populi Romani beneficiis tenebatur non iniuriis bella aut pro sociis aut de imperio gerebantur exitus erant bellorum aut mites aut necessarii regum populorum nationum portus erat et refugium senatus nostri autem magistratus imperatores que ex hac una re maximam laudem capere studebant si prouincias si socios aequitate et fide defendissent. Itaque illud patrocinium orbis terrae uerius quam imperium poterat nominari.*).

34. See *De Off.* 2.13.45. On the civil war, including Cicero's own complicated involvement and Caesar's rise as a despot and assassination, see Mitchell, *Cicero*, 236–72.

35. *De Off.* 2.8.29 (*parietes modo urbis stant et manent . . . rem uero publicam penitus amisimus*).

36. Ibid., 3.22.88.

37. Ibid., 3.26.99–30.110.

38. Ibid., 3.30.110 (*Quare ex multis mirabilibus exemplis haud facile quis dixerit hoc exemplo aut laudabilius aut praestantius.*).

39. Ibid., 3.31.111 (*Nam quod rediit nobis nunc mirabile uidetur illis quidem temporibus aliter facere non potuit. Itaque ista laus non est hominis sed temporum.*).

40. Ibid., 3.6.26 (*Ergo unum debet esse omnibus propositum ut eadem sit utilitas unius-cuiusque et uniuersorum quam si ad se quisque rapiet dissoluetur omnis humana consortio.*).

41. Plutarch, *Sayings of Kings and Commanders* (ed. Wilhelm Nachstädt, *Plutarchi Moralia* 2: 1–109 [1935. Leipzig: Teubner, 1971]).

42. While there has been some debate over Plutarch's authorship of the *Sayings*, I take them as likely genuine. Apart from the contents and theme fitting with Plutarch's other writings, there appears to be an impulse in the first through third centuries CE to collate the sayings of important figures—other examples include the Christian gospels, Diogenes Laertius, and *Pirke Avot*.

43. *Moralia* 172C–D.

44. For example, see the five dozen additional sayings for Agesilaus the Great in the *Sayings of Spartans* (Ibid., 208B–215A) compared to the dozen Agesilaus sayings in *Sayings of Kings* (Ibid., 109F–191D).

45. Ibid., 172E.

46. Ibid., 208A.

47. Ibid., 172D–E.

48. Ibid., 179D (τί δ' ὄφελος . . . ἐὰν ἔχω μὲν πολλὰ πράξω δὲ μηδέν); translation my own.

49. At a series of meetings between 325 and 451 CE, Christianity established particular doctrines about God that some leaders considered unacceptable. Those who did not agree to the new, somewhat sui generis ideas were cut off from the "mainstream" communities or, in the worst cases, exiled.

50. Foucault saw early Christian ascetics as an example of counter-conduct (*Security, Territory*, 204–8).

51. Examine, for example, the *Life of Antony* compared to the *Epistles* of Antony—in the former, the episcopal author Athanasius constructed an Antony who cared deeply about correct belief, whereas the letters suggest an Antony who gave less thought to such things. See Samuel Rubenson, *The Letters of St. Antony: Monasticism and the Making of a Saint* (Minneapolis: Fortress Press, 1995); and David Brakke, *Athanasius and Asceticism* (Baltimore: Johns Hopkins University Press, 1998). On monastic desire to remain out of Christian conflicts more broadly, see William Harmless, "Desert Silence: Why the *Apophthegmata Patrum* is Reticent about Christology" (appendix to *Augustine on Heart and Life: Essays in Memory of William Harmless, S.J.*; ed. John J. O'Keefe and Michael Cameron; http://moses.creighton.edu/JRS/toc /SS15.html). For an overview of some of the conflicts and some of the violence, see Zachary B. Smith, *Philosopher-Monks, Episcopal Authority, and the Care of the Self: The* Apophthegmata Patrum *in Fifth-Century Palestine* (Instrumenta Patristica and Mediaevalia 80; Turnhout: Brepols, 2018), 36–47.

52. Smith, *Philosopher-Monks*.

53. In at least Cicero's case, one may even trace his conservatism to his political patrons, who desired to maintain control over the Republic in the hands of a very few powerful people (see Thomas N. Mitchell, *Cicero: The Ascending Years* [New Haven: Yale University Press, 1979], 10–51).

54. A good overview of appeals to the past in Roman literature at the end of the Republic and the beginning of the Empire may be found in Andrew Wallace-Hadrill, *Rome's Cultural Revolution* (Cambridge, UK: Cambridge University Press, 2008), 213–58. Wallace-Hadrill demonstrates how both the republicans and Augustus appealed to the past to support their arguments about the present and future governance of Rome.

WHEN THE MEMORY OF DAVID IS NOT ENOUGH TO AUTHENTICATE THE TEMPLE IN JERUSALEM

JOEL GEREBOFF

T HE TEMPLE IN Jerusalem has served over the ages as a primary point of importance in Jewish thought and life. The Temple Mount as well bears significance
in both Islamic and Christian traditions, though with quite different meanings
than Jews ascribe to it. As is true for many groups, the origins of a sacred site, including
reports about the efforts of founding figures, give rise to diverse and contested accounts
that in turn connect to the concerns of their authors. The connection of King David
to the actual building of the Temple in Jerusalem is described somewhat differently
already in diverse biblical texts. Although traditions in the Deuteronomistic History
(2 Sam 7, 1 Kgs 8) make clear that Solomon will be and was the person fully responsible for the construction of the Temple, several traditions in the Chronicler already
give David credit for having procured some of the building materials, devised the plans
for the Temple, and appointed its various officiants.

Rabbinic sources similarly assign in varying ways a greater role to David. One tradition appears with slightly different endings and most importantly with two different
descriptions of how David played a role in the ceremony for dedicating the Temple.
In one version, found in the Babylonian Talmud, *Midrash on Psalms*, and other late
midrashim (*Numbers Rabbah*), when Solomon sought to bring the ark into the Temple,
he was unable to do so as the gates of the Temple would not open. Citing and interpreting 2 Chronicles 6:42, this midrash relates that upon invoking *chasdei david* [God's
kindness for David or, alternatively translated, David's good deeds], the gates immediately opened and the ark was successfully emplaced in the Temple. In some versions of
this midrash, citing the next portion of the biblical text, 2 Chronicles 7:1, fire descended
from heaven and consumed the offerings upon the altar. In several studies, Esther Menn
explores how *Midrash on Psalms* includes this midrash along with a large number of

others that serve together to more closely connect the Temple in Jerusalem with David.[1] In some instances, these midrashic comments serve to explain Psalm 30:1, a *mizmor* for the dedication of the House (the Temple) for/by/of David [*mizmor shir chanukat habayit ledavid*]. A different version of this midrash, appearing in three late midrashic texts (dated for their redaction from the late sixth to the ninth centuries)—*Pesiqta Rabbai, Ecclesiastes Rabbah, Exodus Rabbah*—asserts that the fire descended only when David was actually present in the Temple either by the bringing in of his coffin or his revival and attendance at the event. Thus the invoking of David's memory is not seen as sufficient to authenticate the Temple of Solomon and allow for it to function.

This essay explores the background behind these midrashim. Although previous scholarship has offered explanations for the reason for critiquing Solomon and accentuating the positive impact of the invoking of the memory of David, no one has focused on the motif of David's actual presence either in the form of his bones or his actual self. I correlate these traditions with developments in the Byzantine context of the dates of the documents in which these sources appear. My sense is that in part we can see here a development of ideas about relics, an idea attested in several other rabbinic sources that describe either the still-living corpses of rabbis or the coffin of Joseph as contributing to miraculous occurrences.

In addition, the increased if not initial practice of visiting graves of past individuals by Jews to seek their intervention—for example the tomb of the Patriarchs in Hebron—is also first mentioned in sources dating from the period of the composition of these midrashic documents. This particular connection of David's presence at the time of the dedication of the most important Jewish building, the Holy Temple in Jerusalem, may have been formulated in relation to a number of Christian accounts from the fourth century onward that comment on the Temple of Solomon and connect Christian rituals and places to it. In this regard, authenticating the Temple by connecting it more directly with David emerges from both internal Jewish conflicts and those with emergent and ascendant Christianity of the post-Constantinian era.

BIBLICAL TEXTS ON THE DEDICATION OF THE TEMPLE

First Kings and 2 Chronicles provide different accounts of the ceremonies related to the dedication of the Temple. The version in 1 Kings 8:1–66 consists of several sections and is a complex and composite text. It begins with a section (1 Kgs 8:1–9) reporting the assembly of the participants and the procession that ends with the placing of the ark under the wings of the Cherubim in the Temple itself. It (1 Kgs 8:10–13) proceeds to report that Solomon blesses the whole people, declaring that God has fulfilled all the promises made to his father, David, including that his son would build the Temple. Solomon then offers a long prayer and supplication to God (1 Kgs 8:14–21). The narrative (1 Kgs 8:22–53) next relates Solomon's blessing of the assembled group and concludes (1 Kgs 8:54–66) with comments that after eight days all returned to their homes "joyful and glad of heart over all the goodness [*hatovah*] that the Lord had shown to His servant David and His people Israel." According to this narrative, the bringing of the ark into the Temple proceeded along smoothly without any impediments.

The version of these events in 2 Chronicles differs in various ways from this account, but again Solomon is able to bring in the ark without any complications. As noted above, Chronicles assigns a far greater role to David in the planning of the Temple than does the Deuteronomistic version.[2] Here I focus on the conclusion of the narrative. In this version of the events of the dedication, Solomon's long prayer ends (2 Chr 6:40–42) with the following statements: "Now My God, may Your eyes be open and Your ears attentive to prayer from this place and now, Advance, O Lord God, to your resting place, You and Your mighty Ark. Your priests, O Lord God, are clothed in triumph; Your loyal ones will rejoice in [Your] goodness. O Lord God do not reject your anointed one, remember the good deeds of Your Servant David [*zakhrah chasdei David avadekha*]."

In this account Solomon prays that God bring his ark to its resting place, though previously (2 Chr 5:7–10) the narrative stated that the ark already had been brought into the Temple. This seeming contradiction forms a basis for the rabbinic midrashim related to the dedication of the Temple. In addition, here Solomon explicitly prays that God will remember *chasdei David* [David's good deeds, or alternatively, God's kindness to David]. By contrast, I Kings relates that the people returned home filled with joy because of the goodness [*tovah*] that God had shown to David. The Chronicler's version also concludes in a different manner as it refers in 2 Chronicles 7:1 to the descent of the fire from heaven upon the altar. First Kings had made no mention of the fire. The midrashim, to which we now turn, combine in varying ways the emplacement of the ark and the descent of the fire and report that these events did not occur without difficulty at the ceremony of dedicating the Temple, difficulties that were overcome only through either invoking the merits of David or having him physically present at the dedication.[3]

RABBINIC TEXTS ON THE DEDICATION OF THE TEMPLE

We examine two different versions of the rabbinic description of the dedication of the Temple, each appearing in several different documents. In analyzing these texts, we face the challenge of dating rabbinic sources. In general, while attributions of sayings may indicate the date of the formulation of a comment, at present most scholarship dates

sources more conservatively according to the proposed time of redaction of a particular rabbinic midrashic "document." Moreover, determining when a given document
was redacted is also subject to dispute. In many cases these works developed over centuries with various types of revisions made over time, over centuries. Much contemporary analysis explores how the redactional context of a saying or narrative may have
reshaped the tradition to align with the larger concerns of the redactional unit as a
whole and at times of the document itself.

The texts we examine appear in sources generally dated somewhere between the
sixth through the ninth centuries. I do not attempt to trace the development of these
traditions, nor the relationships among them. For my purposes I will treat them as
connected to these centuries and focus on how they involve David in the dedication. After briefly examining these midrashic accounts, I propose factors that may
account for them and how these relate in part to efforts to underscore the importance
of the Temple in Jerusalem, even in a period long after the destruction of the Second
Temple in 70 CE.

Similar versions of the midrashim appear in the Babylonian Talmud and in *Midrash
on Psalms*, works coming from quite different contexts, Babylonia and Palestine, and
slightly different time periods. Although the dates of redaction of these works are not
settled, the sixth to seventh centuries are most likely for the Talmud and as late as the
thirteenth century for the *Midrash on Psalms*, though most scholars propose a stage of
redaction by the eighth century.[4] In this version, only after invoking *chasdei david*—
a phrase, as already noted, that may be translated as "the good deeds of David," or as some
commentators suggest "God's good actions for David"—is Solomon able to conclude
the dedication of the Temple. I first cite the version from the Babylonian Talmud.

BABYLONIAN SHABBAT 30A

A. Another interpretation of "Then I accounted those who died long since more
fortunate than those who are still living" (Eccl 4:2) is in accordance with what Rav
Yehudah said that Rav said: "What is the meaning of that which is written, 'Show
me a sign of your favor, that my enemies may see it and be ashamed' (Ps 86:17).

B. "David prayed before the Holy One, blessed be He, 'Sovereign of the Universe,
forgive me for that sin [with Bathsheba].' He said to him, 'It is forgiven.' He said to
him, 'Show me a sign in my lifetime.' He said to him, 'In your lifetime I will not make
it known; in the lifetime of Solomon your son I will make it known.'

C. "When Solomon built the Holy Temple, he sought to bring the [Holy] Ark (*aron*)
into the Holy of Holies, the gates stuck one to the other.

D. "Solomon uttered twenty four songs (*renanot*), but he was not answered.

E. "He opened and said, 'O gates, lift up your heads, and be lifted up you everlasting
doors, and the King of glory shall enter' (Ps 24:7).

F. "They [the gates] rushed to swallow him [as they said], 'Who is the King of Glory?' (Ps 24:8).

G. "He said to them, 'The Lord, strong and mighty' (Ps 24:8).

H. "He said [again], 'O gates, lift up your heads, and be lifted up you everlasting doors, and the King of glory shall enter. Who is the King of glory? The Lord of hosts, he is the King of glory. Selah' (Ps 24:9–10). But he was not answered.

I. "When he said, 'O Lord God, do not reject the face of your anointed one; remember the good deeds of David your servant' [alternatively: your kindness to David your servant] (2 Chr 6:42), he was immediately answered [and the gates opened].

J. "At that very hour the faces of all of David's enemies turned [black in humiliation] like the bottom of a pot, and all Israel knew that the Holy One, blessed be He, had forgiven him that sin.

K. "And [thus] did not Solomon speak well when he said, 'Then I accounted those who died long since more fortunate than those who are still living'" (Eccl 4:2).

The Babylonian Talmud places the narrative in the context of a discussion of David's seeking a sign from God that he has been forgiven for his sin with Bathsheba. God indicates that he would do this only after David's passing. In addition, the midrash uses this sequence of events to comment on Ecclesiastes 4:2 that the dead are more fortunate than the living. In *Babylonian Shabbat* 30a the story of the bringing of the ark appears in letters C–I. The gates initially stuck together, so Solomon then uttered numerous prayers. This proved ineffective, so Solomon next is described as reciting portions of what is Psalm 24. But the gates not only did not open but, in what may be a later addition to this account, also sought to swallow him. The midrash interprets Solomon's action as if he was describing himself arrogantly as the "King of glory." But even after Solomon makes clear that God is the king of glory, the gates still do not open. It is only when Solomon invokes the good deeds of his father, David—the words found in 2 Chronicles 6:42—that he is successful. The midrash concludes by indicating that these events evidenced God's forgiveness of David (J) and confirmed (K) the truth of Ecclesiastes 4:2 that the dead are better off than the living.

The similar version of the midrash in *Midrash Psalm* 2:10 focuses directly on Psalm 24.[5]

MIDRASH PSALM 24:10

A. "O gates, life up your heads" (Ps 24:7)

B. You find that when Solomon built the holy temple, he sought to bring the Ark into the Holy of Holy, but the gate was too narrow. This gate was five cubits in height and two and a half cubits in width, and the Ark was only a cubit and a half in height. But cannot something that measures a cubit and a half enter into a space of two and a half cubits? Rather, at that time the gates stuck one to the other.

C. Solomon uttered twenty four songs (*renanot*), but he was not answered.

D. He said, "O gates, lift up your heads," (Ps 24:7) but he was not answered.

E. He said again, "O gates, lift up your heads, and be lifted up you everlasting doors, and the King of glory shall enter. Who is the King of glory?' (Ps 24:9–10). But he was not answered.

F. When he said, "O Lord God, do not reject the face of your anointed one; remember the good deeds of David your servant" [alternatively: your kindness to David your servant] (2 Chr 6:42), immediately the gates opened and the ark entered and fire came down from heaven (2 Chr 7:1).

G. Why did Solomon have so much trouble? Because he was arrogant having said, "I have surely built you a house of habitation" (1 Kgs 8:13).

H. When all of Israel saw what had happened, they immediately said, "Surely, the Holy One, blessed be He, has forgiven David of that sin," and immediately their faces turned [black] like the bottom of a pot, for they felt ashamed. As it is written, "Show me a sign of your favor, that my enemies may see it and be ashamed because you, Lord, have given me aid and comfort" (Ps 86:17). You have given me aid in this world and comforted me in the world to come."

Solomon again succeeds at F only when he invokes the good deeds of David. This version also notes, citing the continuation of the narrative at 2 Chronicles 7:1, the fire descended upon the altar at that time. It also explains explicitly at G that Solomon's arrogance occasioned the difficulties.

In contrast to this version of the events, midrashim found in *Ecclesiastes Rabbah* 4:2[6] and *Pesiqta Rabbati* 2:9[7] contain sayings in the name of various sages that describe the invoking of the memory of David as inadequate to overcome the obstacles Solomon faced. These versions discuss the descent of the fire, not the challenge of bringing in the ark.

ECCLESIASTES RABBAH 4:2

A. R. Samuel b. Nahman interpreted the verse ["Then I accounted those who died long since more fortunate than those who are still living" (Eccl 4:2)] in connection with David.

B. When Solomon built the Temple, he sought for fire to descend from heaven, but it did not descend. He offered one thousand sacrifices, but it did not descend. He prayed twenty four prayers, but it did not descend until he recited, "Remember the good deeds of David your servant" (2 Chr 6:42), and immediately [fire] descended, as it is stated, "And when Solomon finished praying, fire descended from heaven" (2 Chr 7:1).

C. R. Yehudah b. Ilai and the rabbis [differ in their interpretation of what occasioned this outcome].

D. R. Yehudah b. Ilai said, "David came to life at that very hour."

E. And the rabbis said, "He [Solomon] brought in the coffin (*arono*) of David."

F. They do not [really disagree]. The one who said that David came to life at that time [is supported by] what David says with his [own] mouth, "O Lord, you brought me up from Sheol" (Ps 30:4), and another verse says, "Do not reject the face of your anointed one" (2 Chr 6:42), [that is] he who is living before you [now]. And the one who says that he brought in his coffin, this is in accord with that which is written, "Remember the good deeds of David your servant" (2 Chr 6:42).

G. And concerning this very occasion it is said, "Then I accounted those who died long since more fortunate than those who are still living" (Eccl 4:2), such as myself [Solomon] and my associates.

PESIQTA RABBATI 2:8–9

A. Another interpretation of "A song of dedication of the house of David" (*shir chanukhat habayit ledavid*) (Ps 30:1).

B. "You [David] will not build a house for me" (1 Chr 17:4) means you will not build it. "Will you build a house for me" (2 Sam 7:5). [The verse is reinterpreted as a statement, not as a question, rendering it to mean "You will build me a house."] For were it not for you, fire would not descend from heaven. How so, when the Temple was built, how many prayers did he [Solomon] arrange, and the fire did not descend.

C. Another interpretation: "Will you will build me a house" (2 Sam 7:5), you will lay the foundation. "You will not build me a house" (1 Chr 17:4) [means] you will not finish it.

D. Said R. Helbo in the name of R. Shila, "He [Solomon] went and brought the coffin of David. His father.

E. "He said, 'Master of the universe. If I do not have sufficient [good] deeds, do it for the good deeds of my father David.' Immediately fire descended from heaven, as it is written, 'O Lord God, do not reject the face of your anointed one; remember the good deeds of David your servant' (2 Chr 6:42).

F. "And what is written after it? 'And when Solomon finished praying, fire descended from heaven' (2 Chr 7:1)."

G. And if you cannot learn from here [these verses] that Solomon brought the coffin of David his father from the grave, [then learn it from the following interpretation].

H. Said R. Berakhiah in the name of R. Helbo in the name of the school of R. Shila, "There is an explicit verse, 'I extol you, O Lord, for you have lifted me up, O Lord, you brought me up from Sheol' (Ps 30:2, 4).

I. "Therefore said Solomon, 'Since it is because of the merit of David my father the
Holy One, blessed be He, did this, I shall recite a song of dedication of the house in
his name—A song of dedication of the house of David'" (Ps 30:1).

According to B of *Ecclesiastes Rabbah*, invoking the memory of David was adequate.
But C–F relate a dispute between R. Yehudah b. Ilai, an Ushan tanna, and the rabbis
on what actually overcame the difficulty. The rabbis hold at E that David's coffin was
brought into the Temple, while R. Yehudah b. Ilai at D indicates a revived David was present. F provides different exegetical bases for these positions, including a citation from
Psalms 30:4. The version of this midrash in *Pesiqta Rabbati* also assigns a similar, and
in fact a more prominent, role to David. This account serves as a comment on Psalms
30:1, a *mizmor shir chanukat habayit ledavid*—a song of dedication of the house of
David. The midrash interprets this biblical text to refer to a song sung at "the dedication of the house, the Temple of David," treating the *lamed* in *ledavid* to associate the
Temple with David. In this version, the comment about bringing in the coffin of David
is reported at D by the fourth generation Palestinian amora R Helbo, who lived in the
second half of the fourth century.

What factors might account for the critique of Solomon and the greater significance assigned to David in these accounts? In addition, what may explain the very
atypical rabbinic comments that the physical presence of a person from the past, either
in the form of his corpse or of the actual revived person, was effective in securing the
completion of the dedication of the Temple? As already noted, previous scholarship has
commented on the first of these questions. One explanation is that primarily exegetical concerns stand behind these accounts—efforts to explain verses in 2 Chronicles 6,
Psalms 24 and 30, and Ecclesiastes 4:2. For example, why did Solomon offer such a long
prayer; what explains the sequence of questions about the king of glory in Psalm 24?[8]

A second and commonly cited explanation of the critique of Solomon is that these
accounts are an indirect way of critiquing the patriarchate, especially Judah Nesiah, a
third century descendent of Judah the Patriarch. David, parallel to the earlier patriarch, Judah the Patriarch, is fine, but his descendent, just like Solomon, is deficient.[9]
A third explanation of the prominence assigned to David, offered by scholars such
as Hananel Mack and Avigdor Shinan, is that these texts align with other rabbinic
efforts to "clean up and enlarge the image of David."[10] Esther Menn in her previously
mentioned articles provides an explanation of the version of the midrash in *Midrash
on Psalms*. She analyzes a number of texts in this document that elevate King David
for the purposes of treating the Temple as a House of Prayer. The editors of *Midrash
on Psalms* saw David as the author of the book of Psalms and sought to highlight the
importance of prayer in a period long after the time of the destruction of the Temple
in Jerusalem. These explanations clearly assign to David a far greater importance in

connection with the Temple and are also part of an effort, found in many rabbinic texts, that like the much earlier efforts of the Chronicler sought to "clean up" the image of King David. But none of these explanations says anything about the odd imagery of the actual presence of David.

I suggest that this notion relates to emerging notions of relics and the importance for Jews of the physical presence of the remains of significant figures from the past, evidenced in a number of rabbinic texts and in traditions about pilgrimage to such location as the Cave of the Patriarchs in Hebron. These practices developed in the Byzantine era after the consecration of what is known now as the Church of the Holy Sepulcher on September 13, 335. Several scholars, including Jeffrey Rubenstein and Ra'anan Boustan, have examined a variety of rabbinic texts, including stories about R. Eleazar b. Simeon, appearing in both the Babylonian Talmud and *Pesiqta de Rab Kahana*, that describe villagers battling over his body, a body that had not decayed and was able to benefit the living.[11] Similarly, a tradition in the Babylonian Talmud (*b. Sotah* 34b) ascribes to the mid-fourth century Babylonian amora Rava a comment that Caleb during his scouting of the land went and prayed for help from the Patriarchs at their grave in Hebron. This burial site is a location not simply to honor and remember the dead but also to seek their intervention and assistance. Although pilgrimage to graves became prominent among Jews in the Islamic period, as demonstrated by Elchanan Reiner, this tradition attests to the idea that praying in the proximity of a "holy person" is efficacious.[12]

I propose, in line with the views of scholars such as Joshua Schwartz, Joshua Levinson, and Eyal Ben Eliyahu, that the tradition about the physical presence of David at the dedication of the Temple may be a rabbinic response to the growing Christian notion of "the Holy Land" and to their ways of speaking of the Temple.[13] Robert Wilken, John Wilkinson, and others have traced the emerging Christian notion of the Holy Land.[14] A key figure in this development is the Church Father Eusebius, who praises Constantine for his efforts. In his *Life of Constantine*, Eusebius says the following about the building of the church complex at the newly discovered site of Jesus's crucifixion and resurrection: "New Jerusalem was built at the very Testimony to the Savior, facing the famous Jerusalem of old, which after the bloody murder of the Lord had been overthrown in utter devastation, and paid the penalty of its wicked inhabitants. Opposite this then the Emperor erected the victory of the Savior over death with rich and abundant munificence, this being perhaps that fresh new Jerusalem proclaimed in prophetic oracles, about which long speeches recite innumerable praises as they utter words of divine inspiration."[15]

In his *Church History*, Eusebius had previously in 317 CE addressed Paulinus the Bishop of Tyre upon the dedication of its basilica by remarking, "Shall I call you a new Bezalel, the master builder of a divine tabernacle, or a Solomon, king of a new and far nobler Jerusalem, or a new Zerubbabel, who adored the temple of God with the glory that was far greater than gold?"[16] Here a builder of a church is compared to Solomon the builder of the Temple, thereby appropriating the biblical imagery to praise him. Finally, the connection between the Temple and the Church of the Holy Sepulcher appears quite explicitly in the Travels of Egeria to the Holy Land in the early 380s. She relays her observations of the Encaenia, the day celebrating the consecration of that church (called the Anastasia here). The date in September was chosen "to coincide with the very day when the cross had been found. You will find in the Bible that the day of the Encaenia was when the house of God was consecrated, and Solomon stood in prayer before God's altar as we read in the Book of Chronicles [2 Chr 6–7]. At the time of the Encaenia they keep the festival for eight days, and for many days beforehand the crowds begin to assemble."[17] Here the consecration of the church is seen as a direct parallel and a replacement for the previous eight-day celebration that took place when Solomon dedicated the Temple.

Egeria also comments on how the Holy Cross was treated by Christians, how it was seen as a relic with amazing powers. She notes that this potent object was kept in a golden and silver box, a coffin, to protect it and was taken out only with much care.[18] Perhaps these traditions that connect key Christian symbols, the Church of the Holy Sepulcher, and the Holy Cross with the Temple of Solomon, may provide some of the background for the rabbinic stories that connect the successful dedication of the Temple either with the corpse of David in his coffin or a revivified David. Although it was in ruins, the rabbis in many ways continue to underscore in many midrashim the unique power and importance of the Temple, its "founder" David, and the Temple Mount.

Later Christian traditions emerging from the period of the emperor Heraclius in the early 600s also ascribe much significance to his successful return of the Holy Cross to Jerusalem in 630 after retrieving it from the Persians, who had conquered Jerusalem and taken it in 614. They compare the Cross to the Ark of the Covenant, and in later versions of Heraclius's activities they describe his initial lack of success in bringing in the cross through the gate through which Jesus had entered Jerusalem. Heraclius managed to bring in the cross in its box only after he humbled himself, stripped off his royal garb, and then approached the gates.[19] Events associated with Heraclius appear to have led to making connections with David by both Jews and Christians. Scholars connect the capture of Jerusalem in 614 by the Persians with the rise of an intense Jewish apocalyptic set of writings, including *Sefer Zerubbabel* and *Sefer Eliyahu*, accounts that describe the success of a Davidic messiah.[20] Heraclius also draws upon the tradition of David, especially evident in a set of golden plates found in Cyprus that appear to appropriate events from the life of David to symbolize the emperor's own achievements. Heraclius also names one of his children David.[21]

Jews familiar with the midrashim cited above and with these accounts of Heraclius' endeavors may well have seen a parallel between the emperor's efforts at returning the Holy Cross in its box and the box containing the corpse of David. David was a living presence for Jews, and the building now even more closely associated with him, the Temple in Jerusalem, the House of David, and the Mount on which it stood remained potent symbols and a presence for Jews for many centuries.[22] They do so as well even until this day. In the hearts and minds of many Jews, as the song based on a comment in the Babylonian Talmud *Rosh Hashanah* 25a says, "David King of Israel, *chai vekayam*—is alive and endures."

NOTES

1. Esther M. Menn, "Praying King and Sanctuary of Prayer, Part I: David and the Temple's Origins in Rabbinic Psalms Commentary (*Midrash Tehillim*)," *Journal of Jewish Studies* 52 (2001): 1–26; Esther M. Menn, "Praying King and Sanctuary of Prayer, Part II: David's Deferment and the Temple's Dedication in Rabbinic Psalms Commentary (*Midrash Tehillim*)," *Journal of Jewish Studies* 53 (2002): 299–323.

2. David Rothstein's comments on 1 Chronicles 22:2–29:25, a unit that describes David's various preparations for building the Temple, capture the overall thrust of the revisions of the Chronicler. "This entire section has no parallel in other biblical sources. The Chronicler composed it to bolster David's image by suggesting that he did everything allowable for building the Temple short of constructing the structure itself. The Chronicler thus presents the construction of the Temple as a two-part venture, begun by David and completed by Solomon. Chronicles repeatedly makes the point that, although David was denied the honor of building the Temple, he did everything in his power to lay its groundwork. Accordingly David prepares the labor force, and raw materials" (David Rothstein, "First Chronicles," in *The Jewish Study Bible* [2nd ed.; ed. Adele Berlin, et al.; New York: Oxford University Press, 2004], 1749).

3. For how Josephus describes the events of the dedication of the Temple, see Christopher T. Begg, "Solomon's Installation of the Ark in the Temple According to Josephus," *Revista Catalona de Teología* 30 (2005): 251–65.

4. For overviews of the scholarship relating to early rabbinic documents and their dates, I draw upon the discussions in H. L. Strack and Günter Stemberger, *Introduction to the Talmud and Midrash* (2nd ed.; trans. and ed. Markus Bockmuehl; Minneapolis: Fortress Press, 1996). In some instances I also note additional discussions of dating. Several scholars have discussed the midrash in the Babylonian Talmud, commenting on its textual features, its literary structure, the redactional impact upon its formulation and meaning. The variations in the manuscripts do not have any significant

impact on the issues explored here. See Gilead Sasson, *A King and Layman: The Sages' Attitudes towards King Solomon* [Hebrew] (Tel Aviv: Resling Publishing, 2013); Gilead Sasson, "Solomon Desired to Bring the Ark into the Sanctuary: The Editing of an Eretz Yisrael Legend in the Babylonian Talmud," in *Iggud: Selected Essays in Jewish Studies*, vol. I [Hebrew] (ed. Ronelah Merdler; Jerusalem: World Union of Jewish Studies, 2005), 329–37; Joseph Heinemann, "On Life and Death: Anatomy of a Rabbinic Sermon," in *Studies in Hebrew Narrative Art throughout the Ages* (ed. Joseph Heinemann, et al.; Jerusalem: Magness Press, 1978), 52–65; Yonah Frenkel, *Midrash and Agadah*, vol. II [Hebrew] (Tel Aviv: The Open University of Israel, 1996), 280–88. The two parallels of this tradition in the Babylonian Talmud, *Mo'ed Qat.* 9a and *Sanh.*107b, do not contain any important differences for this discussion.

5. I use the translation of Esther Menn, "Praying King and Sanctuary of Prayer, Part II," 300–301, which I checked against the Hebrew text.

6. I have translated from the critical edition of *Ecclesiastes Rabbah* in Marc Hirshman, *Midrash Kohelet Rabbah 1–6: Critical Edition Based on Manuscripts and Genizah Fragments* [Hebrew] (Jerusalem: Schechter Institute of Jewish Studies, 2016). Additional discussions of the date and compositional history of this work include Reuven Kiperwasser, "Qohelet Rabbah-Bein Qadum leMeuchar: Iyyun beArikhah," in *Iggud: Selected Essays in Jewish Studies*, vol. I [Hebrew] (ed. Ronelah Merdler; Jerusalem: World Union of Jewish Studies, 2005), 293–314; Reuven Kiperwasser, "Structure and Form in Kohelet Rabbah as Evidence of Its Redaction," *Journal of Jewish Studies* 58 (2007): 283–302; Reuven Kiperwasser, "Toward a Redaction History of Kohelet Rabbah: A Study in the Composition and Redaction of Kohelet Rabbah 7:7," *Journal of Jewish Studies* 61 (2010): 257–77.

7. I used the critical edition of this work by Rivka Ulmer, *A Bilingual Edition of Pesiqta Rabbati: Volume 1, Chapters 1–22* (Berlin: De Gruyter, 2017). Ulmer has published extensively on this work and has discussed dating, compositional structure, and meaning: Rivka Ulmer, "The Jerusalem Temple in *Pesiqta Rabbati*: From Creation to Apocalypse," *Hebrew Studies* 51 (2010): 223–59; Rivka Ulmer, "Construction, Destruction and Reconstruction: The Temple in *Pesiqta Rabbati*," in *The Temple in Jerusalem from Moses to Messiah: In Honor of Professor Louis H. Feldman* (ed. Steven Fine; Leiden: Brill, 2011), 105–24. On the date and editing of this work, also see Arnon Atzmon, "The Original Order of Pesikta de-Rav Kahana," *Journal of Jewish Studies* 70 (2019): 17, n. 39; Norman Cohen, "Structure and Editing in Homiletic Midrashim," *Association for Jewish Studies Review* 6 (1981): 1–20; Tzvi Novick, "Between First-Century Apocalyptic and Seventh-Century Liturgy: On *4 Ezra, 2 Baruch* and Qillir," *Journal for the Study of Judaism* 44 (2013): 356–78 .

8. Frenkel (*Midrash and Aggadah*), Heinemann ("On Life and Death"), and Sasson (*A*

King and Layman) stress these factors and note how redactors refocus the message of the core story.

9. Sandra R. Shimoff, "The Hellenization of Solomon in Rabbinic Texts," in *The Age of Solomon: Scholarship at the Turn of the Millennium* (ed. Lowell K. Handy; Leiden: Brill, 1997), 457–69, has most recently advanced this analysis. Sasson presents a detailed critique of it. Also see Richard Kalmin, "Portrayal of Kings in Rabbinic Literature in Late Antiquity," *Jewish Studies Quarterly* 3 (1996): 320–41.

10. Avigdor Shinana, "King David of the Sages," *Nordisk Judaistik/Scandinavian Jewish Studies* 1–2 (2003): 53–78; Hananel Mack, "The First Temple in Aggadot of the Rabbis," in *Yerushalayim bi-yeme Bayit rishon: Meḳorot, Sikumim, Parashiyot Nivḥarot ve-Homer Ezer* [Hebrew] (ed. David Amit, et al.; Jerusalem: Yad Ben Zvi, 1990), 184–94.

11. Jeffrey L. Rubenstein, "A Rabbinic Translation of Relics," in *Crossing the Boundaries in Early Judaism and Christianity: Ambiguities, Complexities and Half-Forgotten Adversaries: Essays in Honor of Alan F. Segal* (ed. Kimberly B. Startton, et al.; Leiden: Brill, 2016), 314–32; Jeffrey L. Rubenstein, "Hero, Saint, and Sage: The Life of R. Elazar b. Shimon in Pesiqta de Rab Kahana II," in *The Faces of Torah: Studies in the Texts and Contexts of Ancient Judaism in Honor of Steven Fraade* (ed. Michal Bar-Asher, et al.; Gottingen: Vandenhoeck and Ruprecht, 2017), 509–28; Ra'anan Boustan, "Jewish Veneration of the 'Special Dead' in Late Antiquity and Beyond," in *Saints and Sacred Matter: The Cult of Relics in Byzantium and Beyond* (ed. Cynthia Hahn, et al.; Washington: Dumbarton Oaks Research Library and Collection, 2015), 61–81. Another rabbinic tradition, appearing in a range of documents including the tannaitic midrash *Mekhilta de Rabbi Ishmael, Vayehi Beshalach* 4 and also in *Gen Rabbah* 87:8 and in *Midrash on Psalms* 114:9, also describes the impact of the physical remains of an ancestor. These sources assert that the bones of Joseph occasioned the splitting of the Sea of Reeds. This tradition differs in one crucial detail from the midrashim about David's coffin. In this case, the biblical text itself describes how the Israelites took the bones of Joseph with them when they departed Egypt. Thus the presence of the bones of Joseph on their journey through the desert is not introduced into the biblical text, though ascribing miraculous powers to them is a novel point made in rabbinic texts. It is worth noting as well that while the versions in the earlier documents, *Mekhilta* and *Gen Rabbah*, claim it is the bones of Joseph that had the miraculous impact, in the version in the late *Midrash on Psalms* the coffin [*aron*], the same word found in the traditions about David's presence at the dedication of the Temple, causes the splitting of the Sea. Simcha Raphael, *Images of Joseph's Bones in Torah and Midrash* (Philadelphia: Da'at Institute, 2013), analyzes these traditions in depth.

12. An analysis of the text from the Talmud appears in a longer discussion of the development of the concept of the "merits of the ancestors" in Uri Ehrlich, "Ancestors' Prayers
for the Salvation of Israel in Early Rabbinic Thought," in *Jewish and Christian Liturgy
and Worship: New Insights into Its History* (ed. Albert Gerhaus, et al.; Leiden: Brill,
2007), 249–56; Uri Ehrlich,"Bein 'Zekhut Avot' le'achriyut avot': Pereq Bemachshevet
hatefilah bitequfat hachazal," in *By the Well: Studies in Jewish Philosophy and Halakhic
Thought Presented to Gerald J. Blidstein* [Hebrew] (ed. Uri Ehrlich, et al.; Beer-sheva:
Ben-Gurion University Press, 2008), 13–23. Eyal Ben Eliyahu, "The Rabbinic Polemic
against Sanctification of Sites," *Journal for the Study of Judaism* 40 (2009): 260–80,
contends that although the rabbis objected to the practice of visiting gravesites, earlier
popular practice from the first century indicates that such places were sites of visitation
as the presence of the remains of prophets were buried there. Most scholars rely on
the later dating of the text *The Lives of the Prophets* in David Satran, *Biblical Prophets
in Byzantine Palestine: Reassessing the Lives of the Prophets* (Leiden: Brill, 1995), and
assign a later date to grave visitation. Elchanan Reiner studies the expansion of Jewish
pilgrimage to grave sites during the Islamic period in *"Aliyah va-'aliyah le-regel le-Erets
Yisra'el: 1099–1517"* [Hebrew] (Ph.D. diss., The Hebrew University, 1988). Also see
Yoram Tsafrir, "Jewish Pilgrimage in the Roman and Byzantine Periods," *Jahrbuch
fur Antike und Christenthum* 20 (1995): 369–76; Catherine Herzer, *Jewish Travel in
Antiquity* (Tubingen: Mohr Siebeck, 2011); Allen Kerkeslager, "Jewish Pilgrimage
and Jewish Identity in Hellenistic and Early Roman Egypt," in *Pilgrimage and Holy
Space in Late Antiquity Egypt* (ed. David Frankfurter; Leiden: Brill, 1998), 99–225.
On objections to such practices and the notion that gravesites can serve as loci of
mediation to the divine and heavenly forces, see Shraga Yechezkel Lichtenstein,
"The Rambam's Approach Regarding Prayer, Holy Objects and Visiting Cemeteries"
[Hebrew], *Hebrew Union College Annual* 72 (2001): 1–34.

13. Joshua Schwartz, "The *Encaenia* of the Church of the Holy Sepulcher, the Temple of
Solomon and the Jews," *Theologische Zeitschrift* 43 (1987): 265–81; Joshua Levinson,
"There Is No Place Like Home: Rabbinic Responses to the Christianization of
Palestine," in *Jews Christians and the Roman Empire: The Poetics of Power in Late
Antiquity* (ed. Natalie B. Dohrmann, et al.; Philadelphia: University of Pennsylvania
Press, 2013), 99–120.

14. Robert L. Wilken, *The Land Called Holy: Palestine in Christian History and Thought*
(New Haven: Yale University Press, 1992); John Wilkinson, "Jewish Influences on the
Early Christian Rite of Jerusalem," *Le Museon: Revue D'Etudes Orientales* 92 (1979):
347–59; E. P. Sanders, "Jerusalem and Its Temple in Early Christian Thought and
Practice," in *Jerusalem: Its Sanctity and Centrality to Judaism, Christianity and Islam*
(ed. Lee Levine; New York: Continuum, 1999), 90–103. Jerusalem and the significance, or lack thereof, of Solomon's Temple, or more generally the Temple Mount, a

term first used extensively in rabbinic sources, become foci of treating places in the Holy Land as holy. These issues are discussed in a number of studies by Yaron Eliav, especially *God's Mountain: The Temple Mount in Time, Place and Memory* (Baltimore: Johns Hopkins University Press, 2005); and in David Goodblatt, "The Temple Mount: The Afterlife of a Biblical Phrase," in *Le David Maskil: A Birthday Tribute for David Noel Freedman* (ed. Richard Elliott Friedman, et al.; Winona: Eisenbrauns, 2004), 91–101.

15. Eusebius, *Life of Constantine* III 33 (trans. Averil Cameron; New York: Oxford University Press, 1999), 135.

16. Eusebius, *Church History (Historia Ecclesiastica)* 10.4.2–3 (trans. G. A. Williamson, Penguin Books: New York 1990).

17. Egeria, *Egeria's Travels to the Holy Land* 48.1–2; 49.1 (trans. John Wilkinson; Jerusalem: Ariel Publishing House, 1981), 146–47.

18. There are many studies of the related issues of the development of Christian notions of relics, including that of the Holy Cross, and pilgrimage, as well as of Christian appropriation of the symbolism of the Temple of Solomon during the Byzantine and subsequent periods. An excellent collection of studies of the history of relics is Cynthia Hahn et al., eds., *Saints and Sacred Matter: The Cult of Relics in Byzantium and Beyond* (Washington: Dumbarton Oaks Research Library and Collection, 2015). On traditions of the Holy Cross, see Barbara Baert, *Heritage of Holy Wood: The Legend of the Cross in Text and Image* (Leiden: Brill, 2004). An excellent study of early Christian pilgrimage is Bruria Bitton-Ashkelony, *Encountering the Sacred: The Debate on Christian Pilgrimage in Late Antiquity* (Berkeley: University of California Press, 2005). Christian appropriation of symbolism associated with the Temple of Solomon appears in Jonathan Bardill, "A New Temple for Byzantium: Anicia Juliana, King Solomon, and the Gilded Ceiling of the Church of St. Polyeuktos in Constantinople," in *Social and Political Life in Late Antiquity* (ed. William Bowden, et al.; Leiden: Brill, 2006), 339–70; Ekaterina Kovalchuk, "The Encaenia of St. Sophia: Animal Sacrifice in a Christian Context," *Scrinium* 4 (2008): 161–203; Ekaterina Kovalchuk, "The Holy Sepulchre of Jerusalem and St. Sophia of Constantinople: An Attempt at Discovering a Hagiographic Expression of the Byzantine Encaenia Feast," *Scrinium* 6 (2010): 263–338; Robert Ousterhout, "New Temples and New Solomons: The Rhetoric of Byzantine Architecture," in *The Old Testament in Byzantium* (ed. Paul Magdalino, et al.; Washington: Dumbarton Oaks Research Library and Collection, 2010), 223–54; Rina Talgam, "The Representation of the Temple and Jerusalem in Jewish and Christian Houses of Prayer in the Holy Land in Late Antiquity," in *Jews, Christians, and the Roman Empire: The Poetics of Power in Late Antiquity* (ed. Natalie B. Dohrmann, et al.; Philadelphia: University of Pennsylvania Press, 2013), 222–48; Oliver Larry Yarbrough, "Early Christian Jerusalem: The City of the Cross,"

in *Jerusalem: Idea and Reality* (ed. Tamar Mayer, et al.; New York: Routledge, 2008), 67–85; Amnon Linder, "Jerusalem as a Focus of Confrontation between Judaism and Christianity," in *Vision and Conflict in the Holy Land* (ed. Richard I Coen; New York: Saint Martin's Press, 1985), 1–22.

19. The literature on Heraclius is extensive, with some of the following including detailed discussion of George of Pisidia's *Restitution Sanctae Crucis*. See Mary Whitby, "Defenders of the Cross: George of Pisidia on the Emperor Heraclius and His Defenders," *Mnemosyne Supplementum* 181 (1998): 247–76; Mary Whitby, "George of Pisidia's Presentation of the Emperor Heraclius and His Campaigns," in *The Reign of Heraclius (620–641): Crisis and Confrontation* (ed. Gerri J. Reinik, et al.; Leuven: Peeters, 2002), 157–73; Mary Whitby, "A New Image for a New Age: George of Pisidia on the Emperor Heraclius," in *The Roman and Byzantine Army in the East* (ed. Edward Dabrowa; Krakow: Drukarnia Uniwersytetu Jagiellońskiego, 1994), 197–225; Marlin Mundell Mango, "Imperial Art in the Seventh Century," in *New Constantines: The Rhythm of Imperial Renewal in the Byzantium 4th–13th Centuries* (ed. Paul Magdalino; Hampshire: Variorum Ashgate, 1994), 109–37; Jan Willem Drijvers, "Heraclius and the *Restitutio Crucis*: Notes on Symbolism and Ideology," in *The Reign of Heraclius (620–641): Crisis and Confrontation* (ed. Gerri Reinik, et al.; Leuven: Peeters, 2002), 175–90; Cyril Mango, "The Temple Mount AD 614–638," in *Bayt Al-Maqdis: Abd al-Malik's Jerusalem* (ed. Julia Raby-Johns; New York: Oxford University Press, 1992), 1–16; Stephan Borgehammar, "Heraclius Learns Humility: Two Early Latin Accounts Composed for the Celebration of *Exaltatio Crucis*," *Millennium: Jahrbuch zu Kultur und Geschichte des Ersten Jahrtausends* 6 (2009): 145–201; Christina Maranci, "The Humble Heraclius: Revisiting the North Portal at Mren," *Revue des Etudes Armeniennes* 31 (2008): 167–80.

20. Martha Himmelfarb, *Jewish Messiahs in a Christian Empire: A History of the Book of Zerubbabel* (Cambridge: Harvard University Press, 2017); Martha Himmelfarb, "*Sefer Eliyahu*: Jewish Eschatology and Christian Jerusalem," in *Shaping the Middle East: Jews, Christians, and Muslims in an Age of Transition 400–800 CE* (ed. Kenneth G. Holum, et al.; Bethesda: University of Maryland Press, 2011), 223–38; Woute Jan van Bekkum, "Jewish Messianic Expectations in the Age of Heraclius," in *The Reign of Heraclius (620–641): Crisis and Confrontation* (ed. Gerri J. Reinink, et al; Leuven: Peeters, 2002), 95–112. Christian writers at the time subsequently asserted that Jews supported the Persian invasion and massacred many Christians. Discussions of these matters appear in Averil Cameron, "Blaming the Jews: The Seventh-Century Invasions of Palestine in Context," in *Melanges Gilbert Dagron* (ed. Vincet Deroche; Paris: Association des amis du centre d'histoire et civilization de Byzance, 2002), 57–78; and Elliot Horowitz, "The Vengeance of the Jews Was Stronger Than Their Avarice:

Modern Historians and the Persian Conquest of Jerusalem in 614," *Jewish Social Studies* 4 (1998): 1–39.

21. Heraclius' appropriation of King David is discussed in Suzanne Spain Alexander, "Heraclius, Byzantine Imperial Ideology, and the David Plates," *Speculum: A Journal of Medieval Studies* 52 (1977): 217–37.

22. Muslims also treated the Temple Mount as holy and over time built the mosque of Al Aqsa and the Dome of the Rock there. A rich discussion of these issues appears in Pamela Berger, *The Cross and the Temple: The Dome of the Rock as Image of the Ancient Jewish Sanctuary* (Leiden: Brill, 2012).

FROM ACOSTA AND SPINOZA TO ARENDT TO LAURENCE AND AYLON

Verbiage and Visual Art as Instruments of Dissent in Modern Jewish Thought

ORI Z. SOLTES

INTRODUCTION: DISSENT AND THE RABBINIC TRADITION

RABBINIC LITERATURE DESIGNED to interpret God's words offered from the outset multiple perspectives on any given issue. Rarely would an interpretive question yield fewer than two or three answers. For instance, when in *Midrash Rabba* on Genesis 1:1 the question is asked regarding the phrase "in the beginning God created the heavens and the earth," one rabbi (or "school") argues that heaven was created first, a second rabbi (or "school") counters that it was earth, and a third rabbi argues that they were created simultaneously.

Through the centuries discussion, disagreement, and dissent were part of the framework defining Jewish authority. The consequence of this pattern, together with the fact that Jews were so dispersed and separated, and rarely with any political power, meant that the concept of "heresy" did not functionally exist within Judaism: individuals could not easily be accused of dissenting dangerously from rabbinical authority. As a practical matter, Jews in Paris were not likely to know much about Jews in Fez and therefore not be offended by Moroccan Jewish Passover gastronomy, much less be able to accuse their coreligionists of heresy or to do something to them because of it.

Even if Rhineland rabbis could strongly dissent from Iberian rabbis regarding the appropriate treatment of Jews seeking a return to the fold after having been forced into Christianity, at a practical level each rabbinic group could at most decide only for its own constituents what was "proper Judaism"—and what might be done to correct improprieties. In any case, the rabbinic focus was almost inevitably on behavior, on proper and improper conduct, on being a "proper Jew" through one's actions, not one's thoughts and beliefs.

This contrasts strongly with Christianity, which — politically hegemonic and contiguous by the late fourth century and increasingly powerful in the centuries that followed — offered an ongoing partnership between (even if there were constant conflicts between) political and religious leadership. And Christian religious leadership tended to be more focused on the world to come than on this world, on the possibilities of heaven and hell, salvation and damnation (Judaism's language, Hebrew, does not even have proper terms for "hell" and "damnation") than on the world of the here and now. Most important within the matrix of "proper Christianity" is one's beliefs: understanding properly what and how God is; who is or are the primary intermediator(s) between God and oneself; and how, in the past, present, and future, God relates to humanity.

FROM THE INQUISITION TO URIEL ACOSTA'S EXCOMMUNICATION

During the period of the evolving rabbinic Babylonian and Palestinian gemaras, Church leaders were debating the nature of God: at the Council of Nicaea in 325 CE, the position articulated by Athanasius, that God is Triune — the Father, Son, and Holy Spirit are co-substantial — prevailed over Arius's stated position that the Father is separate from and superior to the Son (i.e., that Jesus was not divine). The Arian view, however, did not simply disappear — there was an operating Arian baptistery in Ravenna as late as 526, and it was not until 589 that the Visigothic king, Reccared, pushed his Iberian kingdom to embrace triune instead of Arian Christianity. So Church authorities struggled against what they termed "heresy" — essentially defined as being within the circle of belief but misbelieving (as opposed to those outside the circle, who were sufficiently spiritually misguided to be termed "infidels" or "faithless").

As the medieval period moved forward and eventually Arianism disappeared, other forms of heresy took its place, and the problem itself remained unsolved. Nine centuries after the Council of Nicaea, the Dominican and Franciscan monastic orders received papal imprimatur in the early thirteenth century, in part to serve as instruments in rooting out heretics. These preaching orders established boards of inquiry — first in northern Italy, then in Southern France and in Southern Italy and Sicily — to inquire into the faith of professing Christians so that the preachers might correctively teach the misguided. As this mechanism moved through the following two hundred years or so, the Dominicans in particular became fierce pursuers of the spiritually mistaken — and along the way picked up methods of physical torture in Sicily to help the interrogations that they imported most particularly into Spain.[1]

There, where Jews had been resident since at least the second century—rolling with the changes from pagan to Arian to Catholic to Muslim hegemony and, in the centuries of the *Reconquista*, often playing a relatively comfortable role as go-betweens in the interface between Muslim and Christian Iberians—conditions radically changed after 1391. In that year (for reasons beyond this discussion) riots began on Ash Wednesday in Sevilla against the Jewish community and spread through much of Christian Spain, continuing with ongoing if sporadic intensity until 1415. By then, perhaps a third of the Jewish population had left, a third stayed and remained openly Jewish. A third converted to Christianity, but we don't know and cannot know how many of these *conversos* were or became genuinely practicing and believing *nuevos cristianos* [New Christians].

As a practical matter, for the Church in Iberia in the fifteenth century, the most prevalent form of heresy became the "Judaizing heresy": once baptized, a *converso* who was found—or merely accused of—lighting candles on Friday evening or fasting on Yom Kippur or eating unleavened bread on Passover was considered heretical. All of the ugliness that had accumulated since Sicily in developing Boards of Inquisition climaxed with the centralization of the Spanish Inquisition in Sevilla under the directorship of Tomas de Torquemada in 1483—two years after the first *auto da fe* in that city entertained the public with the burning at the stake of seven *conversos*. Torquemada, all four of whose grandparents were Jews, had a powerful personal, emotional, and psychological reason for pushing the inquisitional envelope.

He was also personal confessor to "the most Catholic Queen," Isabel of Castilla, whose marriage to Ferdinand of Aragon in 1474 had de facto unified Christian Spain for the first time in more than seven centuries. Ferdinand's maternal grandmother was Paloma, a Jewess of Toledo, giving him an important psychological need to support the inquisitional process, both to be an appropriate spouse to "the most Catholic queen" and because the partnership between church and state enriched both (one of the first steps of the inquisitional authorities when arresting someone accused of heresy was to confiscate all of his or her material goods—which typically ended up divided between the two entities).

What would evolve as centuries of inquisitional process failed to solve the problem of heresy, but a second step toward its solution, was the expulsion of all openly practicing Jews from Spain (in 1492), and shortly thereafter, from Portugal (1496–1497). Many of these Jews gained refuge within the Ottoman Turkish world, or—ironically enough—in papal lands from southern France to Italy. Some ended up in the Netherlands or Germany. Over the following few hundred years, *conversos* desirous of returning to openly Jewish lives followed in a small but steady trickle—particularly by the late sixteenth century, when the seven northern Dutch provinces asserted their independence from the Catholic Habsburg Spain–dominated empire.

Among this group was Gabriel/Uriel Acosta (ca. 1585–1640) from Porto, Portugal—a cleric, no less, but from a *converso* family, whose ongoing study of the New Testament and Hebrew Bible led him to conclude that Christianity was spiritually misbegotten. At first secretly returning alone to Judaism—perhaps after the death of his father—he eventually revealed his secret to his family, and all of them (his three brothers, his mother, and he) decided to flee Portugal (there may also have been financial reasons for the sudden departure) and so arrived in Amsterdam and Hamburg by 1614. As an individualistic thinker, however, and a recent devotee of Torah study, Acosta soon began to feel that the Judaism to which he had returned and its rabbinic leadership were falling wide of the mark indicated in the Hebrew text. There is an irony here: his expectations for Jewish life were based strictly on a literal reading of what he saw in the Torah, as often through history Christians have assumed that Judaism is strictly Torah-guided without recognizing the centuries of rabbinic commentary and interpretation that have shaped Judaism as a dynamic, ever-evolving organism. So Acosta's view of proper Judaism is more Christian—or at least Karaite—than mainstream Jewish, even after his conversion.

Acosta composed a tract, eleven *Propositions against Tradition*, that was published in Venice and Hamburg in 1616. He argued (among other theses) that 1, the use of phylacteries is not prescribed in the Torah; 2, circumcision as it is currently practiced corrupts the injunction commanding it in the Torah; 3, adding extra holy days while in exile (a second day to Rosh Hashanah and an eighth day to both Sukkot and Passover, for example) is also contrary to the prescription in the Torah and therefore a sin; 6, the command to punish "an eye for and eye and a tooth for a tooth" should be taken literally and not yield to being replaced by monetary compensation from victimizer to victim; 7, oral teachings (i.e., the discussions in the rabbinic tradition) are fundamentally illegitimate, only written laws (i.e., what is in the Torah) are valid; 11, benedictions are illegitimate, since they do not derive directly from the Torah.

If Acosta's Mosaic view may be seen as derived from the Christological mentality that he imported into his analysis of Judaism, the same might be said for the response to his publication. He apparently engaged in public disputes with Sephardic rabbinic leaders (i.e., rabbis whose roots, like his, were also in Spain or Portugal), in which he referred to them as Pharisees, viewing them also from a New Testament, not rabbinic, perspective. The consequence of this oppositional, defiant—seriously dissenting—behavior was that he was excommunicated in 1618. More precisely put: the rabbinic leadership published a statement that extended from Venice to Hamburg banning him from the community and ordering the community to exclude him from intercourse with them. This form of forced separation is referred to as a *niddui* in Hebrew. It is a limited writ of excommunication, in both time and meaning: Acosta's exclusion was for a month, and he was required to pay a fine to the community.

A few years later, in 1623, by which time he was living in Amsterdam, he was publishing a new work, in which his view of the rabbinic authorities as Pharisees in the negative, New Testament sense was amplified: the very title of the work was *An Examination of the Traditions of the Pharisees*. In this booklet he argued against the notion of reward and punishment beyond this world, contradicting the prevailing wisdom among the Sephardic rabbinate.[2] The response of the communal leaders, Rabbis Saul Levi Morteira and Manasseh ben Israel, was to accuse Acosta of denying God. Children were incited to hound him in the streets, yelling "heretic" and "apostate" at him. Needless to say, the import of both the *niddui* and this sort of harassment is a far cry from the torture and death meted out and the eternal damnation promised by the inquisitional and papal authorities within the Church, but the influence of the Catholic methodology on the Sephardic leadership is clear.

This second writ that banned Acosta from the community was formally delivered on May 15. Its text included the injunction that "nobody, whoever it might be, is permitted to talk with him, neither man nor woman, neither relatives nor strangers, nobody may show him favor or otherwise be in contact with him, under penalty of becoming included within the same ban and being excluded from our congregational fellowship. And to his brother we grant a period of grace of eight days in which to complete his separation from him." The idea is one of complete, if temporary, isolation from the community.

The rabbinic leadership also threatened Acosta with further action: that of bringing his case before the Christian (Dutch Reformed, essentially a branch of Calvinism) magistrate, as subverting the Christian Church (for which the immortality of the soul and its suffering or salvation in the eternal afterlife were essential doctrines) and not only Judaism. They apparently did this, since there follows a record of Acosta having spent some eight to ten days in prison and paying a three-hundred-florin penalty (he was released on May 31, 1624, so the entire process took over a year to complete). He was still affected by the *niddui* and ultimately fled Amsterdam and settled again for a time in Hamburg but found himself ostracized by the Sephardic community there as well. Eventually he felt that he had no choice but to return to Amsterdam, around 1631—he asserted that he would go back to being "an ape amongst the apes" (a less complimentary form of "doing in Rome as the Romans do") but seems to have found it difficult to really be one of them. In any case, his nephew accused him of abrogating the kashrut laws shortly thereafter, which seems to have led to a renewal of the *niddui* against him.

Moreover, he continued to speak out in ways found outrageous by the community. Thus he openly questioned whether the laws of the Torah were truly divinely sanctioned or whether Moses simply composed them. Ultimately, he asserted that all religion is humanly contrived and overrun with empty ceremonies and rituals that are meaning-less to God. For God resides in nature—which is peaceful and harmonious—whereas religion is stamped with blood, strife, and incessant violence. Moreover, two would-be proselytes to Judaism came forth to accuse him of trying to dissuade them from their path. In response, the horrified rabbinate demanded of him that he read a statement of recantation that they drew up and that he submit to a public whipping. His refusal led to a fuller and more definitive writ of excommunication by 1633: a *heirem*, which banned him from the community for seven years, dooming him to virtual isolation, shunned by his family and his loved ones, regardless of where he was living.

If even the *heirem* was far less extreme than a Catholic writ of excommunication (most obviously, it lacks the force of eternal damnation into a fiery hell), for Acosta it was psychologically and emotionally powerful enough that he eventually returned to Amsterdam—yet again—in 1640, desperate for reconciliation. He begged for mercy and reinstatement within the community. The conditions of that reinstatement were threefold: that he read a "confession" publicly; that he submit to a public flogging of thirty-nine lashes (administered while the rabbinic leadership chanted Psalms of Praise to God); that, as a consummate act of humbling himself, he lay across the threshold of the synagogue as every member of the congregation walked through the doorway, tramping on him as they passed through it.

He submitted to all of this and thus was "welcomed" back into the community, but he was so demoralized and depressed that he could not live with himself for much longer. He penned a brief autobiography, *Example of a Human Life*, in which he talked about his experience as a victim of intolerance—so much then for greater tolerated dissent in early modernity than in the ancient and medieval pasts—and one last time addressed the matter of the Laws of Nature, which, he contended, contain the best of the laws found in Judaism, Christianity, and Islam alike.[5] He obtained a pair of pistols with which he apparently intended to shoot both his cousin and himself (it is not clear why his cousin was in his sights), but the gun aimed at his cousin misfired. He managed to shoot himself, dying of his wound.

BARUCH (BENEDICT) SPINOZA: FROM *NIDDUI* TO *HEIREM*

That year (1640), Baruch (Benedict) Spinoza was turning eight years old. His family had most directly derived from *conversos* in the town of Espino in Galicia (northwest-ern Spain, just north of Portugal), but may also have had Portuguese and even French branches to it—and may have included among its members Don Diego d'Epinoza, a

Grand Inquisitor, which would simply add another thread of irony to the tapestry of this narrative. In any case, his father, Michael, a merchant of modest means, seems to have come in the 1620s from Galicia. Baruch was born on November 24, 1632, in the Jewish quarter of Amsterdam. Spinoza's mother, Hannah Deborah, Michael's second wife, died in 1638, when Baruch was only six years old. A few years later, in 1642, his father married a third time to Esther De Espinosa, whose family came from Lisbon (so even if Baruch's bloodlines did not include a Portuguese branch, the step-side of his family certainly did).

As a young lad at the Talmud Torah—a school for Jewish boys, who were still taught separately from their Christian neighbors, in which he studied Hebrew and Aramaic by way of the Hebrew Bible and the rabbinic tradition (the tradition that Uriel Acosta had rejected summarily when he became a Jew)—he showed splendid promise to become a rabbi. His most important teachers were none other than Rabbi Saul Levi Morteira and Manasseh ben Israel, who, as the key rabbinical figures in the Sephardic community of Amsterdam, had overseen the various excommunication processes involving Acosta. They shared the hope that Baruch would himself become a rabbi, and as he grew older he added to his repertoire a strong interest in the medieval Jewish rationalist philosophers, such as Maimonides, Gershonides, and Chasdai Crescas, and an interest in but apparent contempt for the mystical tradition of the kabbalists. Nonetheless, kabbalah and in particular the doctrine of the *sephirot* would have an influence on his thinking.

Manasseh ben Israel was the instructor who introduced Spinoza to kabbalah. He was also the individual who, visiting England in the 1650s, convinced Oliver Cromwell to publish an edict in effect rescinding the 1290 expulsion of the Jews. Morteira was a fanatical and conservative ecclesiastic. In retrospect, it was only a matter of time until conflict would erupt between these teachers and their pupil, brilliant and modest—but unafraid of expressing his rationalist viewpoint. It should be noted too that in 1648, when Spinoza was 16, several important events transpired within the world of Christians and Jews. In that "messianic" year, in which the Thirty Years War ended, two different individuals—David Reubeni, from central Europe, and Shabbetai Tzvi, of Ottoman Greece and Turkey—declared themselves to be the messiah. They stirred up, especially in Shabbetai's case, an enormous expectant reaction across the European Jewish world.

Meanwhile, by about 1651, the young Dutch Jew began to study the work of the French Catholic modernist philosopher René Descartes. Three years later, with the death of his father and no means—his family, his stepsister, and her husband, a zealous follower of Rabbi Morteira, had all but cast him off at this point—he began to teach in the private humanistic school run by an ex-Jesuit and freethinker, Franciscus van den Enden, with whom he also studied Latin and through whom he came into contact with the thought of Saint Augustine, the medieval Scholastics, Christian Renaissance thinkers, and modernists such as Thomas Hobbes. (Van den Enden himself would go to Paris later, in 1661, to further his own studies of Cartesian philosophy, where he became implicated in a plot to assassinate King Louis XIV.)

When Spinoza's father died in 1654, a struggle ensued between Spinoza and his half-sister, Rebecca, over an inheritance, and in her deposition before the court she referred to him as a "renegade." More precisely, his brother-in-law denounced him as an apostate and a heretic to the rabbinical authorities. These were led by Rabbi Morteira—Mannaseh ben Israel was in England—who was himself presumably already disappointed that Spinoza had not followed the spiritual path that he had foreseen for him and was acquainted with the intellectual vector along which the young thinker seemed to be traveling.

Spinoza decided to fight for his inheritance. From all that can be determined, his motive was not the money itself, but rather the principle: that justice be done in the matter of his father's will. But rather than acceding to a trial and judgment to be held before and through the rabbinic leaders—a Jewish *Bet Din*, theoretically emulating the sorts of *Batei Din* described in the Talmud's tractate *Sanhedrin*—he brought the case before the Dutch governmental (i.e., Christian) court. Such an act insulted the sense of authority of the rabbis and also provoked their fear, since to have internal community strife aired to outsiders might lead, they thought, to a curtailing of Jewish rights within that outside world.

Within the *Bet Din* that was nonetheless convened at the insistence of Rebecca and her husband, Rabbi Morteira was in the uncomfortable position of confronting the pupil whose brilliance he knew so well and whose freethinking had strayed so far from the course that he had expected and intended for him. Witnesses were called, since for someone to be found guilty of heretical thinking there needed to be a minimum of two witnesses who could attest to it. In other words, the case was being treated as a capital crime, since removal from the community was viewed as tantamount to death. As in the case of Uriel Acosta, two erstwhile acquaintances of Spinoza came forth and confirmed the "fact" that he had uttered blasphemous ideas in their presence. Morteira interrogated Spinoza, requesting either denial or confirmation of the testimony offered by his two "friends."

Apparently disheartened by this betrayal by friends, Spinoza refused to respond, neither confirming nor denying. The result was a thirty-day ban from visiting the synagogue and from receiving visits from fellow Jews—a *niddui*—together with a pleading, demanding, threatening request that he clean up his philosophical-spiritual act and renounce his heretical views. He remained silent in the face of the sermon delivered to him by the court. He found his inheritance case twisted into a heresy case before the *Bet Din*, which case was lost by his refusal to comply with its demand that he speak up. On the other hand, having won the inheritance case before the Christian court but then turning over the money to his half-sister, Spinoza began his life of increasing isolation from the Jewish community and of increasing interest in modernist thought.

Toward the end of the following year, on December 5, 1655, there is a record, nonetheless, of Spinoza reading from the Torah in the synagogue. Around the same time, van den Enden tried to convince him to take on a more substantial teaching position at his school, but Spinoza refused. One might suppose from the grounds of his later refusal to accept a teaching position at the university that this was because he was wary of being beholden to any institution that might then expect him to think and teach in a particular manner—or perhaps he simply wanted to devote more time to his own thinking. Since he needed so little to live on, Spinoza may well have reasoned that a more substantial teaching job would get in the way. He ended up making his modest living as a grinder of lenses.

In any case, the hostility toward him and his views, and possibly his outspokenness about those views as he began more firmly to formulate them, led to the convening of another *Bet Din*. This one took place without his even agreeing to be present.[4] Yet a crowded congregation filled the synagogue lit by black candles, where on July 27, 1656, a fuller ban—a *heirem*—was pronounced against him. The text of the *heirem* gives us a sense of how far the Sephardic rabbinate in Amsterdam had come toward seeing itself as an instrument of God to which God in turn hearkened—in a manner reminiscent of the inquisitional authorities in place for the Catholic Church since the thirteenth century. It reads in part:

> Obtaining . . . more information every day of the horrible heresies which he practiced and taught, and of the monstrous actions which he performed, and as they had many trustworthy witnesses who in the presence of the same Espinoza reported and testified against him and convicted him . . . they now excommunicate him with the following ban:

>> After the judgment of the Angels, and with that of the Saints, we excommunicate, expel, curse and damn Baruch d'Espinoza with the consent of God, Blessed be He, and with the consent of this Holy Congregation . . . with all the curses that are written in the Torah. Cursed be he by day, and cursed be he by night; cursed be he when he lies down and cursed be he when he rises up; cursed be he when he goes out and cursed be he when he comes in. The Lord will not pardon him; the anger and wrath of the Lord will rage against this man, and bring him all the curses that are written in the Book of the Torah, and the Lord will destroy his name from under the Heavens, and the Lord will separate him to his injury from all the tribes of Israel with all the curses of the firmament.

So these rabbis clearly at least intended their constituents to imagine them to be operating with God's cooperation and approval. Their tone is quite Christological right from the start, with their invocation of angels and saints. On the other hand, we recognize their usage of a key passage from the Torah (Deut 6:7), part of the *ve'ahavta*.

One might ask: what was it exactly about Spinoza's beliefs that so exercised everybody? We might assume that the content of his thought as it is found in his writings distressed members of the community or its rabbinic leaders. Certainly his short treatise, *God, Man and His Well-Being*, which discusses the issue of how we can have knowledge of God and thereby knowledge of truth, might have contained ideas that were deemed heretical. But he wrote this treatise between 1656 and 1660, after his excommunication, so his views were in any case only available orally at the time of both trials, the first one when he remained silent before Rabbi Morteira's interrogation and the second one when he was not even present before the *ma'amad* [rabbinical court].

That short treatise contains in seed form what would be the centerpiece of perhaps his greatest work, the *Ethics*, on which Spinoza spent the last fifteen years of his life—beginning his writing not before 1662, a good six years after the *heirem* was pronounced against him. In both the short and the long works God is associated with Nature. Put otherwise, Spinoza articulated a form of panhenotheism—a concept often confused with pantheism. Where the latter finds gods everywhere, the former finds the one [*heno*] God [*theos*] in all [*pan*] things. More specifically, Spinoza began to articulate the notion that God is Nature in the process of "naturing" [*natura naturans*] and what the creation process yielded is nature "natured" [*natura naturata*]: thus God is both separate from and yet identical with the universe.

While such an idea is not in fact so far from the Jewish and Christian notion that God breathes Itself into the first human and as Adam and Eve's "progeny" we are "besouled" thereby—we all have a bit of God within us—Spinoza offers two problems for the conventionally thinking Jew or Christian. One is that what I am calling "besoulment" encompasses more than merely humans. By implication, to ascribe souls to other than humans might be considered as heretical as, say, to argue that the earth moves around the sun rather than that the sun and all other heavenly entities revolve around the earth.

The other problem for most of Spinoza's contemporaries could be that what he describes essentially eliminates the "personality" ascribed by Judaism and Christianity to God and with that elimination he eliminates the notion of a personal relationship between God and ourselves: *natura naturans* cannot easily be imagined to be "talking" to Moses and delivering to him commandments at Sinai, much less hearkening to our daily prayers. The "personalization" of God by treating "God" as a—personal—"name" enables "my God" versus "your God" thinking—and with it, concepts of heresy, schism, and infidelism, together with religious violence and wars. We are far less likely to be driven into that sensibility if we refer to the creator as nature: *natura naturans.*

Spinoza observed, moreover, that our embrace of the Bible and its teachings is based on belief, which should not be confused with reason; there is no rational proof of God as the deliverer of the Torah to Moses. He also argued that in our tight embrace of the God of Scripture—a God of laws and commandments—we have lost hold of the God of Life that he articulates as continuous *natura*—that is, continuous in the barely discernible form of the nonetheless extant boundary between *naturans* and *naturata.*

The difficulty for us with all of this, however, is twofold. First, that new ideas and disagreement of ideas were a constant in earlier Jewish intellectual history. So the very fact of the process against Spinoza (as against Acosta and others) offers a unique moment in Jewish history, in which this particular branch of Jewish leadership is so paranoid as well as methodologically influenced by the very institution that is the central source of its paranoia that it acts in an unprecedented manner.

The second difficulty is that Spinoza hadn't written any of his "heretical" thoughts down until well after the time of his excommunication, so it is difficult to know what those who accused him actually had before them as proof of his heretical thinking. They clearly practiced an inquisitional methodology of embracing hearsay-based assertions, favoring the prosecution without worrying overly much about arguments for the defense. We might suppose that if, in the case of the first "trial," his sister and brother-in-law had money as a motive, in the case of subsequent "trials" it was the anger and frustration as righteous indignation of Rabbi Morteira and his colleagues that blinded them to the absurdity of the situation—aided and abetted by Spinoza's refusal either to return to the path that they envisioned for him or even to rise to the bait of his pathetic accusers.

Equally intriguing is the issue raised by the fact that, when he did write down his thoughts, he used Latin. As the universal language of science and philosophy in his era, Latin would have made his thought accessible to intellectuals across religious and political lines. So one might posit that in their concern that the non-Jewish majority would read Spinoza's writings and suppose from them that the Jewish minority was a group that not only denied the Christhood of Jesus but the Godhead in any form, the Sephardic leadership panicked and cast him out. But for fear related to the fact of his writing "publicly" in Latin to be the determining factor, he would already have had to write before the two trials leading to the *niddui* and *heirem* respectively had taken place. And there seems to be little likelihood that that had transpired.

So we are back to the more fundamental, word-of-mouth, gossip-based, jealousy-driven accusation and testimony and a condemnation supported by the refusal to defend himself. Where the rabbis were concerned, there may truly have been concern for the community's safety in general and in particular with regard to the possibility of reimposing the Inquisition upon it in the event of a Spanish or Portuguese return to power over the Netherlands. Casting out a Spinoza might be presumed to make the community less likely to attract the interest of the Inquisition in such an event.

They would have had at least one legitimate reason for that concern. The Dutch had been engaged for nine years in a war with the Portuguese for which the key focus in the end was the city of Recife, on the coast of Brazil. In the very year of Spinoza's father's death and the inheritance struggle with his stepsister and her husband, 1654, the victorious Portuguese among other things took Recife. Some of the *conversos* who had resumed their openly Jewish lives in the Dutch colony, who would now face the Inquisition, fled. They ended up not in Amsterdam but in New Amsterdam, marking the virtual beginning of the Jewish community in North America.

In spite of the totality of the *heirem* against him, Spinoza seems to have been largely unaffected by it (in this, as in other ways, he was different from Acosta) and content to live a pretty isolated life. He did respond to the charges by way of a theological essay, his *Apologia*, which the community was forbidden to read, of course. Many of his former Christian associates also began to avoid him, since the views he espoused—or was said to espouse—were as offensive to them as they were to Jews. Among those who did not abandon him was Franciscus van den Enden, in whose home Spinoza lived during the next few years (and with whose daughter, Clara Maria, Spinoza was, according to some overly romanticizing sources, in unrequited love).

He subsequently moved to Ouderkerk, just outside Amsterdam. By 1660, he had moved on to Rhynsburg, near Leiden. He kept up correspondence with a close circle of friends and fellow scholars and wrote some of the most important treatises in philosophy and theology of the seventeenth century. He died peacefully, in his sleep, on February 21, 1677, and was buried in the cemetery of the New Church in Amsterdam, although he never renounced his Judaism or became a Christian.

In one of his letters to Henry Oldenburg we get a brief summary of issues that are discussed in his *Ethics*, such as his comment "God, whom I define as a Being consisting in infinite attributes, whereof each is infinite or supremely perfect, after its time. You must observe that by attribute I mean everything, which is conceived through itself and in itself, so that the conception of it does not involve the conception of anything else ... by God we mean a Being supremely perfect and absolutely infinite."

In the same letter to Oldenburg, Spinoza also went on to respond to his colleague's inquiry regarding "errors that I detect in the Cartesian and Baconian philosophies." In this we recognize him as a key figure in the shaping of modern Western thought—some have asserted that Spinoza is the father of modern Western thought—so what might have been dissent within the rabbinic Jewish world was part of a process of laying down tracks for the larger world that gradually saw itself as not Christian, but post-Christian and secular.

MODERNITY, THE HOLOCAUST, AND HANNAH ARENDT

We may point to any number of ways in which "modernity" succeeded in separating itself from medieval thinking and behavior—from the industrial and scientific revolutions to the diverse acts of emancipation of Jews in the late eighteenth and early nineteenth centuries. On the one hand, extraordinary advances in science and technology would bring the world crashing down around the ears of the West with the Great War of 1914–1918—if its cause was less religion than politics and economics, it was no less fierce in articulating the unique human capacity for cruelty and destruction against other humans.

As modernity hurtled forward, the small-scale trauma for Spinoza's Sephardic Jewish community exploded into a trauma for the entire Jewish world within two decades after the Great War, as the Holocaust swept across Jewish life and consciousness. The new technology of gas that had reshaped the horror of war at Verdun and the Somme in 1916—through which, in each battle, half a million men were destroyed on both sides of the national divide—was applied to civilians, who were destroyed in unprecedented numbers at killing centers at sites like Maidanek and Auschwitz-Birkenau.

The aftermath of the Holocaust is particularly noteworthy for the degree to which it was ignored—perpetrators certainly did not wish to be reminded or to have others reminded of what they had done; the allies, who had fought so hard to defeat the Germans but manifested far less concern about ending the Nazi Holocaust of Jews, did not want to be reminded of that large gap in their glory; survivors preferred to get on and try to reshape their lives rather than obsess about the worst era of their lives.

This began to change in 1961, with the capture and very public trial of Adolph Eichmann, who functionally shaped the Final Solution to the Jewish Problem that anchored the Holocaust. With remarkable alacrity, the subject of the Holocaust moved from offstage to center stage: books began to proliferate and—often in lieu of broader Jewish studies programs—Holocaust programs entered the academic world as courses and even departments. Among the books that emerged early was the work of journalistic social philosophy by Hannah Arendt: *Eichmann in Jerusalem: A Report on the Banality of Evil.* What began as a series of *New Yorker* articles achieved a large—and largely negative—notoriety, particularly within the Jewish community, for what was interpreted as an insensitive blindness to the suffering of Hitler's victims and an overly simple equation of their psychological position with that of their Nazi victimizers: that "evil" is banal and easily enacted by anyone, and not unique to Nazis at the Holocaust level or at any level.

Arendt's critics asserted that her coverage of the Eichmann trial reflected motivations aside from those of mere reporting—or rather, that she used her reporting as a stepping-off point for other issues that interested her, such as exposing the Jewish leadership during the Holocaust as morally flawed and offering a focus on German guilt and on larger philosophical questions regarding the nature of totalitarianism. Indeed, she presented a critical view of the judicial procedures in the Israeli courtroom, asserting that larger issues that should have been set aside were not, in order to facilitate the building of the case "on what the Jews had suffered, not on what Eichmann had done."[5]

Arendt wondered whether in the end justice was served and whether we learned anything from the proceedings and their outcome. She asserted that the trial obscured "the lesson that this long course in human wickedness had taught us—the lesson of the fearsome word-and-thought-defying banality of evil." Further, in proceeding toward her theme of the everyday banality of evil, at least *in potentia*, Arendt placed emphasis on Eichmann's own banality: she dwelt on his shallow intellect, his cliché-filled speaking patterns, and his great capacity for self-deception and detachment from reality.

Given how iconic the Holocaust and its eventually heroized surviving victims were becoming, particularly through the Eichmann trial, Arendt would appear to be an early dissenter with regard to the engagement of that subject. The question—raised by some of her critics—was whether she offered dissent or mere criticism. And was it criticism of Judaism as if from without, as opposed to self-criticism from within? Was it dissent or criticism as opposed to self-loathing? It was easy to accuse her of *selbsthasse*: self-hate.[6]

As a Jew who moved comfortably in the exhilarating upper stratosphere of German academia—she was romantically involved and in love with her professor, Martin Heidegger, to the extent that his distinct Nazi leanings were completely ignored by this otherwise very astute thinker—she was believed by many to have retained a profound anger, not at the Germans, whose embrace of Nazism led to her becoming a refugee and forced her to leave that world behind (although she relocated to the Institute for Advanced Studies at Princeton University, as opposed to having to clean bathrooms or drive a taxicab), but at the Jews: had she not been Jewish, she would not have been pushed out as she was.

This is speculative, of course, and her involvement in Jewish organizations soon after she arrived in the United States might also be seen to militate against this perspective regarding her motivations. The point for the purposes of this discussion is that the views espoused in Arendt's book dissented distinctly from the normative appraisal of the Holocaust and its surviving victims and their victimizers. That, like Spinoza, she was a philosopher raises the question of how much she may be seen to be following a line of thinking independent of the Jewish community and critical of its leadership that began with Acosta and Spinoza and resonated three centuries later. If New York—or, more broadly, American—Jewry had possessed the mechanism for a *heirem* in the 1960s, it is fair to suggest that she would have been subject to one.

SUBVERSIVE QUESTIONS OF MODERN JEWISH ART AND THE PAINTINGS OF GEOFFREY LAURENCE

During the same three centuries of evolving modernity in the realms of philosophy and political thought, the visual arts were also moving forward, particularly for Jews. From Salom Italia, the mid-seventeenth century lithographer and illuminator, best known for his portraits of rabbinical figures—including the most famous, Manassah ben Israel—to the mid-nineteenth century genre scenes of Moritz Oppenheim and Mauritzy Gottlieb and the landscapes of Camille Pissarro, and from the distinctive portraits of Amadeo Modigliani to the luminous abstract expressionist masterpieces of Mark Rothko and Barnett Newman, Jews moved gradually but inexorably from the edges to the center of Western art. By the twentieth century the pace of engagement had expanded exponentially and by the last third of the century—from the time period soon after the Eichmann trial forward—explosively, in painting, sculpture, architecture, and a range of other modes of visual expression.

With that explosion there also emerged a distinctive question that continues to be frequently asked by Jewish artists today: where do I (and my art) fit into Western art, so much of the history of which in the past fifteen centuries has been Christian art? Works like Barnett Newman's *The Name II* (1950) and Susan Schwalb's entire *Creation* series from the mid-1990s both use the triptych form familiar in Christian art, with its triune God symbolism, but radically transform the overt subject matter—turning to complete abstraction, among other things—to recast that form's symbolic language in Jewish terms. Others play on recognizable Jewish symbols, such as the seven-branched menorah—or more subtle ones (I am thinking, for example, of paintings and sculptures by Ruth Mordecai in the 1970s and beyond, into the new millennium), like the arched form that is associated with the "Syrian Gable" of ancient synagogues at sites like Kfar Bar-Am and Capernaum.[7]

So too, by the 1970s, a growing array of Jewish artists—almost any Jewish artist worth his or her salt—began to feel compelled to address that consummate Jewish trauma, the Holocaust. Survivor artists, like Alice Lok Cahane in her series, *Rainbows from the Ashes*, or Kitty Klaidman—who turned to the subject only after a 1989 family visit back to the small Slovakian town in which she was hidden, as a small child, with her brother and parents—used their mixed media works as instruments of both reflection and healing. Second-generation artists, like Kitty's daughter, Elyse, painted fiercely expressionist works that bubble with barely suppressed anger.[8]

Artists like R. B. Kitaj and Judy Chicago—she is renowned for her feminist work, in particular her iconic installation *The Dinner Party*—found themselves aware only by the late 1960s, somehow, of the enormous catastrophe. Ohio-born Kitaj turned from American themes to those that embedded the issue of the Holocaust and its iconic oven chimneys into a constant reflection on Jewish historical experience. Chicago, on the other hand, together with her husband, photographer Donald Woodman, created an enormous multimedia work called *The Holocaust Project* (1993).[9]

Among the bolder artists to address this subject—in a subversive, dissenting manner—is Santa Fe–based painter Geoff Laurence (b. 1950). The son of survivors—his father so scarred by the experience that, in a differently angled and more obvious act of *selbsthasse* than some see in Arendt, he refused to allow his wife to use garlic in her cooking: "It stinks of the ghetto!"—Laurence grew up virtually afraid of his Jewish identity. He recovered it as he was developing as an artist, and among the subjects that he has intermittently addressed is the Holocaust, beginning with a small mixed-media installation, *Inheritance*, composed with fragments of objects brought to America by his father from that era.

Laurence's most astonishing painting focused on this subject, however, is called *ISWASWILLBE* (2000), which offers a wry and disturbing comment on one of the painful consequences of the Holocaust: it will be several more generations before it will be possible for us to disentangle the term "Jew" from the term "Nazi" or even the term "German"—particularly given an environment in which too often in, say, academic settings, "Holocaust studies" has become the mainstay or the even the only component of "Jewish studies" courses, programs, and events.

In Laurence's painting, two figures stand before the viewer on the front part of a stage, its curtains pushed back, baroque style, to reveal the figures. One of these is a Nazi officer, attired in full uniform, with jackboots and leather. He presents the second figure, arm around his shoulder, to the viewer—as if that second figure is being stage-managed or directed by the Nazi officer. That second figure is a skeleton, and around its shoulders is what we can easily recognize as a *tallit*—a Jewish prayer shawl.

Thus the message is clear: Jew and Nazi (Jew and German, Jew and Austrian, Jews and those from all the places where Nazism flourished) are inextricably interconnected on the stage of history. Judaism has come to the front and center of that stage in the more than half century since Auschwitz, but the irony is that if and when that position is dependent only on the matter of the Holocaust, it is the Nazis who become the impresarios—and the form of Judaism that they hoped to skeletonize has in fact been reduced to a skeleton of the robust living creature that had marched so dynamically across the stage of history for millennia.

Geoffrey Laurence, *ISWASWILLBE*, oil on canvas, 2000.
(Permission granted by Geoffrey Laurence.)

The bright light cast upon this pair illumines a circle of bright red (the color of the curtain) framed in deep shadowy black. The colors red and black in combination (which colors are echoed on the Nazi uniform) are the colors of Nazi flags but also a traditional Renaissance symbol of purgatory: the painful yet hopeful process of ascent from hell to paradise—but this is a drama for which such an ascent is hardly a given. The stage lights of Laurence's visual and conceptual theater are harshly focused, sharpening the details and the edges of his characters and the questions that their performance forces upon us. He asks whether on the stage that is the life where we all act our parts for better and for worse, whether on the stage of the next generation and the generation after that, we will act in concert to produce a theater of ongoing tragedy or arrive finally at a conclusion in which we might live happily, even if thoughtfully, ever after.[10]

This work is hardly in lockstep with the authoritative mainstream visual address of a once ignored, now iconic subject. Nor is it the only time when Laurence has been subversive in his imagery. His 1999 *Tefillin* [Prayer phylacteries] addresses the question of Jewish artists within Western Christian art while embedding in it a question asked with increasing parallel passion by Jewish women artists like Schwalb, in her previously mentioned *Creation* series, or like Judy Chicago's colleague in pioneering feminist art, Miriam Schapiro, in her *My Home* series. That question is "Where do I as a Jewish woman artist fit in—to Western art, with or without Christian emphases, which has been so female-artist-exclusive over its history? And to Judaism, which traditionally excludes women from fundamental ritual aspects of the faith, such as reading publicly from the Torah or reciting the kaddish [mourner's prayer] after one's father's death?"[11]

Laurence is one of the few significant male artists to echo that query in this painting, conceived as a vertical triptych—and thus revisiting the "Christian art" issue by reconceiving that familiar form, but with figurative imagery. The "figures" however, are parts of an anonymous, unidentifiable, naked female body—not a woman, but her body or body parts—alluding, tongue-in-cheek, to the long history of naked women, from Praxiteles's sculpture (ca. 340–330 BCE) of his girlfriend, Phryne, as "Aphrodite"; to *Venuses* by Titian and Giorgione; to their disturbing reflex in Manet's *Olympia*; to Matisse's various *Odalisques*. All of these images and many others like them have been contrived by male artists for the visual delectation and pleasure of male viewers. Laurence's work finalizes the removal of humanity in which the viewer isn't interested anyway, by eliminating a face and reducing the figure to sumptuous eye candy.

There is more, however: he has bound (pun intended) a leather thong in and around those body parts. Most Jews, at least, would immediately recognize that thong—and connect it to the painting's title as the leather strap of the *t'fillin* [phylacteries] that traditional Jewish males wrap around their right arm and around the upper part of their heads during morning prayers, on every day but the Sabbath. In both cases, the straps are attached to, extend from, small boxes (one on the upper arm; the other on the forehead, just above the eyes) with prescribed passages from the Torah written on parchment within them. The boxes and wrapped-around leather straps respond to and fulfill an injunction found within those prescribed passages: "Thou shall bind them for a sign upon thy hand and they shall be as frontlets between thine eyes" (Deut 6:8). But only men do this. In traditional Judaism, only men are permitted to do this, which means that women are excluded from fulfilling this commandment, as they are from so many others.

The most sacred of actions wraps itself around the most secular of presentations of a woman—a kind of *Playboy* centerfold, its three foldout parts each within its own frame. Moreover, given the nipple ring in the bottommost painting in the triptych, one can surely associate the image with sexual bondage. So the commandment to bind it and such bondage pun on and play with each other in this subversive work that dissents from the standard, straightforward adulation in authoritative tradition of the glories of fulfilling divine commandments without worrying about the question of who is included and who excluded from the rewarding pleasure of fulfillment.[12]

Geoffrey Laurence, *Tefillin* (detail, bottom panel), acrylic on
wood, 1999. (Permission granted by Geoffrey Laurence.)

HELÈNE AYLON AND VISUAL
DISSIDENCE AGAINST TRADITIONAL
RABBINIC ADJUDICATION

This is an issue taken up with an extended emphasis by Helène Aylon (1931–2020) an
Orthodox-raised woman who married at seventeen but was widowed at thirty. She
began her career as an artist with a focus on environmentalist issues before beginning
to produce art that combined environmental matters with feminist concerns. The
distinct turn toward the interweave of the Jewish question vis-à-vis Western art with
the female question within art and within Judaism began to percolate in a particular
manner just before her son's wedding, when they went out to the cemetery to visit
his father's (her husband's) grave—and she noticed, perhaps for the first time, that
the inscription referred to him as the son of his own father, but with no mention of
his mother.

She realized that her traditional wedding contract, her *ketubah*, connecting her to
her husband at the beginning of their life together, mirrored this feature, in offering
both of their names, but also referring only to their respective fathers and not to their
mothers—and that the traditional illuminated *ketubah* that her own son was asking
her to create for him would necessarily also make no mention of her, who had borne
and singlehandedly raised him.

The culmination of the thinking process that this induced was a nine-part series of installations created over a thirty-seven-year period called *The G-d Project*. Beginning in 1990–1996, each component became an act of subversion that would engage tradition and traditional texts and challenge their traditional readings. Thus, for instance, in the fourth part of the series—her 1999 *Epilogue: Alone with My Mother*—she placed five spread-open books on five tables: the five books of the Torah in book (not scroll) form. In each she had scrupulously gone through the texts and struck through, with a pink highlighter pen, words and passages that promote or can be construed to promote violence, particularly against women. She asserted that God could never have spoken such words and phrases or delivered such commandments, that these must be the result of the male-dominated redaction (editing) and transmission process, and that in eliminating these unacceptable passages she was liberating God from the shackles of that process.

The entire series culminated in 2007 with a room-sized installation called *All Rise*. With this work our own discussion spirals full circle to where it began—with the observation that the rabbinic tradition inherently entertains dissent in its discussions—but as a spiral, rather than simply a circle, it begins a new spin: a spin that dissents from more than two millennia of tradition. In Aylon's installation, three high-backed chairs sit on a platform approached by three steps. The chairs represent the three judges who, according to tractate *Sanhedrin*, should make up a standard *Bet Din* that adjudicates everyday matters (as opposed to the twenty-three-person *Bet Din*, which deals with capital crimes, or the Great Sanhedrin, the *Bet Din HaGadol* of seventy-one persons). For tractate *Sanhedrin* is that extended text within the ultimate Jewish, human-contrived textual legal authority, the Talmud, in which, among other things, the question is asked and discussed regarding who may and who may not serve as judges or witnesses in a *Bet Din*.

In providing an ascent, the three steps of Aylon's installation allude to authoritative ideas and structures in the Judaean-Jewish tradition, such as the Temple, with its threefold courtyard, or a text like that of the Talmudic tractate, *Pirke Avot* (2:1), that "on three things the world stands: Torah, service and good works." The platform and its chairs are flanked by two flags—made of pink pillowcases.[13] Three brass plaques adorn the surfaces above the chairs, and the latter are decorated with fringes that resemble the fringes on a *tallit* [prayer shawl] traditionally worn by Jewish males (but not females) in prayer.

On the railing before the platform are two lengthy inscriptions that explain what this installation is about and how it serves as a profound offering of dissent within and against the authority-shaping of the rabbinic tradition. The first inscription notes that the *Shulhan Arukh* and *Mishneh Torah* forbid women from serving as judges or giving evidence in a *Bet Din*. It further alludes to Joseph Karo (author of the *Shulhan Arukh*) and to Maimonides (a preeminent medieval Jewish philosopher), suggesting that their exclusion of women—"and minors and idiots and slaves (among others)"—for such roles misrepresents God's intentions (and the Divine Name is rendered as G-d, following the Orthodox tradition of not saying or writing the ineffable Name of God, even in the circumlocution of an English translation). And so, in contradiction of and as an antidote to that historical exclusion, the artist observes that she has created "an imaginary female court of law also known as a Bet Din."

The second inscription offers a "petition for an apology in absentia, as it were" to be made to all of those women who might have been judges but were forbidden from offering religious/legal opinions—which opinions will never be known—that they, women who are judges and judges who are women, be finally addressed as "your honor." Thus "all women will be honored and the Name of G-d will be honored." And she notes the Jewish year—5768—and "rest[s her] case."

The installation dissents, then, not from the structural idea of the *Bet Din* but from its makeup as all male throughout rabbinic history, and with that ongoing makeup a fundamental lack of *kavod*—the Hebrew word for "honor," the root consonants of which comprise the word *kaved*, "heavy"—and thus a fundamental lack of weight is traditionally accorded to women. Assumed to lack weight, gravitas, women have been subject not only to standard exclusions, as from reading the Torah publicly and reciting kaddish for their fathers—and mothers—but also from studying kabbalah and in matters specifically handled by a traditional *Bet Din*, such as the right to petition successfully for key life changes: a divorce, for instance. Aylon asks: Is it not about time that *Batei Din* included women among their constituencies?

Dissent is to ask questions and to offer disagreement with authority, with the mainstream, with the majority. What begins within rabbinic Judaism as a kind of norm yields—from Acosta and Spinoza to Arendt to Laurence and Aylon (among others)—increasingly diverse verbal and visual ways of questioning rabbinic Judaism and its authoritative format and of disagreeing with mainstream Jewish thinking as that thinking has itself continued to evolve through whatever we might term the "modern" age.

Aylon's dissident installation addresses the question of extent or limitation to the very concept of dissent within the traditionally conceived rabbinic tradition. As a practical if speculative matter, one might wonder whether the *Bet Din* faced by Spinoza might have treated him differently had its constituents been female or at least included women. Aylon's work offers a particular furthering of the insistent push toward "modernity" that began with Spinoza, offering universal yet very specific Jewish implications in the context of both thought and visual art.

NOTES

1. See Cecil Roth, *A History of the Marranos* (New York: Harper & Row, 1966), ch. II, IV, and V.

2. The question of what happens after death, what sort of an afterlife there might or might not be, and whether and how reward and punishment might play out in that posthumous realm had been discussed and debated in fact by the rabbis (and is found in rabbinic literature) as far back as the time when the Pharisees and Sadducees and subsequently the "schools" of Hillel and Shammai, respectively, were operative—before the time of Jesus.

3. See Uriel Acosta, *A Specimen of Human Life* (New York: Bergman, 1967).

4. Nor was Manasseh Ben Israel present, since he was still in England meeting with Cromwell and would not return to the Netherlands until 1657.

5. Hannah Arendt, *The Trial of Eichmann: A Report on the Banality of Evil* (New York: Viking, 1963), 6. It should be noted that Gideon Hausner, chief judge of the court, in his long book on the Eichmann trial extensively discussed the many ways in which the court exercised itself in order to make sure that Eichmann received a fair trial. See Gideon Hausner, *Justice in Jerusalem* (New York: Schocken, 1968), ch. 18, 19, 20.

6. For the most renowned critical discussion of this work, see Gershom Scholem's last (1963) letter to Arendt—written presumably with the intention that it be made public published (which it was)—and which marked the end of a more than thirty-year friendship—in *The Correspondence of Hannah Arendt and Gershom Scholem* (ed. Marie Luise Knott; trans. Anthony David; Chicago: University of Chicago Press, 2017).

7. For more detail on these artists and works, see Ori Z. Soltes, *Tradition and Transformation* (New York: Canal Street Studios, 2016), 294–97, 421–22, 482–83.

8. Ibid., 396–400, 448–50.

9. Ibid., 407–9, 422–24.

10. Ibid., 489–90. See also Geoffrey Laurence, *The Holocaust Series* (Santa Fe: Lomnitz, 2010), 25–30.

11. Soltes, *Tradition and Transformation*, 422.

12. Ibid., 489.

13. Alas, Helène Aylon died due to complications brought on by Covid-19 as this essay and volume were being prepared for print, and before I was able to reach her for permission to show an image of this work, or to fully quote her two inscriptions in the form in which she wrote and placed them in it. One may be found in Soltes, *Tradition and Transformation*, 486.

JEWISH LAW AND THE LAW OF THE STATE

A Study in Authority and Dissent

GIL GRAFF

INTRODUCTION: "THE LAW OF THE KINGDOM IS LAW"

THROUGHOUT THE TWO and a half millennia that have passed since the end of the first Jewish commonwealth (586 BCE), Jews and Judaism have confronted the challenge of relating to the demands of the ruling power. In the spirit of accommodation to the law of the state, Jeremiah counseled the Judeans exiled to Babylonia to "seek the peace of the city whither I have caused you to be carried away captive, and pray unto the Lord for it; for in the peace thereof shall ye have peace" (Jer 29:7). Similarly, Nehemiah advised the Judeans living under Persian rule to accommodate themselves to their subjugation, for God had willed that their overlords "have power over our bodies, and over our cattle, at their pleasure" (Neh 9:37). Living at a time of Roman rule, Rabbi Hanina, declared: "Pray for the welfare of the government, for were it not for the fear of it, men would swallow each other alive" (*Avot* 3.2).

Not until early in the third century CE was a legal principle addressing the issue of the Jews' relationship to state law formulated. In the three words *dina de-malkhuta dina* [the law of the kingdom is the law], the Babylonian *amora* [Talmudic sage] Samuel enunciated a doctrine that was to become the basis for defining church-state relations in Jewish law.[1] There are but four references to the principle in the Talmud (*Ned.* 28a; *Git.* 10b; *B.K.* 113 a–b; *B.B.* 54b–55a), none of which sets forth a legal foundation for the dictum.

As did Babylonian Jewry, the European Jewish communities of the Middle Ages enjoyed substantial control over the conduct of their legal affairs. As long as Jews exercised such autonomy, the principle *dina de-malkhuta dina* remained limited in the scope of its application; it was invoked primarily in the realms of taxation, confiscation, and the execution of bills in non-Jewish courts. Its application was defined by rabbinic authorities. The principle served not only as a means of accommodation to the will of the monarch; it was also interpreted to provide a legal basis for resistance to the arbitrary demands of the ruling power. Unjust decrees were pronounced *gezelah de-malkhuta* [robbery by the kingdom] and were deemed beyond the scope of the king's authority. *Dina de-malkhuta dina* thus reflected elements of both authority and dissent.

After briefly examining the Talmudic origins and various bases adduced for Samuel's statement, this essay explores the scope of the principle's application in medieval times through its use by the Assembly of Notables convened by Napoleon in 1806. Over these more than fifteen hundred years, changing notions of law and the Jews' standing in society contributed to an evolving definition of *dina de-malkhuta dina*. Consistent with the general trend toward the acceptance of positive law in the thirteenth and fourteenth centuries and in response to the reality of the *servi camerae* [servants of the royal chamber] status to which the Jews were reduced in the aftermath of the Crusades, determinations of *gezelah de-malkhuta* — the basis for resistance to unjust decrees — significantly diminished over time.

During the long span of years between the third and eighteenth centuries, there was remarkable uniformity in the range of issues arising in connection with *dina de-malkhuta dina*. This is in great measure attributable to the legal authority that characterized Jewish life until the emancipation. From the perspective of medieval kings, the law of the land governed the Jews; the king, however, chose to accord his Jews significant communal autonomy. From the Jewish perspective, *dina de-malkhuta dina* gave limited recognition to foreign law, based on Jewish law.

With the erosion of the corporate society of medieval Europe and the emergence of the modern state, the legal autonomy enjoyed by Jewish communities since the initial formulation of Samuel's dictum came to an end. Starting in the eighteenth century — and brought to a head by Napoleon — the state increasingly encroached on domains previously reserved to the jurisdiction of the Church. In this new historical milieu, the principle *dina de-malkhuta dina* again evolved, providing the legal framework for Jewish accommodation to modern Western society. The extent or limit of its application became a matter of vigorous debate between Jewish traditionalists and religious reformers. This internal debate over *dina de-malkhuta dina* reflected a larger narrative of authority and dissent with respect to the continuing role and scope of Jewish law in modern society.

LEGAL BASIS OF *DINA DE-MALKHUTA DINA*

The Talmudic references to *dina de-malkhuta dina* affirm the ruler's authority to collect customs (*B.K.* 113a), appropriate palm trees for the construction of bridges (*B.K.* 113b), require written deeds of sale to effectuate land transfers (*B.B.* 54b), confiscate and sell land for failure to pay the land tax (*B.B.* 55a), and ordain that forty years' unchallenged occupancy of land establish an impregnable claim of ownership (*B.B.* 55a). Samuel's statement is also brought in his name to afford legal recognition to bills executed by non-Jewish courts, with the specific exclusion of divorce and manumission (*Git.* 10b).

The Talmud is silent as to the legal foundation of the principle *dina de-malkhuta dina*. During the medieval period, however, a number of bases for the principle were proposed. Rashi (1040–1105) predicated Samuel's statement on the commandment obligating non-Jews to enact laws to preserve social order. Although all humankind ("the sons of Noah") was obligated to maintain order in the world, the nations of the world were not expected to observe the strictures of Jewish marriage and divorce law. Hence the specific exclusion of writs of divorce from the jurisdiction of non-Jewish courts is readily understandable (Rashi, *Git.* 9b). Other scholars viewed the principle as a matter of implicit, contractual agreement between the king and his subjects. Thus, Maimonides (1135–1204), in codifying the law that the principle applies to the edicts of a king whose sovereignty is demonstrated by the circulation of his coins as common, local currency, avers that the inhabitants of that country have accepted him and take it for granted that he is their master and they are servants to him (Maimonides, *Yad, Gezelah,* 5:18). Similarly, Rashi's grandson, R. Samuel b. Meir (1085–1174), commented: "For all the citizens accept the king's statutes and laws of their own free will" (Rashbam, *B.B.* 54b). Rabbi Nissim of Gerondi (ca. 1310–1375) explained the contractual basis of *dina de-malkhuta dina* more starkly: because the king owns the land, the Jews are obligated to obey the conditions he establishes for residence thereon (Ran, *Ned.* 28a). Yet another basis for the contract was the principle that a king acquires total sovereignty over his subjects through military conquest (Rashba, *Yev.* 46a).[2] A third rationale for *dina de-malkhuta dina* was first put forward by Rabbi Ya'akov Tam (ca. 1100–1171), younger brother of the Rashbam (Rabbi Samuel b. Meir). Rabbeinu Tam based the rule on the right of the court to uproot a law of the Torah in matters of civil law, *hefker bet din hefker* (*Git.* 36b, *Yev.* 89b). Another view analogized the authority of the ruler to the power of a king of Israel (*Hidushei ha-Ritba, B.B.* 55a).[3] A fifth view based the legal underpinning of the principle on the halachic validity of customary law (*Aliyot de-Rabbeinu Yonah, B.B.* 55a).[4] Salo Baron aptly observed that, in the Middle Ages, "*Dina de-malkhuta dina* was more frequently invoked than clarified."[5]

LIMITATIONS ON THE SCOPE OF
DINA DE-MALKHUTA DINA

A fundamental principle, upon which all authorities agreed, was that *dina de-malkhuta dina* recognition extended only to monetary matters [*mamona*] and not to religious ritual prohibitions [*issur ve-hetter*]. Another universally accepted axiom was that the law of the kingdom must apply equally to all the kingdom's inhabitants (Maimonides, *Yad, Gezelah* 5:14; *Sh. Ar, H.M.* 369:8). But if a law fell equally upon all Jews, even though it was discriminatory against Jews as a class, it was at times upheld (*She'elot u-Teshuvot Maharik* 194).[6] This qualification reflected the feudal realities of European Jewish life; the principle was not so qualified by the rabbinic authorities living under Moslem rule.[7]

In the spirit of medieval jurisprudence, most of the *rishonim* [early medieval Jewish legal authorities] limited the application of *dina de-malkhuta dina* to ancient law, excluding new legislation enacted by the king (*Ḥiddushei ha-Ritba, B.B.* 55a). With the developing trend toward the recognition of positive law in the later Middle Ages, there were changes in the Jewish legal position with regard to new legislation.[8] A distinction was made, however, between legally warranted taxes (those within the scope of *dina de-malkhuta dina*) and taxes considered *gezelah de-malkhuta* [robbery by the kingdom] and hence avoidable.[9]

Though the king was by no means bound by rabbinic pronouncements, a rabbinic declaration that an act was *gezelah* had implications within the Jewish community. If property were stolen, one who later came into its possession would not be considered the rightful owner. A Jew could not benefit from the unlawful confiscation of another Jew's property. To this extent, the principle *dina de-malkhuta dina* was not only one of accommodation but also one of resistance and dissent.

RESORT TO NON-JEWISH COURTS

The issue of the validity of bills executed in non-Jewish courts was a matter of substantial rabbinic discussion during the Middle Ages. A *mishnah* [oral teaching recorded early in the third century] in *Gittin* [Talmudic tractate Divorce] permitted recourse to non-Jewish courts for the limited purpose of executing certain bills (*Git.* 10b). However, a further *tannaitic* [material attributed to the sages quoted in the Mishnah] passage absolutely forbade seeking judgment before a non-Jewish tribunal: "It has been taught: R. Tarfon used to say: In any place where you find heathen law courts, even though their law is the same as the Israelite law, you must not resort to them since it says, 'These are the judgments which thou shalt set before them,' [Exod 21:1] that is to say, 'before them' and not before heathens" (*Git.* 88b). The Ashkenazic *rishonim* [early rabbinic authorities] insisted upon the exclusive jurisdiction of rabbinic courts for Jewish litigants,[10] and this provision was successfully solicited from the secular powers in the Jews' corporate charters.

At a synod at Troyes, about 1150, Rabbeinu Tam and other authorities, with the assent of a large group of northern French and possibly western German rabbis, decreed:

1. We have voted, decreed, ordained and declared under the *ḥerem* [ban] that no man or woman may bring a fellow-Jew before Gentile courts or exert compulsion on him through Gentiles, whether by a prince or a common man, a ruler or an inferior official, except by mutual agreement made in the presence of proper witnesses

2. If the matter accidentally reaches the government or other Gentiles, and in that manner pressure is exerted on a Jew, we have decreed that the man who is aided by the Gentiles shall have saved his fellow from their hands, and shall secure him against the Gentiles . . . and he shall make satisfaction to him and secure him in such manner as the seven elders of the city will ordain. . . .

3. He shall not intimidate the seven elders through the power of Gentiles. And because the masters of wicked tongue and informers do their deeds in darkness, we have decreed also excommunication for indirect action unless he satisfy him in accordance with the decision of the elders of the city.[11]

The continuing prohibition against recourse to non-Jewish tribunals was not only rooted in the struggle to preserve judicial autonomy but also in a belief that these forums were fundamentally corrupt and unfair. Thus even for the purpose of accepting a document drawn in a non-Jewish court as evidence of a sale, Maimonides required that it be established that the judges and witnesses in the court in question did not accept bribes (*Yad, Git.* 1.5).

Over time, owing both to external pressures and to the internal weakening of rabbinic authority, the exclusive jurisdiction of Jewish tribunals over cases involving Jews began to erode. In an effort to combat this trend, a synod of the heads of various German Jewish communities gathered at Frankfurt in 1603 decreed:

It is a common offense among the people of our generation to refuse to obey Jewish law and even to compel opposing litigants to present themselves before secular courts. The result is that the Holy Name is profaned and that the Government and the Judges are provoked at us. We have therefore decided that anyone who sues his neighbor in secular courts shall be compelled to free him from all the charges made against him, even though the courts decided in favor of the plaintiff. A person guilty of taking a case to Gentile courts shall be separated from the community of

Israel, shall not be called to the Torah, and shall not be permitted to marry until
he repents and frees his fellow from the power of the Gentile courts. If the defen-
dant was compelled to undertake expenditures in order to bring the infraction of
this ordinance before the Jewish courts, the offender shall be compelled to bear
the expense.[12]

Notwithstanding the forceful tone of the ordinance, the problem it addressed does
not appear to have been solved, as evidenced by continuing rabbinic fulminations
against recourse to non-Jewish courts throughout the eighteenth century. Implicit
in the choice of non-Jewish courts was dissent from the authority of rabbinic courts.
The erosion of rabbinic authority was exacerbated by the fact that the charters granted
the Jews in the seventeenth and eighteenth centuries substantially eliminated rabbinic
judicial authority in other than ceremonial and ritual matters.

THE NAPOLEONIC PHASE: BACKDROP
TO THE ASSEMBLY OF NOTABLES

In France, the abolition of corporate society as part of the Revolution led to the
phenomenon of the Jew as state citizen. This new standing vis à vis the state called
for a redefinition of *dina de-malkhuta dina*. Although the French Revolution eventually extended citizenship to the Jews, it was Napoleon who demanded a definitive
pronouncement on the relationship between Jewish law and the law of the state.

In dealing with the institutions of religion in French society, Napoleon sought
above all a means of subordinating them to the state; this began with the Church.
Long before his rise to prominence, Napoleon had written:

It is axiomatic that Christianity, even the reformed kind, destroys the unity of the
State: (1) because it is capable of weakening as well as of inspiring the trust which
the people owe the representatives of the law; (2) because, such as it is constituted,
Christianity contains a separate body which not only claims a share of the citizens'
loyalty but is able even to counteract the aims of the government. And, besides, is
it not true that that body (the clergy) is independent of the State? Surely this is so,
since it is not subject to the same rules. Is it known for defending the fatherland,
law, and freedom? No. Its kingdom is not of this world. Consequently, it is never
civic-minded.[13]

During his second campaign in Italy in 1800, Napoleon began negotiations with
Pope Pius VII toward a concordat between the Catholic Church and the French state.

His position was ostensibly rooted in Gallicanism, which maintained that the Church in France had ecclesiastical liberties independent of papal jurisdiction. Unlike earlier expressions of Gallicanism, however, Napoleon's version permitted state involvement in Church affairs. Notwithstanding the compromising nature of the first consul's demands, the pope was anxious to reach an accord that would rescue the Church in France from the precarious position it had occupied during the more radical phase of the Revolution and from which it had not recovered.

The agreement that emerged provided that Catholic clergy would henceforth be nominated by the first consul and only then be consecrated by the pope. Salaries of the Catholic clergy would be paid by the state. Bishops could control churches necessary for worship, and the Church would be permitted to receive bequests and endowments. It was agreed, however, that the holders of former Church properties nationalized during the Revolution would not be disturbed in their possession. The pope further agreed that the French government could issue such police regulations for religion as it deemed necessary. Pursuant to this last provision, Napoleon enacted Organic Articles for the Catholic Church at the same time he published the concordat with the pope in 1802.

The Organic Articles provided that Catholic seminaries were to employ exclusively French teachers and to profess the principles of Gallican liberties. No papal bull was to enter the country without government approval. In addition, there would be one catechism for all France. This uniform catechism emphasized that the Church was to be in the service of the state. It read in part:

Q. What are the duties of Christians with respect to the princes who govern them, and what are in particular our duties toward Napoleon I, our Emperor?

A. Love, respect, obedience, fidelity, military service, tributes ordered for the preservation and defense of the Empire and of his throne; we also owe him fervent prayers for his safety and for the spiritual and temporal prosperity of the State.

Q. Why do we have these duties toward our Emperor?

A. First, by bountifully bestowing talents on our Emperor both in peace and war, God has established him as our sovereign and has made him the minister of His power and His image on earth. To honor and serve our Emperor is therefore to honor and serve God himself. Secondly, because our Lord Jesus Christ . . . taught us what we owe to our sovereign. . . . He has ordered us to give to Caesar what belongs to Caesar.

Q. Are there not special motives which must attach us more strongly to Napoleon, our Emperor?

A. Yes, for he is the one whom God has given us in difficult times to re-establish the public worship of the holy religion of our fathers and to be the protector of it. He has re-established and maintained public order by his profound and active wisdom; he defends the State with his powerful arm; he has become the Lord's anointed through the consecration which he received from the pontifical sovereign, head of the universal Church.

Q. What must one think of those who may fail in their duty toward our Emperor?

A. According to the apostle Paul, they would resist the established order of God himself and would be worthy of eternal damnation.[14]

Similar articles were drafted and implemented for the regulation of Protestants in France. The government named all Protestant seminary teachers, paid ministers' salaries, and assumed the right of approving all Church doctrinal decisions. Only French nationals could serve as clergymen, and they were forbidden to have relations with any foreign authority.[15]

In January 1806, while returning from his German campaign, Napoleon stopped briefly in Strasbourg, where he gave audience to several deputations of farmers and landowners who brought claims against Jewish usury. On that backdrop, he called for an assembly of principal Jews that, among other things, was to seek out ways "to replace the shameful expediency to which many among them have devoted themselves from father to son for many centuries."[16] Napoleon's prefects in the various lands under his rule were to select deputies from among the rabbis, landholders, and other distinguished Jews in their district; the deputies so designated—eventually numbering 111—were to arrive in Paris by July 10, 1806, and await further instructions.

On July 22, Napoleon communicated the text of questions to be put to the Assembly, with the objective of "reconciling the belief of the Jews with the duties of Frenchmen, and to make them useful as citizens."[17] A clear symbol to the challenge of the state to the place of religion in the life of the Jews was the insistence that the Assembly convene for its first session on Saturday, July 26.[18] *Dina de-malkhuta dina* was to figure prominently in addressing the matters raised by Napoleon, as highlighted below.

DINA DE-MALKHUTA DINA AS INVOKED BY THE ASSEMBLY OF NOTABLES: THE JEW AS STATE CITIZEN

Napoleon's commissioners presented twelve questions to the Assembly:

1. Is it lawful for Jews to marry several women?
2. Is divorce allowed by the Jewish religion? Is divorce valid, even when not pronounced by courts of justice and by virtue of laws that contradict the French code?
3. Can a Jewess marry a Christian, or a Christian woman a Jew? Or does the law order the Jews to marry only among themselves?

4. In the Jews' eyes, are Frenchmen considered as brethren or as strangers?

5. In either case, what relations does their law prescribe for them toward Frenchmen who are not of their religion?

6. Do the Jews born in France, and treated by the laws as French citizens, acknowledge France as their country? Are they bound to defend it? Are they bound to obey its laws and to follow all the provisions of the Civil Code?

7. Who appoints the rabbis?

8. What police jurisdiction do rabbis exert among Jews? What judicial power do they exert among them?

9. Are these forms of election, this police jurisdiction, requested by their law or only sanctioned by custom?

10. Are there professions which are forbidden to Jews by their law?

11. Does the law of the Jews forbid them to take usury from their brethren?

12. Does it forbid them, or does it allow them, to take usury from strangers?[19]

The Assembly adopted a declaration that was to precede its responses. The declaration read:

> The assembly, impressed with a deep sense of gratitude, love, respect, and admiration for the sacred person of his Imperial Majesty, declares, in the name of all Frenchmen professing the religion of Moses, that they are fully determined to prove worthy of the favors His Majesty intends for them, by scrupulously conforming to his parental intentions; that their religion makes it their duty to consider the law of the prince as the supreme law in civil and political matters, that, consequently, should their religious code, or its various interpretations, contain civil or political commands, at variance with those of the French Code, those commands would, of course, cease to influence and govern them, since they must, above all, acknowledge and obey the laws of the prince.[20]

At first glance, the declaration seems to be a simple expression of the principle *dina de-malkhuta dina*. A careful reading, however, reveals that its scope is not limited to monetary matters [*mamona*]. The broad statement that the Jewish religious code is subordinate to the state's civil and political laws makes no distinction between monetary and ritual matters [*mamona-issura*]. Nonetheless, the basis of authority for the civil-religious distinction is clearly Jewish law.

In its reply to the first question, the Assembly asserted that, though polygamy had at one time been practiced among the Jews, the *herem de-Rabbeinu Gershom*[21] [ban decreed by the authority of R. Gershom, ca. 960–1028] had banned the practice and it no longer existed among European Jewry. Implicit in this response is the statement that a rabbinic synod is empowered to enact legal measures binding upon the Jewish

people. This statement is double-edged: first, it calls into question the religious authority of a non-rabbinic assembly; second, it suggests the possibility of convening a duly
authorized synod to enact new regulations. In any case, it is clearly grounded in internal Jewish legal principles.

The second response opened with a declaration that a Jewish divorce was valid
only if previously pronounced by the French Civil Code. Although no Jewish law was
violated by securing a prior civil decree, the absence of such a decree had never been
held to impair the validity of a properly issued *get*. This extension of *dina de-malkhuta
dina* to an issue of family law required a halachic rationale and, for this purpose, the
Shulḥan Arukh [Code of Jewish Law] was invoked:

> According to the Rabbis who have written on the civil code of the Jews, such as
> Joseph Caro in the *Even ha-Ezer* [a section of the *Shulḥan Arukh*], repudiation is
> valid only in case there should be no opposition of any kind. And as the law of the
> state would form an opposition, in point of civil interests—since one of the parties
> could avail himself or herself of it against the other—it necessarily follows that, under
> the influence of the civil code, rabbinical repudiation cannot be valid. Consequently,
> since the time the Jews have begun to enter into engagements before the civil offi-
> cer, no one, attached to religious practices, can repudiate his wife but by the law of
> the state, and that prescribed by the law of Moses.[22]

The Bible requires a bill of "cutting off" to effectuate a divorce (Deut 24:1). Based
upon this requirement of a total severance of the marital relationship, the rabbis held
that if at the time of the issuance of a *get* [Jewish legal divorce document] there remained
an as yet unfulfilled condition, the *get* was ineffectual (*Sh. Ar., Even ha-Ezer* 137, 143).
The Assembly declared that a failure to comply with state law would leave the marital
tie unsevered because one of the parties could attack the *get* as incomplete. This halachic
support is novel in acknowledging that noncompliance with state law might provide a
halachic basis for challenging the validity of a *get*; it established concurrent jurisdiction
between state and religion in marriage and divorce law. As a final rationale for extending
dina de-malkhuta dina to the field of family law, the response invoked the contractual
theory of *dina de-malkhuta dina*: the rabbis, having sworn allegiance to the sovereign,
agreed thereby to incorporate his demands into their juridical proceedings.

The sixth question, concerning the obligation of military service and of conforming
to the laws of the Civil Code, struck at core issues in complaints alleging the Jews' abuse
of citizenship. The Assembly's answer affirmed the Jews' duty to defend their country.
Rabbi Ishmael of Modena, who was eighty-three years old at the time the Assembly
convened, did not attend the proceedings but formulated responses to Napoleon's
questions, presumably as a guide to the Italian deputies. While affirming the obligation
of military service, Rabbi Ishmael underscored the limits of *dina de-malkhuta dina*:

"Samuel has said *dina de-malkhuta dina.* . . . But ritual matters are not included in this, for surely the king grants permission to all inhabitants of his state to fulfill the practices of their law, each one according to their religion."[23] Rabbi Ishmael—as the Assembly of Notables—acknowledged that the era of rabbinic jurisdiction over civil matters had come to a close; yet there remained a sphere in which traditionalist rabbis might resist the encroachment of state authority.

SUMMARY AND DENOUEMENT

During the corporate phase of Jewish life, European Jewry enjoyed far-ranging judicial authority. Under such conditions, *dina de-malkhuta dina* was narrowly applied. The principle was not strictly one of accommodation; it provided a rationale for resistance to unjust decrees. It served as a basis for dissent against the authority of rulers deemed to be acting *ultra vires* [that is, beyond their legal power].

Consistent with the general trend toward the acceptance of positive law in the thirteenth and fourteenth centuries and in response to the reality of the *servi camerae* status to which the Jews had been reduced in the aftermath of the Crusades, application of the concept *gezelah de-malkhuta* significantly diminished. The king's law, whether preserving "good old law" and whether equitable or not, was law, at least in the commercial sphere. Even so, the basis for extending the principle's application was ostensibly rabbinic decision. By the seventeenth century, there was a marked decline in the exclusive jurisdiction of rabbinic courts in Western Europe; recourse to courts operating under the king's law became increasingly common. In matters of religious prohibition [*issura*], however, rabbinic jurisdiction remained unchallenged.

Jews were first accorded equality of citizenship in revolutionary France. Napoleon demanded a clear statement of the Jews' relationship to the state, summoning an Assembly of Jewish Notables (followed immediately by a Sanhedrin to formalize its pronouncements) to relate to this subject. Recognizing and accepting the collapse of Jewish legal autonomy, the Paris Assembly and successor Sanhedrin asserted only the continuing validity of Jewish ritual law, specifically in matters of marriage and divorce. This new definition of synagogue-state relations can be seen as the ultimate stage in a process that began as early as the thirteenth century. Once the absolute power of the king to legislate in the commercial sphere was acknowledged, the abdication of all but ritual jurisdiction was conceivable. The total loss of communal autonomy subjected even the ritual authority of the rabbinate to voluntary compliance by individuals following the French Revolution.

Jewish religious reformers in the decades following the Assembly of Notables were to carry the principle *dina de-malkhuta dina* to what they saw as its logical conclusion. Matters involving interpersonal relations, particularly if regulated by the state, were civil [*mamona*]; only the private matter of religious belief was beyond the scope of *dina de-malkhuta dina*.²⁴ Such practices as strict Sabbath observance and special family law usages, they argued, retained no compelling place in Jewish life in the modern state. This conclusion, invoking *dina de-malkhuta dina*, effectively turned Samuel's dictum on its head; it evoked vigorous, traditionalist response. Two centuries later, revisiting debates over the scope and application of *dina de-malkhuta dina* during an era of dramatic change serves as a significant backdrop to understanding divergent expressions of Judaism that have since evolved.

ACKNOWLEDGMENTS

This essay draws substantially upon the author's book *Separation of Church and State: Dina de-Malkhuta Dina in Jewish Law, 1750–1848* (Tuscaloosa: University of Alabama Press, 1985), with the permission of University of Alabama Press.

Readers interested in further exploration of *dina de-malkhuta dina* might also consult Leo Landman, *Jewish Law in the Diaspora: Confrontation and Accommodation* (Philadelphia: Dropsie College, 1968); and Shmuel Shilo, *Dina de-Malkhuta Dina* [Hebrew] (Jerusalem: Hebrew University, 1974).

I acknowledge with appreciation the technical assistance of Chen Bain in preparing this essay for publication.

NOTES

1. Jacob Neusner suggests that Samuel's dictum emerged out of the favorable situation enjoyed by Babylonian Jewry under Sassanid rule and the apparent friendship between Samuel and the Sassanid ruler, Shapur I. Jacob Neusner (*A History of the Jews in Babylonia*, vol. 2 [Leiden: Brill, 1966], 64–70).

2. Solomon ben Abraham Aderet, ca. 1235–1310.

3. R. Yom Tov ben Avraham Asbili, ca. 1250–1330.

4. R. Yonah ben Abraham Gerondi, ca. 1200–1263, found in *Shitah Mekubbezet*.

5. Salo W. Baron, *A Social and Religious History of the Jews*, vol. 5 (Philadelphia: Jewish Publication Society, 1957), 77.

6. R. Joseph Colon, ca. 1420–1480.

7. Shalom Albeck, "*Dina de-Malkhuta Dina be-Kehillot Sefarad*," *Abraham Weiss Jubilee Volume* (New York: Shulsinger Bros., 1964), 110.

8. The attitudes of medieval rabbinic authorities to notions of natural and positive law are

explored in Baruch Finkelstein, "The Law of the State is the Law: The Nature of Law in Jewish Jurisprudence," *The Review of Rabbinic Judaism* 19 (2016): 256–74.

9. See, e.g., *Teshuvot Maharam* (Rabbi Meir of Rothenburg, ca. 1215–1293), no. 128. In certain cases, taxation beyond ordinary limits was accepted, as, for example, "for great needs," such as financing a war *(Haggahot Mordecai, B.B.* no. 659).

10. In Spain, rabbinic jurisdiction was in some respects more limited than in Western Europe, and in other respects it was greater. Most Jewish courts in Spain were empowered to adjudicate criminal cases with the full support of the state's coercive force. Jewish courts used the prisons of the country to compel obedience to their orders. Floggings, fines, imprisonment, excommunication, and, in extreme cases, mutilation or death were among the penalties imposed by the Jewish courts. *She'elot u-Teshuvot ha-RI*, 122; *She'elot u-Teshuvot Ribash*, 232; *She'elot u-Teshuvot ha-Rosh*, 8, 17.

11. Louis Finkelstein, *Jewish Self-Government in the Middle Ages* (New York: Feldheim, 1964), 155–56. The "seven elders" were community leaders sometimes referred to as *parnassim*; Israel Abrahams, *Jewish Life in the Middle Ages* (London: E. Goldston, 1932), 68–69.

12. Finkelstein, *Jewish Self-Government*, 257–58.

13. Quoted in J. Christopher Herold, *The Mind of Napoleon* (New York: Columbia University Press, 1955), 103.

14. Quoted in Robert B. Holtman, *The Napoleonic Revolution* (Philadelphia: Lippincott, 1967), 130.

15. On Napoleon's relations with the Church, see ibid., 121–38.

16. The text of Napoleon's remarks and decree can be found in his *Correspondance* (Paris, 1863), 12:411–12, no. 10291, and in English translation in Simeon J. Maslin, *Selected Documents of Napoleonic Jewry* (Cincinnati: Hebrew Union College Jewish Institute of Religion, 1957), document I-A.

17. Napoleon, *Correspondance*, 12:571–72, no. 10537.

18. The deputies met for Sabbath services that morning and proceeded to the meeting, which was called for eleven o'clock.

19. The questions are found in Napoleon, *Correspondance*, 12:572, no. 10538. The translation here is from Simon Schwarzfuchs, *Napoleon, the Jews and the Sanhedrin* (London: Routledge & Kegan Paul, 1979), 56–57.

20. Diogene Tama, *Transactions of the Parisian Sanhedrin* (trans. F. D. Kirwan; London: 1807; rpr. Farnborough, 1971), 149–50.

21. An eleventh century rabbinic ordinance so called after Rabbeinu Gershom *Me'or ha-Golah* [Light of the Dispersion], ca. 960–1028, under whose authority the ordinance was issued.

22. Tama, *Transactions*, 153–54.

23. Baruch Mevorach, *Napoleon u-Tekufato* (Jerusalem: Mosad Bialik, 1968), 115. Moses Mendelssohn had, one generation earlier, distinguished between elements of the Mosaic constitution, which were no longer applicable since the dissolution of the nation's civil bonds, and the religious laws that were strictly binding. Moses Mendelssohn, *Jerusalem and Other Writings* (trans. Alfred Jospe; New York: Schocken, 1964), 104.

24. See, in this connection, excerpt from Samuel Holdheim's *On the Autonomy of the Rabbis* (1843), in Michael Walzer, Menachem Lorberbaum, Noam J. Zohar, eds., *The Jewish Political Tradition*, vol. 1: Authority (New Haven: Yale University Press, 2000), 454–58.

"THE TERRIBLE ANIMAL KNOWN AS THE MASSES"

The Status and Authority of the Community Rabbi in Nineteenth Century Eastern Europe

MOTTI ZALKIN

Wᴴᴬᴛ ɪs ᴀ rabbi? A scholar? A teacher? An adjudicator? A judge? An educator? A preacher? A community leader? A social worker? A psychologist? An arbitrator? It is reasonable to assume that if we ask this question of ten different people, we will get ten different answers. Many Jews have their own rabbi. But in the present context, it's not the actual rabbinic figure they are related to in one way or another that matters, but rather their perception of the essence of the term. However, while examining the term "rabbi," we must first remember the basic distinction between a rabbi as a scholar, who is ordained for his knowledge of halachah, and a rabbi as a person who plays a public and social role, certainly if this activity is carried out in a formal framework such as a community rabbinate.

Indeed, along the spectrum between these two options there is a wide variety of other possibilities, but it seems that the dominant perception that has taken root in the Jewish world since the High Middle Ages is that of a community rabbi. Yet, this concept, or rather this essence, is a relatively new phenomenon in Jewish society. As Israel Yuval has shown, this institution appeared only in the fifteenth century in Central European Jewish communities.[1] Since then, the community rabbinate has undergone many changes in all its aspects.[2] In this context, I have tried to examine the institution of the nineteenth century community rabbinate in Eastern Europe, the region where 80 percent of the world's Jews lived.

To do this, I first reconstructed the biographies of about fifteen hundred rabbis, focusing on those who served in the small and medium communities in the Lithuanian Jewish cultural arena—that is, in today's Lithuania, Latvia, Belarus, and northeastern Poland.[3] The reason for focusing on rabbis of small communities was not only that this group never received proper attention in the historical research, but also because it was the largest group within the contemporary rabbinical world. In this way, I wanted to avoid the methodological failure that characterized many of the studies on the rabbinate in the Middle Ages and in the modern era, mainly the attempt to draw broad conclusions and offer insights concerning all contemporary rabbis, based on a very limited sample of only the most prominent and well-known rabbis of the time. In this essay, I focus on what I consider the most significant challenge these community rabbis faced—namely, the question of their public authority, which accompanied them throughout their entire rabbinical career.

According to traditional hagiography, especially that of the ultra-Orthodox school, the community rabbi was the ultimate local religious authority, dominating most aspects of local Jewish life, with regard not only to purely halachic issues, such as kashrut, Shabbat, and family life, but also public matters such as education and relations with non-Jewish authorities. However, given the variety of sources available to us, this concept has nothing to do with the real status of the community rabbi and his degree of authority. Until the mid-nineteenth century, all crucial aspects of the community rabbinate—that is, the selection process of the community rabbis, their appointment, and their employment contract as well as their possible dismissal—were dominated by a small group of the local political-economic elite.[4] The local Jewish community elites perceived themselves as the sole and exclusive center of power concerning all aspects of local community life, certainly those of public significance. Extending significant authority to the rabbi, especially in public matters, inevitably reduced the elite groups' degree of social and political authority and control. Thus, the members of this group did everything in their power to avoid this situation or to minimize its probability as much as possible—for example, by an indefinite postponement of the appointment of a new community rabbi, sometimes for a period of several years.[5] Moreover, even when a community rabbi was appointed, the elite members who controlled the rabbi's selection process made sure that the elected candidate would not threaten their exclusive control of local public life, as described by Rabbi Yehuda Leib Margaliot, who at the end of the eighteenth century was the rabbi of several Jewish communities in Poland:

> In their haughtiness, the leaders and rulers of the community would never appoint a famous, respectable, and righteous rabbi. This would require them to submit to him, and to give him the power to punish wrongdoers for their crimes. They prefer to appoint a rabbi who will submit to them, one with no power, and when the rabbi wishes to correct some matter pertaining to the community's daily life, everything will be done only by consulting them. He will have to speak to them softly, and flatter them [in order to convince them] to cooperate with him.[6]

Likewise, when, in mid-nineteenth century, about twenty-five candidates ran for every vacant rabbinical position, it was not difficult to find the candidate who would suit this approach of the local elites. In this way the local community hierarchy was clarified already in the first place.

The degree of control of the local elite over the community rabbinate can be demonstrated through the content of the rabbinic contracts. For example, the contract granted by the Verona Jewish community to Rabbi Yohanan ben Seadia in the year 1539 states: "In matters of public affairs, the rabbi is bound to agree to any regulation of the community leadership."[7] Similarly, according to the regulations of the Jewish community in Vilnius (Vilna), "when the leaders of the community call the rabbi to participate in a meeting, for whatever purpose, he must come immediately without any delay. It goes without saying that he may not refuse to attend any meeting that deals with any judgement or public issue."[8]

Thus, even if no one publicly challenged the rabbi's authority to rule in accordance with the halachah, a system of checks and balances was established, as was ruled by the Berlin Jewish community: "In any rabbinic court case or ruling, the rabbi must be accompanied by two judges who will be appointed by the leaders of the community."[9] Similar restrictions were imposed on the rabbi as to the amount of fine he was allowed to impose as a penalty in a rabbinic court,[10] as well as to his authority to represent the community before the authorities.[11]

However, these restrictions were not limited to the rabbi's involvement in various aspects of public life. Many communities prohibited the rabbi from engaging in business of any kind, as well as traveling anywhere without obtaining prior permission from the competent community institution.[12] Similarly, the rabbi had to accept upon himself various restrictions regarding the daily lives of his family members, such as the possibility of appointing them to public positions, and his involvement in legal proceedings in which they are involved.[13] This subordination had crucial implications from both the personal and family perspective of the rabbi, mainly because of the fear that if he did not comply with these regulations, his term in office would not be renewed at the end of the period prescribed by the rabbinate's contract or would be terminated without prior notice.[14] It should be remembered that in such a case, in addition to losing his source of income, he might develop a bad reputation as a rabbi who did not accept the authority of the community institutions, which would make it much more difficult for him to win a rabbinic position in any other Jewish community.

Therefore, most community rabbis had no choice but to accept the authority of the local elites, even when it involved giving up their personal dignity and respect for the institution of the rabbinate.[15] This was apparently the reason that during the nineteenth century most community rabbis refrained from confronting the local community elites when the Jewish communities were instructed to submit to the authorities the lists of Jewish recruits for the Russian army.[16] This reality is largely consistent with what Newton Malony and Richard Hunt defined as "Push," a situation in which the cleric feels a lack of control over the space in which he operated.[17]

Indeed, when a certain rabbi dared to confront the centers of power of his community—for example, when his ruling, though formulated according to Jewish law, had any kind of implication for the economic situation or the public status of those who were among the local elite—they would not hesitate to remind him of the local political hierarchy: "The rabbis totally depend on the leaders of the community. When, for example, one of the community leaders is angry with the rabbi for not respecting him, or provoking him with his regulations, he will act to fire him, will fight him and harm his livelihood, until the rabbi would honor him properly."[18]

One of the best examples to illustrate the problematic and complex situation of the community rabbi with regard to his ability to exercise his halachic authority is his relationships with the local butchers and slaughterers. It should be borne in mind that the rabbi was, at least theoretically, the supreme halachic authority regarding the issue of kosher food sold in the community, and especially concerning slaughtering. According to the accepted practice in most East European Jewish communities, butchers would buy the cows alive, transfer them to slaughtering, and then sell the meat in their shops. When doubt arose about the kosherness of a slaughtered cow, the rabbi had the sole authority to approve or disapprove the meat. When the rabbi ruled that the slaughtered cow was not kosher, the butcher had no choice but to sell this cow to a non-Jewish butcher or directly to the non-Jewish population, at a much lower profit than he would get for kosher meat. Given that the percentage of nonkosher cows from all the cows slaughtered was close to twenty-five,[19] each purchase of a cow was accompanied by the risk of considerable financial loss.

To avoid a great loss of money, some butchers sold nonkosher meat as kosher, disregarding the rabbi's ruling.[20] I do not intend to claim that most butchers ignored the laws of kashrut and were willing to sell nonkosher meat to the Jewish population, although, as Assaf Kaniel showed in his groundbreaking study, a high percentage of observant Jews in interwar Warsaw consciously consumed nonkosher meat only because they could not afford the high price of kosher meat.[21] Nevertheless, it can be assumed that this situation contained a clear potential for confrontation between the rabbi and the local butchers, certainly in cases when the question of whether a certain cow was kosher or not was not unequivocal, or when the rabbi had repeatedly disapproved the kosherness of cows purchased by a certain butcher.

Against this backdrop, disagreements between community rabbis and butchers were quite common.[22] However, in this case it was not a confrontation between two sides of equal status. Not only were the butchers usually members of the local political and economic elite, but they also had complete control over the rabbi's economic situation. For various reasons, both those related to contemporary formal regulations and those deriving from the community's financial structure, the rabbi's salary was not paid directly from the community budget but through the collected "meat tax." Traditionally, the communities imposed this special tax on the butchers for each slaughtered cow.[23] However, these funds were not transferred to the treasurer of the community but directly to the rabbi as his salary.[24]

Against this background, one can clearly discern the negative correlation between the extent to which the rabbi was adhering to the laws of slaughter and the koshering of the slaughtered cows and his economic situation. As the number of cases in which the rabbi disapproved of the kashrut of slaughtered cows was increased, his economic situation deteriorated.[25] The butchers did not hesitate to postpone the payment of his weekly salary, sometimes for several days, sometimes for a week or a month. In some cases, they even stopped paying him at all.[26] The difficult economic reality that many rabbis experienced had severe implications for their ability to function in the public sphere, as Rabbi Naftali Freund wrote with great pain:

> The rabbi's blood will pour like water until he gets to see his thin salary, and he is the target of the arrows of every insolent and wretched man. These rabbis, which are at the lowest economic level, how can we hope that they will stand guardedly in the war against sinners? If there is no flour, there is no Torah![27]

In practice, the community rabbis had almost no effective tools to deal with this reality. From the point of view of the community leaders, the situation of a rabbi who was dependent on them was preferable, and it is reasonable to assume that even if he approached them with a complaint regarding his salary, they would not respond in the affirmative, as it turns out from the following text:

> Notices were posted in the town's synagogue, on behalf of our rabbi, who complains to the leaders of the community about his bitter and hasty situation. He is starving and unable to provide food for his family. He begs the rich to be kind enough, to pay attention to his very well off condition, and find some source from which he can make a living, at least minimally.[28]

In such a case, the rabbi can hardly be seen as an authoritative figure, to say the least.

The desire to limit the rabbi's authority was not unique to the elite groups. It was also prevalent in other local social strata. The middle class, and even the lower strata members of the community, usually shared the same attitude toward the rabbi, despite the rabbi's attempt to position himself as not only a moral and spiritual model but also as such that without his daily guidance the Jew cannot live in accordance with halachah.

However, in the eyes of those who belonged to these social strata, the rabbi was generally perceived just as a scholar who specializes in solving daily halachic problems, such as food kosherness and Sabbath regulations. When it came to questions relating to broader aspects of private and public life, such as educational worldview and moral questions or public conduct, many community members did not give special weight to the rabbi's opinion and therefore rarely consulted him.[29]

Indeed, as the political power of the middle classes and even of the lower strata increased, especially in the second half of the nineteenth century, so did their involvement in the subject at the center of our discussion.[30] Traditionally, the ordinary Jew did not dare to challenge, at least publicly, the authority of the leaders of his community for fear of harm. However, the stronger the self-confidence of those who belonged to the middle and lower social strata, as well as their willingness to take a leading position in shaping the social and political reality, the weaker the status of those with traditional authority, especially the rabbi. Thus, most often the community rabbi served as an alternative easy and convenient target, for instance in cases of public dissatisfaction with some policies of the community institutions. The status of the rabbis deteriorated to such an extent that sometimes they had to defend themselves against a campaign of public slander, and there were even rabbis who felt helpless while members of the community challenged their halachic authority.[31]

An echo of the deep sense of affront felt by many contemporary rabbis arises from Rabbi Abraham Zakheim's subsequent remarks, which largely reflect the situation of the community rabbinate in Eastern Europe in the second half of the nineteenth century:

> Any rude can harm the rabbi as seen in many communities in our country. Rabbis are afraid of some individuals who oppose them, because they did not do what they were expected to do, or because they lost the rabbi's trial, or other such matters, and all for the sake of envy and respect. Therefore, the rabbis are afraid to intervene in public issues, because it is impossible to please everyone.[32]

One of the only means left to the rabbis to preserve their status was what was known as a "judicial strike." Rabbis who felt that their halachic authority had been significantly threatened, or whose wages were not paid for a long period, adopted the idea of strike as an instrument to stop this process and perhaps even regain some of their lost authority. When the rabbi also served as a judge, the threat of strike was sometimes also extended to the jurisdiction sphere.[33] In the background of this move was the assumption that a society that adheres to the laws of kashrut, Shabbat, family purity, and the like is incapable of functioning without proper halachic guidance. However, because of the possible ramifications of such a drastic move and certainly because of the fear that some people would unknowingly eat nonkosher meat or violate other halachic prohibitions, this step would involve difficult deliberations, as described by Rabbi Eliyahu David Rabinowitz-Te'omim:

> It was hard for me, and despite the fact that well-known rabbis already adopted this option from time to time, yet I did not dare to do so until I asked the most important rabbi of our time, Rabbi Isaac Elhanan Spector. His answer was that it is not only permissible, but he himself also adopted this solution while serving in small communities, and it is customary in many Jewish communities.[34]

However, despite Rabbi Rabinowitz's feeling that he was taking a drastic step, in practice this move had little or no effect at all. In a society in which not only did classical social structures become less and less relevant, but also secularization rapidly spread, the willingness to accept any authority, including religious authority, was significantly reduced.

Despite all that has been said so far, it seems that there is still room to question whether the concept of "honor of the Torah," embodied in the figure of the rabbi, had no importance in the consciousness of many of the time. Despite the temptation to attribute this phenomenon solely to the processes of secularization that Jewish society has undergone since the late nineteenth century, this explanation does not stand up to the test of historical reality. For limiting the authority of the community rabbi, sometimes to the point of disrespect, was not an exceptional phenomenon even in previous periods. Therefore, it seems that the answer to this question can be found, at least in part, in the figure of the late nineteenth century community rabbi.

Two interrelated realities that took place during this period contributed significantly to the decline in the status of the community rabbinate: rabbis who were not worthy of this position and the fierce competition for every available rabbinical position. In these cases, and they were probably quite a few, the nature of the rabbi became clear to all, for example with regard to his halachic authority and thus to the capacity of his ruling. Against this background, it was quite easy for members of the Jewish community to cross the conscious barrier with regard to the duty to respect the rabbi, to obey his rulings, and to treat him as a religious leader.

Toward a conclusion, it seems impossible to escape the question of why, if the situation of the community rabbinate was as described here, so many contemporary young scholars actually opted for this career. This can be explained of course by the high level of unemployment that prevailed in the western provinces of the Russian Empire during the period under discussion. However, it seems that during their years of study in the yeshiva, a spiritual and social space that was largely disconnected from the prevailing daily reality, most of these young scholars did not even conceive the possibility that in real life—that is, outside the yeshiva study hall—the rabbi's authority could be in doubt. No doubt that if they had asked themselves this question before embarking on the course that would lead them to the pulpit, many of them would have opted for another way.

NOTES

1. Israel Jacob Yuval, *hakhamim bedoram* (Jerusalem: Magnes, 1989).

2. See, for instance, Chimen Abramsky, "The Crisis of Authority within European Jewry in the Eighteenth Century," in *Studies in Jewish Religious and Intellectual History* (ed. Siegfried Stein and Raphael Loewe; Alabama: University of Alabama Press, 1979), 13–28; Yaron Ayalon, "Rethinking Rabbinical Leadership in Ottoman Jewish Communities," *Jewish Quarterly Review* 107 (2017): 323–53; Gershon Bacon, "hakhevra hamasortit betmurot ha'itim: hebetim betoldot hayahadut ha'ortodoxit bepolin uberussia 1850–1939," in *kiyum va-Shever* (ed. Israel Bartel and Israel Gutman; Jerusalem: Shazar, 2001), 453–91; Roger Berg, *Historie du rabbinate Francais 16–20e* (Paris: Cerf, 1992); Jay R. Berkovitz, "harabbanut haortodoxit betsarfat: ben massoret lereforma," in *ortodoxya yehudit* (ed. Adam Ferziger, Aviezer Ravitzky, and Yosef Salmon; Jerusalem: Magnes, 2006), 381–93; Mordechai Breuer, *edah udeyokanah, ortodoxya yehudit bareikh hagermani 1871–1918* (Jerusalem: Shazar, 1991); Menachem Friedman, "The Changing Role of the Community Rabbinate," *Jerusalem Quarterly* 25 (1982): 79–99; Abraham Greenbaum, "The Russian Rabbinate under the Czars," *Studies in Jewish Civilization* 16 (2005): 1–7; Yosef Hacker and Yaron Harel, eds., *lo yassur shevet miyehudah: hanhaga, rabbanut ukehilah betoldot Yisrael* (Jerusalem: Bialik, 2011); Michael L. Miller, "Crisis of Rabbinical Authority: Nehemias Trebitsch as Moravian Chief Rabbi, 1832–1842," *Judaica Bohemiae* 4 (2007–2008): 65–91; Ismar Schorsch, "Emancipation and the Crisis of Religious Authority: The Emergence of the Modern Rabbinate," in *Revolution and Evolution: 1848 in German History* (ed. Werner Mosse, et al.; Tübingen: Mohr, 1981); Simon Schwarzfuchs, *harabbanut betzarfat badorot ha'akharonim* (Ramat Gan: Bar Ilan University Press, 2000); Shaul Stampfer, "Inheritance of the Rabbinate in Eastern Europe in the Modern Period—Causes, Factors and Development over Time," *Jewish History* 13 (1999): 35–57; Adam Teller, "Tradition and Crisis? Eighteenth-Century Critiques of the Polish-Lithuanian Rabbinate," *Jewish Social Studies* 17:3 (2011): 1–39; Eric Zimmer, *gakhaltan shel khakhamim: perakim betoldot harabbanut begermania bame'ah ha-16 uvame'ah ha-17* (Beer Sheva: Ben Gurion University Press, 1999).

3. For studies on the community rabbinate in other parts of Central and Eastern Europe,

see Gershon Bacon, "Rabbis and Politics, Rabbis in Politics: Different Models within Polish Jewry," *YIVO Annual of Jewish Social Science* 20 (1991): 39–59; Haim Gertner, *Harav veha'ir hagedolah* (Jerusalem: The Zalman Shazar Center, 2013); Michael L. Miller, *Rabbis and Revolution: The Jews of Moravia in the Age of Emancipation* (Stanford: Stanford University Press, 2011); Rachel Manekin, "Gaming the System: The Jewish Community Council, the Temple, and the Struggle over the Rabbinate in Mid-Nineteenth-Century Lemberg," *Jewish Quarterly Review* 106:3 (2016): 352–82; Michael Silber, "hebetim beyerushat harabbanut bayahadut haortodoksit behungaria bame'ot ha-19 veha-20," in *hayerusha barabbanut ba'et hakhadasha* (ed. Eric Zimmer; Ramat Gan: Bar Ilan University Press, 1996), 9–15; Adam Teller, "The Laicization of Early Modern Jewish Society: The Development of the Polish Communal Rabbinate in the 16th Century," in *Schöpferische Momente des Europäischen Judentums in der frühen Neuzeit* (ed. Michael Graetz; Heidelberg: Winter, 2000), 333–49.

4. Jay Berkovitz, "Patterns of Rabbinic Succession in Modern France," *Jewish History* 13 (1999): 59.

5. Shaul Stampfer, "The Missing Rabbis of Eastern Europe," in *Families, Rabbis and Education* (ed. Shaul Stampfer; Oxford: Littman Library, 2010), 282–95.

6. Judah Margaliot, *Beit Middot*, Shklov 1786, 42.

7. Yesha'ayahu Sonne, "avnei binyan le'toldot hayehudim be'Verona." *Kovetz al yad* 3 (1941), 152, 168, 169, 182. See also David Kaufmann, "Extraits de l'ancien livre de la communaute de Metz," *Revue des Etudes Juives* 19 (1889), 124–28; Pinhas Wetstein, *kadmoniyot mi'pinkesa'ot yeshanim* (Krakow: Fisher 1892), 18–19.

8. Shmuel Yoseph Finn, *kiryah ne'emana* (Vilna: Funk, 1915), 37.

9. Yoseph Meisel ed., *pinkas kehilat Berlin* (Jerusalem: Mass, 1962), 30. See also Avigdor Berger ed., zekhor le'avraham (Holon: yeshivat eliyahu, 1999), 532–34.

10. David Kaufmann, "pinkas k"k Bamberg," *kovetz al yad* 7 (1895), 25, 27; Dov Avron, *Acta electorum communitatis judaeorum posnaniensium* (Jerusalem: mekize nirdamim, 1967), 327.

11. Shimon Bakhrakh ed., *takanot ha'na'asot mi'shelukhei hakehilot be'asefat hava'ad Hagadol* (Ofen, 1869), 12.

12. Menahem Mendel Biber, *mazkeret legedolei ostraha* (Berdichev: sheftel, 1907), 314; Avraham Shmuel Herschberg, *pinkas Bialystok* (New York: Geselschaft far geschichte fun Bialystok, 1949), I, 104; Israel Heilpern ed., *Constitutiones congressus generalis judaeorum moraviensium 1650–1748* (Jerusalem: mekize nirdamim, 1952), 111.

13. Shlomo Buber, *kiryah nisgavah* (Krakow: ha'eshkol, 1903), 9, 10, 112; Heilpern, 1952, 111; Sonne, 1941, 177; Meisel, 1962, 108.

14. Judah Liva, *Netivot Olam* (Prague, 1595), "Netiv Hadin," ch. 2.

15. Ibid.

16. Mordechai Zalkin, "bein bnei elohim libnei adam: rabbanim, bakhurei yeshivot vehagiyus latzava harussi bame'ah ha-19," in *shalom umilkhama batarbut hayehudit* (ed. Avriel Bar-Levav; Jerusalem: Shazar, 2006), 165–222.

17. Newton Malony and Richard Hunt, *The Psychology of Clergy* (Harrisburg: Morehouse, 1991).

18. *Hakarmel* 7, no. 46.

19. Moshe Nahum Yerushalimsky, *Be'er Moshe* (Warsaw: Baumritter, 1901), "Kevod Hakhamim," para. 13.

20. Jacob Emden, *She'elat Yavetz* (Lemberg 1884), II, para. 24; Yekutiel Yehuda Grunwald, *ha'shokhet ve'hashekhita basifrut ha'rabbanit* (New York: Feldheim, 1956), 24–26.

21. Assaf Kaniel, "Bein hilonim, masortiyim veorthodoxim: shemirat mitzvot bere'i hahit-modedut im 'gezerat hakashrut' 1937–1939," *Galed* 22 (2010): 75–106.

22. Judah Landa, *Nodah beyehudah* (Lwow: Fleker 1859), Yoreh De'ah, para. 1; Zadok ben Yehoshua, *Siftei Tzadik* (Vilna: Katzenelenbogen, 1889), introduction.

23. Isaac Levitats, *The Jewish Community in Russia 1772–1844* (New York: Columbia University Press, 1943), 52–57.

24. Vladimir Levin, *From Revolution to War* (Jerusalem: Shazar, 2016), 353

25. Aharon Moshe Toibesh, *Toafot Re'em* (Zholkiev: Hoffer, 1855), Yoreh De'ah, para. 3; Shalom Shakhna Perlow, *Mishmeret Shalom* (Warsaw: Baumritter, 1895), II, Yoreh De'ah, para. 245.

26. Barukh Epstein, *Mekor Barukh* (Vilna: Romm, 1928), III, 1186; Eliyahu David Rabinowitz-Te'omim, *seder Eliyahu* (Jerusalem: Mossad Harav Kook, 1984), 62; *Hazefirah* 7, no. 25; Ibid., 19, no. 52.

27. *Kol Ya'akov*, June 25, 1908.

28. *Hamelitz* 31, no. 45.

29. *Hakarmel* 8, no. 17.

30. *Hamelitz* 31, no. 62.

31. *Hamelitz* 19, no. 89; Judah Margaliot, *Beit Middot* (Shklov 1786), 42.

32. Abraham Zakheim, "Bemi ha'asham?," *Hapisgah* 10, 86

33. *Hamelitz* 26, no. 107

34. Rabinowitz-Te'omim, *seder Eliyahu*, 64–65.

THUMBING MENDELSSOHN'S NOSE AT THE NAZIS

Hans Pfitzner's Symphony in C,
Op. 46 (1940)

THEODORE ALBRECHT

I N TODAY'S GERMANY or Austria, if you mention the composer Hans Pfitzner (1869–1949) to a classical music lover,[1] you are likely to be greeted by skeptically raised eyebrows because . . . he was a Nazi composer, wasn't he? People who can no longer whistle a tune of his (if they ever could) have the vague impression of an obscure composer who somehow collaborated in Hitler's regime or at least willingly remained in Germany throughout World War II. If you do a little research and look up Pfitzner in sundry standard musical encyclopedias, you will probably find mildly embarrassed biographical entries[2] that are not likely to alter that perception. But by that time, your momentary curiosity will have been satisfied, and you can happily go back to enjoying your Bach, Mozart, and Beethoven.[3]

In fact, the answer to "the Pfitzner Question" is not so simple. Even though he composed Romantic music—symphonies, concertos, chamber music, operas, and songs—that falls easily, warmly, and happily upon our ears, he was a complex personality with strongly nationalistic (though not necessarily National Socialistic) leanings, a cynical, sometimes bitterly self-contradictory musician with a fondness for all sorts of humorous wordplays and puns that are often misunderstood by German speakers and are almost unfathomable by English speakers who—paralleling their search of musical encyclopedias—give up in favor of easier linguistics, less philosophical, political, and polemic baggage, or more immediately available music.

In this essay, however, we shall explore the Lutheran Pfitzner's lifelong friendship with the Jewish-turned-Catholic journalist Paul Cossmann (1869–1942), as well as several inside references—both verbal and musical—that never make their way into encyclopedia articles but give us a momentary smile of satisfaction that Pfitzner was never a Nazi composer.

TWO FRIENDS

Cossmann was born in Baden-Baden, in southwest Germany, on April 6, 1869. His father, the Jewish cellist Bernhard Cossmann (1822–1910), had been hailed as "the Joachim of the violoncello" in his youth.[4] The elder Cossmann had been principal cellist at the Moscow Opera but moved back home so that his son could be educated "as a German in Germany." In 1876 he moved to Frankfurt to help found Dr. Hoch's Conservatory and become professor of cello there.[5]

Pfitzner had been born on May 5, 1869, in Moscow, Russia, where his Lutheran Protestant father, Robert, was first violinist in the same theater as Cossmann's father. When young Pfitzner was two, his father also moved back to Germany to become concertmaster at the Frankfurt Opera. Thus, the two fathers were friends, and their two sons were destined to become friends while they were still schoolboys.

UNIVERSITY AND CONSERVATORY EDUCATIONS

At the University of Frankfurt Cossmann studied natural sciences and philosophy, but he had literary and political leanings and decided on a career in journalism. In 1903 he moved to Munich to found the *Süddeutsche Monatshefte* [South German monthly], which soon became one of the leading cultural journals in Germany. One of Pfitzner's great disappointments came when Cossmann left the Jewish faith and converted to Catholicism in 1906, especially when it led the journalist to favor Bavaria's separation from Protestant northern Germany and alliance with Catholic Austria.[6]

Meanwhile, Pfitzner had entered the Conservatory in Frankfurt in 1886, studying piano with James Kwast and composition with Iwan Knorr, and Cossmann penned some of the poems that Pfitzner used for his earliest songs. After leaving the Conservatory in 1890, Pfitzner taught at Coblenz on the Rhein, and then in 1897 moved to Berlin to take a post at the Stern Conservatory. Life in the Prussian capital, however, was not nearly so pleasant without the companionship of pixie-cute Maria (Mimi) Kwast, the partially Jewish daughter of his old teacher James Kwast. The elder Kwast opposed Pfitzner's romance with his daughter, and so, in May 1899, Cossmann and several other friends smuggled Mimi out of Frankfurt to Berlin, where Pfitzner was waiting. From here they fled to England, where they were married on June 10. The elopement caused a fair number of humorous comments at the Frankfurt Conservatory, and a

British fellow student composed the following ditty in English, German, and Frankfurt dialect: "So let us think / Of Humperdinck / Of Mimi and of Hänschen! / They ran away. / Oh weh! Oh weh! / Was gibt es doch für Menschen!"[7]

COSSMANN'S JOURNALISTIC AND POLITICAL CAREER TO 1933

When Cossmann founded the *Süddeutsche Monatshefte* in 1903, he enlisted the aid of Pfitzner to write a musical column for it. With the advent of World War I, the periodical took on a more political and national tone, advocating victory for Germany and its allies. Once they lost the war, Cossmann and his journal continued the patriotic tone, railing against the Treaty of Versailles, complaining about the war debt imposed upon them, and later promoting the "stab-in-the-back" myth that the German army had been betrayed by foreigners and especially by the financially influential Jews. Typical of the confused times of the Weimar Republic, Cossmann also gave space to the opponents of the rising Nazi powers, arguing for "Truth," whatever its source.

Cossmann had never married, was reputed to be unusually kind, and became an indefatigable promoter of charitable causes.[8] Even so, when the Nazis came to power, Cossmann was imprisoned without a trial in March 1933, first at Stadelheim Prison in south Munich and then at the brand new Dachau concentration camp for political opponents to the regime, nine miles northwest of Munich, which opened on March 22.[9]

PFITZNER'S MUSICAL CAREER

In 1907, Pfitzner moved from Berlin to Strassburg to conduct opera and to teach at the conservatory there. During his decade in the Rhenish city, he composed an opera, *Palestrina*, that he termed a "musical legend." The legend tells of a time (ca. 1560) when the Catholic Church wanted to abolish polyphonic (multivoiced) music, and so the composer Giovanni Pierluigi da Palestrina (ca. 1525–1594) came forth with a polyphonic *Missa Papae Marcelli* [Mass for Pope Marcellus] of such beauty and reverence that it moved the ecclesiastical hierarchy to retain that style of music.[10] Pfitzner wrote his own libretto, including a memorable scene in which a dozen musical masters from the past descend from on high, urging him to compose the mass that would save church music. When the Jewish Bruno Walter conducted its premiere in Munich in 1917, *Palestrina* was hailed as a "second *Parsifal.*"[11]

With the end of World War I, the German Pfitzner felt that he could no longer remain in a French Strasbourg and he ultimately moved to Berlin, where he was offered a teaching position at the Prussian Academy of the Arts. Like Robert Schumann

(1810–1856) and Hugo Wolf (1860–1903) before him, Pfitzner had long admired the Romantic poetry of the Prussian Joseph von Eichendorff (1788–1857), and in June 1920 he began assembling a text from his *Aphorisms* and other poems. The result was a ninety-minute cantata, *Von deutscher Seele* [From the German soul], for solo voices, chorus, organ, and orchestra, divided into three parts: "Man and Nature," "Life and Singing," and "Songs." It was premiered in Berlin on January 27 (Mozart's birthday), 1922.

The cantata's finale begins with a lullaby of consolation: "Sleep, my dear one, sleep; / hear the fountain's gentle splashing / through the flowers on the lattice. / How lovely and warm is your breathing! / We have come home from the war, / through stormy night and rain. / God stood by us in our need. / Now in the moonlight above, / sleep peacefully; the land is truly free."

This leads to triumphant words of hope for the future: "When the waves rage below, / mankind's spirit is confounded. / But above, the shepherd of the waves / lifts a fiery beacon homewards. / Hold fast the rudder, leave fear behind. / God's hand guides / these waves to transport you / and the stars to protect you."

When heard in a historical context, *Von deutscher Seele* might even be considered as an anti-war statement. Unfortunately, however, it has not traveled well: few conductors outside of German-speaking lands will program it because of its nationalistic title.[12]

Earlier harmonious contacts led Pfitzner, in 1925, to become "professor for life" at the Academy of Music in Munich, the Bavarian capital. Despite his own crotchety and cantankerous nature, Pfitzner and Mimi had enjoyed a happy marriage, from their earliest days together in Berlin to later times with their three children. In April 1926, however, the delicate Mimi died after an operation, leaving Pfitzner a broken and bitter man. Even though he resumed teaching soon after her death, it was not until his sixtieth birthday in 1929 that Pfitzner became fully active again. Shortly thereafter, however, the worldwide economic depression prevented the amount of musical activity that he could once again undertake.

And with the Great Depression came the swift rise of the opportunistic National Socialist Party . . . and Adolf Hitler.

FRIENDS AT ODDS WITH THE NAZIS

At the beginning of 1933, the Nazis, who had been growing in power over the last several years, suddenly but "peacefully"—by means of a national election—took over the reins of government in Germany. Bowing to external influences beyond his control, the aging President Paul von Hindenburg (1847–1934) appointed Adolf Hitler as chancellor in January. By March, Hitler had assumed dictatorial powers and wielded them with a vengeance. Bruno Walter, Otto Klemperer, and other Jewish friends of

Pfitzner's found themselves either dismissed from their positions or their musical activities curtailed severely.

Even closer to Pfitzner's home and heart, Paul Cossmann was summarily imprisoned in Stadelheim Prison without trial on March 6, 1933.[13] Pfitzner likened this action to the tyranny portrayed in Beethoven's opera *Fidelio*, but "without the benefit of the rescue fanfares."[14] He indignantly complained to Heinrich Himmler and ultimately went through the weakening President Hindenburg to arrange Cossmann's release several months later.[15] Witnessing these events, Hitler never forgave the aging composer this affront.[16]

The retaliatory blow came in May 1934: Pfitzner found himself removed from his lifetime teaching position at the Munich Academy, supposedly "due to approaching old age." Ailing in body but keen in mind, the composer could do little on his own behalf. Had Pfitzner emulated so many of his colleagues, he would have left Germany for safety abroad. But no: Germany was home; Germany was where Mimi was buried; and besides, Pfitzner himself did not want to die in a foreign country.[17]

In June 1934, Pfitzner applied for a state pension. Denying the application, Hermann Goering, the Führer's right arm, wrote Pfitzner that an investigation had indicated that he did not need the money. He virtually accused the composer of swindling. With feisty pluck, Pfitzner replied on January 30, 1935: "I shall preserve your letter as a cultural document of inestimable value and a companion to the swift kick that the Bishop of Salzburg could administer to Mozart with impunity. Heil Hitler!"[18]

Almost needless to say, Pfitzner was summoned before Goering within the week. The minister threatened him with imprisonment in a concentration camp but let him go home "contritely" . . . and with no pension.[19]

Some small compensation for Pfitzner's forced retirement had again been engineered by the ailing President Hindenburg, who arranged for the city of Frankfurt to award Pfitzner its highly coveted Goethe Prize and Goethe Medal during August 1934, the same month in which Hindenburg himself died.[20] With his protector in Berlin gone and at a most uneasy peace with the Nazis, Pfitzner now found himself with no regular income.

SHAKESPEARE AND MENDELSSOHN

To be sure, Pfitzner could have ingratiated himself with the Nazis by composing the "decorative, propagandistic, and demagogic" music they preferred. They approached him to compose music for William Shakespeare's *A Midsummer Night's Dream* to replace that by Felix Mendelssohn (1809–1847), popular since the 1840s but now banned. The first systematic German translation of Shakespeare's plays was made by Johann Joachim Eschenburg from 1775 to 1782. A second attempt was made by August

Wilhelm Schlegel from 1797 to 1801, to be completed by Ludwig Tieck from 1825 to 1833. In general, the Eschenburg edition was more literal; the Schlegel-Tieck edition was more poetic, and it became the standard German edition.

Mendelssohn of course was the grandson of the Berlin silk merchant, banker, and philosopher Moses Mendelssohn (1729–1786). Moses's son Abraham continued the family's banking business, but, in order to make his own children (Franziska, called "Fanny," and Felix) more acceptable in northern German society, had them baptized into the prevailing Lutheran faith at an early age.[21] After his years as a child prodigy, Felix became director of the Leipzig Conservatory and one of Germany's most prominent composers. His Symphonies Nos. 3 (*Scottish*), 4 (*Italian*), and 5 (*Reformation*), as well as his Violin Concerto and *Hebrides Overture*, became standard works on orchestral programs around the world, and his oratorio *Elijah* was not only performed frequently but also imitated internationally by other composers.

In 1826, at age seventeen, Mendelssohn wrote an almost magical Overture to Shakespeare's popular *Midsummer Night's Dream*, and in 1842 he was commissioned to compose music (a total of thirteen sometimes brief movements) to be used throughout the play. He accommodated with music consistent in style with his Overture, and Shakespeare's play (in the Schlegel-Tieck translation) with Mendelssohn's music became a standard—and beloved—pairing in theatrical performance.[22] An orchestral suite consisting of the Overture, Scherzo, Nocturne, and Wedding March (and perhaps another movement or two) began appearing frequently on concert programs. The Wedding March was often used worldwide to conclude matrimonial ceremonies. But no longer in Germany after 1933.

While it is generally recognized that the Nazi ban on Mendelssohn's music took its toll in the concert hall and the wedding service, it also dug deeply into musical life among the everyday middle class, aspects that are seldom considered by academic musicologists. During and after the Napoleonic Wars, Germans, as part of their resistance against the French, began organizing singing societies, performing unaccompanied choral songs featuring patriotic themes: love of the German mountains, valleys, forests, and women; love of the hunt, drinking, good fellowship, and so on. The Liedertafel movement, begun in Berlin in 1809, spread south and west, while the similar Liederkranz movement from Zürich and Stuttgart in the 1820s began moving north, culminating in a *Sängerfest* [singers' festival] in Frankfurt in 1838 and eventually a German *Sängerbund* [singers' league]. They held periodic regional and national music festivals made up largely of middle-class amateur singers, mostly with no special training beyond school, church, and their own enthusiasm. At first there were men's choruses [often called by the generic name *Männerchor* or *Gesangverein*], soon joined by women's choruses [similarly *Damenchor*]. These were often family affairs: the men might rehearse on a Tuesday evening, the women on a Thursday evening, and both men and women together in a mixed chorus on Friday evening.[23]

By 1928 there were an estimated 1.5 million members of these singing societies worldwide, with a great number in the United States. In Germany itself, the national *Sängerbund* alone numbered 600,000 individual members, with thousands of societies in every city and town.[24]

Among the male choruses, one of their favorite pieces—something that they could sing by heart from an early age—was the strophic song *Der Jäger Abschied* [The hunter's farewell], to a sentimental text by Joseph von Eichendorff:[25] "Who built you, o beautiful forest, so high up there? / I want to praise that Master / as long as my voice sounds. / Farewell, o beautiful forest." The final stanza read: "What we have silently praised in the forest, / we will honor when we depart. / The ancients remain true to you / until the last song fades away. Farewell, God protect you, o beautiful forest, o German forest."[26]

Similarly, the women's choruses had a favorite unaccompanied work, to a biblical text, that they too had memorized at an early age—*Hebe deine Augen auf*: "Lift thine eyes, o lift thine eyes / to the mountains, whence cometh help. / Thy help cometh from the Lord, / the maker of heaven and earth. / He hath said thy foot shall not be moved. / Thy Keeper will never slumber. / Lift thine eyes, o lift thine eyes / to the mountains, whence cometh help."[27]

Suddenly in 1933, whether their texts originated with Eichendorff or in the Bible, both the men's "Hunter's Farewell" and the women's "Lift Thine Eyes" were banned in Nazi Germany because in both cases their composer was the Jewish Mendelssohn.[28]

Therefore, when the Nazis offered Pfitzner a commission to write new music to Shakespeare's *Midsummer Night's Dream*, he courageously replied that he found Mendelssohn's music absolutely congenial and a success upon which he could never improve. Instead, his works during the Nazi years became increasingly abstract in nature: the chamber music, the Cello Concerto, the symphonies—all contrary to the ideals espoused by the regime.[29]

Hitler regarded Pfitzner as a belligerent pest and truly wished to place a ban on his works.[30] But the little malcontent was in fact one of the most honored composers in a Germany that was losing many of its most prominent musicians because they were Jews, and so Hitler begrudgingly relented as long as the old man kept his mouth shut about political matters.[31] As a result, Pfitzner began a series of concert tours and guest appearances as a conductor and stage manager, mostly of his own works, but at least it kept bread on the table. He also recorded from time to time, including orchestral excerpts from his operas *Palestrina*, *Das Herz*, and *Das Christ-Elflein*, in addition to his highly Romantic interpretations of Beethoven's Symphonies Nos. 1, 3 (*Eroica*), 4, 6 (*Pastorale*), and 8.[32]

COSSMANN AFTER HIS RELEASE

Pfitzner's friend Cossmann had now retired from public life altogether. He had already suffered from a heart condition when he was sent to Stadelheim in April 1933. Later, still a prisoner, he was transferred to a hospital from which he was released in poor health after nine months of arrest. He secluded himself in suburban Isartal, near Munich, withdrawn and concerned with his philosophical writings. By 1938, at age sixty-nine, the once vital Cossmann was "a broken man," but Pfitzner still came often to visit him.[33]

DEVELOPMENTS IN FRANKFURT

Meanwhile, in 1929 Clemens Krauss left Frankfurt for Vienna after a glorious five-year stay. He had conducted the Opera and had led the concerts of the Museum Society, whose orchestra was the augmented opera orchestra playing on the stage of the *Saalbau* [auditorium or concert hall] rather than in the fifty-year-old Opera, three blocks away. Krauss's successor was the Jewish Czech Josef Turnau (1888–1954),[34] a singing actor who brought a promising young conductor, Hans Wilhelm Steinberg, to head the musical activities.[35] Together they supported operetta and community outreach to bring money to the Depression-plagued house. They staged progressive new productions of Alban Berg's *Wozzeck*, Maurice Ravel's *L'Heure Espagnole*, Giuseppe Verdi's *Macbeth*, and many others over the next three seasons.[36]

In March 1933, however, the new Nazi mayor of Frankfurt, Dr. Friedrich Krebs (1894–1961), removed Turnau, Steinberg, and many other Jewish members of the singing and acting ensembles from their positions. Krebs then installed Hans Meissner (1896–1958) as general manager. Meissner had been born in Frankfurt and, as a theater man, had led the local Art Theater before moving to a similar position in Polish Stettin. Until mid-March Meissner had been a member of the Social Democratic Party, but upon his appointment in Frankfurt he obediently joined the Nazi Party. He had to walk a narrow line—on one hand he was dependent upon the ruthless Krebs for his position and the success of his programs. On the other hand, Meissner protected several members of his company, such as actor Joachim Gottschalk, who had a Jewish wife.[37]

Meissner met Pfitzner for the first time in August 1934, when the composer came to Frankfurt to accept the Goethe Prize.[38] He surely knew the trouble that Pfitzner was having with Hitler. Nonetheless, he courageously envisioned a bold plan, something he termed "an act of justice."[39] He would stage a new production of one of Pfitzner's operas each year for the next five years, until 1939, when, for the composer's seventieth birthday, they would all be in the repertory. Pfitzner would be on hand too to supervise the productions, thus giving him not only the honor but also the necessary honorarium on which to live.

Meissner began the series with Pfitzner's most frequently performed—and therefore most politically acceptable—opera, *Palestrina*, during the 1935–1936 season, with *Das Herz* [The heart, possibly the most controversial] the following year. In 1937, Meissner, along with the new music director Franz Konwitschny (1901–1962), continued to add to the Pfitzner operas in the repertory—*Der arme Heinrich* [Poor Heinrich] in 1937–1938, *Die Rose vom Liebesgarten* [The rose from the garden of love] during the next season, and finally *Das Christ-Elflein* [The little Christmas elf] projected for 1939–1940.[40]

HONOR, DISHONOR, AND BITTER PUNS

In the meantime, however, Pfitzner had gotten himself back into hot water with the Nazi regime. After keeping a low profile for two years, while the Nazis concentrated their attacks on Paul Hindemith,[41] Pfitzner had been proclaimed a Cultural Senator of the Reich in 1936.[42] During the same year, he was elected an honorary member of the Accademia di Santa Cecilia in Rome, shortly after Germany and Fascist Italy created their Axis.

But the little pest began once more to peck at Hitler's patience. On one occasion, when Pfitzner was to conduct a radio concert, a uniformed representative was sent to meet the composer, who arrived in a visibly bad mood. To make pleasant conversation, the envoy quickly began to tell the latest political joke: Hitler had just had his first personal meeting with Benito Mussolini[43] and had been a little nervous about a face-to-face confrontation with the Italian leader. In order to give himself courage, Hitler had tried to be funny and asked his adjutant: "Should I call him *Duce* or *Sie-tsche*?" Instead of chuckling at the joke, Pfitzner shot back: "For me, they are both *Er-sche!*"

This dynamite-laden proliferation of pronominal puns warrants a fuller explanation. The radio representative's original joke was based on *du* and *Sie*, the second-person familiar and polite pronouns, respectively. Would Hitler address Mussolini with the familiar or the polite form of "you"? And he linked the informal *du* with Mussolini's title: *Duce* [leader or the near English cognate Duke], pronounced "doo-chay" in Italian. And he added "tsche" [pronounced "chay"] as the designation for address using *Sie* [pronounced "zee" in German] to result in *Sie-tsche* [pronounced "zee-chay"]. The quick-minded and sharp-tongued Pfitzner transferred the pun to the third-person, masculine pronoun *er* [meaning "he" and pronounced "air" in German] and likewise added a parallel suffix to make the word *Er-sche* [pronounced "air-sheh" in German], literally that both of them are a third-person "he." But *Er-sche* sounds like *Ärsche*, the plural of *Arsch* [meaning "ass," as in one's posterior]. Therefore, what Pfitzner was saying, in effect, was, "for me, they are both asses!"[44]

But historically, the pun has even deeper meaning. In the days of great monarchies, the superior noble would not address his social inferiors as *du* but instead would use the deflective third-person *er*—the form that Pfitzner used here. Therefore, he was also saying that both Hitler and Mussolini were his—Pfitzner's—social inferiors.

On one occasion, Pfitzner was seated in a public place—a restaurant—with a group of acquaintances when the conversation turned to racial characteristics as defined by the Nazis, including "round-skulled" [*rundschädelig*] for Aryan Germans and "long-skulled" [*langschädelig*] for Jews. Whereupon Pfitzner interjected sarcastically: "Well, let's hope that Hitler isn't *lang schädlich*!" [meaning that he hoped that Hitler would not be *schädlich*—harmful—for very long].[45]

On still another occasion, while conversing in the crowded lobby of Frankfurt's Hotel Carlton, Pfitzner blurted out: "You know what Hitler is? The greatest criminal of all time!"

FRANKFURT'S DILEMMA AND
FRIENDLY SOLUTION

Hitler's response was predictable. In 1939 as May 5, Pfitzner's seventieth birthday, approached, the Führer forbade any national celebration of the event and ordered that any such plans be canceled immediately.[46]

This turn of events placed Hans Meissner in an unenviable position. His Frankfurt cycle of five Pfitzner operas was 80 percent realized, with the one remaining, *Christ-Elflein*, far advanced in the planning stages. Consulting with conductor Franz Konwitschny, he decided to go ahead with plans for a "Pfitzner Festival Week," to be celebrated strictly on the local level of course.[47]

Incredibly enough, Berlin paid scant attention when the event finally took place in May 1939. Pfitzner, however, was overjoyed. Among his operas in production that week was a revision of *Die Rose vom Liebesgarten*, premiered on his birthday. On that day too the Frankfurt Opera and the Museum Society named him an honorary member, and during the same week the Hoch Conservatory, his alma mater, gave a concert of his music.[48]

Not only had Frankfurt done more than any other city to celebrate Pfitzner's birthday, but, for the first time in over a dozen years, he was relatively happy with life in general because he was going to get married again—to Amalia (Mali) Stoll, a woman half his age.

TRAGEDY AND ESCAPE

Pfitzner's happiness, however, was not destined to last for long. On May 19, 1939, only two weeks after his birthday, his daughter Agnes (Agi) committed suicide. The publicity surrounding the event suggested that it was caused by unhappiness at home. Distraught, Pfitzner asked Paul Cossmann for a statement that the Pfitzner children had enjoyed a harmonious childhood. Whether he suspected the rumor to be true or whether he feared that a public proclamation from a Jew on Pfitzner's behalf might hurt the composer, Cossmann declined the request. Furiously, Pfitzner broke with him.[49]

The composer then considered travel to Switzerland to revive his spirits, but on June 16, the antisemitic musical author Walter Abendroth (1896–1973) advised him: "As I have often told you, be silent and refrain from giving any unthinking or bitter opinions! Every word that you say will be observed and reported. Your entire life's work could be boycotted, so behave yourself in Switzerland as if you were already in a concentration camp!"[50]

Instead of Switzerland, Pfitzner spent part of his summer in the cultural capital of Weimar, where the poet Goethe (1749–1832), although born in Frankfurt, had worked from 1775. The poet Friedrich Schiller (1759–1805) had also worked here, as had the pianist, composer, and conductor Franz Liszt (1811–1886). Pfitzner made a day trip to the *Kickelhahn* mountain, eleven miles southwest of Weimar, where Goethe had written his serene *Wanderers Nachtlied* [Wanderer's night song], a poem known to every German school child.[51] On August 11, Pfitzner reported to Abendroth, "I couldn't help writing a 1939 version," and included a biting parody of Goethe, whose birthplace he had visited only three months before.[52]

A SYMPHONY IS BORN

In the fall Pfitzner went back home to Munich, where the Nazis were indeed watching his activities and conduct.[53] Over the winter of 1939–1940—out of gratitude to Frankfurt—he composed Symphony in C, Op. 46, constructed of three relatively short movements, fast-slow-fast (the old eighteenth century *sinfonia* sequence), to be played without pause. On March 29, 1940, he wrote to Walter Abendroth concerning his progress: "I am rather busily at work on a score of a Symphony in C Major. The second movement, a short Adagio, has already been finished for some time; the first is about half done. At the moment, however, I am writing the third movement, a Presto Finale, which has an abundance of notes."[54]

The Symphony in C—described as "three movements in one" and dedicated *An die Freunde* [To my friends]—had its premiere in Frankfurt's *Saalbau*, with Franz Konwitschny conducting the Museum Society's Orchestra, on October 11, 1940.

Within the week—on October 13, 14, and 15—Wilhelm Furtwängler, conductor of the Berlin Philharmonic and also on an uneasy footing with the Nazis, programmed Pfitzner's Symphony with his orchestra,[55] and Pfitzner himself recorded it in Berlin before the year was out.[56] It was performed widely in Germany over the next few years, until the end of World War II. The first performance of Pfitzner's Symphony in C in the United States was given by the Northland Symphony Orchestra, Kansas City/Parkville, Missouri, conducted by Theodore Albrecht on December 11, 1983.[57]

THE DEDICATION "AN DIE FREUNDE"

Like his contemporary Richard Strauss (1864–1949), Pfitzner had now reached an Indian Summer of composition; not since the *Palestrina* Preludes had he composed such graceful orchestral music—well-crafted and enjoyable in performance. And yet, in this pleasant Symphony in C is concealed, ever so subtly and yet cynically, a protest against the Hitler regime. Here is where our newly found awareness of Pfitzner's puns can be helpful.

The first clue is the dedication or subtitle: *An die Freunde* [To my friends]. Those friends were certainly his colleagues in Frankfurt who had supported him, even when he was at odds with the Nazis. But the dedication finds deeper meaning in a pun. With the mere deletion of an "n," *Freunde* [friends] becomes *Freude* [joy], and the dedication now becomes *An die Freude*, the Ode to Joy by poet Friedrich Schiller that Beethoven used in his Symphony No. 9, with its message "*Alle Menschen werden Brüder*" [All mankind will be brothers]—a philosophy hardly being practiced in Germany at the time.[58]

WORDS ABOUT MUSIC

The Symphony's first movement [*Allegro moderato*] opens with a heroic theme in the horn that can be interpreted as a simple fanfare figure or one whose arching melodic contour is derived from the baritone's opening recitative in the Finale of Beethoven's Symphony No. 9: "*O Freunde, nicht diese Töne!*" [O friends, not these tones!]. Indeed here is a connection with the dedicatory subtitle. Soon the theme is taken up by the entire orchestra.

The movement's secondary theme is gentler, almost plaintively lyrical, but beginning with a series of repeated notes, leading to a rising motive, very similar to the secondary theme in the first movement in Beethoven's *Eroica* Symphony.

The second movement is a slow Adagio [*Sehr langsam*] with a long, broad, almost sobbing melody for English horn that might be interpreted as Pfitzner's lament, either for his beloved Germany under the Nazi yoke or for his beloved wife Mimi. But in his letter to Walter Abendroth on March 29, 1940, Pfitzner indicated that the Adagio (then described as "short") had been written first, suggesting that it reflected his more immediate anguish over his daughter Agi's suicide.[59] Here too is an echo of the contemplative music in his opera *Palestrina*, which portrays the artist's troubled place within society.

As the sounds of the English horn die away, the audience is awakened by a sudden loud cymbal crash to begin the third movement [Presto]. Its energetic rhythm is derived from the Finale of Felix Mendelssohn's famous Symphony No. 4 (*Italian*): Poom poom poom poom POOM! ta da-da-da poom, ta da-da-da poom, and so on. Pfitzner's version skips Mendelssohn's first five introductory notes and starts with the endlessly repeated rhythmic figure, a saltarello melodic motive, and its triplets: ta da-da-da poom, ta da-da-da poom, ta da-da-da poom, ta da-da-da poom. Over this, the trumpet proclaims a simple staccato melody that descends and ascends again, reminiscent of Mozart's mocking, nose-thumbing trumpet motive in the Coda, the final section, of his otherwise serious Piano Concerto in D minor, K. 466.

As the movement progresses, the violoncellos and contrabasses take the Mendelssohnian-Italian ostinato motive and turn it into a fugal theme, joined by the remainder of the orchestra, reminiscent of the Trio, the middle section of the third movement of Beethoven's famous (and defiant) Symphony No. 5 in C minor. With increasing humorous ferocity, this thematic combination rollicks forward until Pfitzner adds a triumphantly joyous restatement of the first movement's principal theme, ending the Symphony in C in a blaze of glory that defies the composer's seventy years.

But Mendelssohn's music—so thinly disguised here—was banned in Nazi Germany. Pfitzner himself had noted this, years before, in conjunction with *A Midsummer Night's Dream*. This was not a substitute but rather a musical pun akin to Pfitzner's verbal inventiveness, a reminder to audiences deprived of Mendelssohn's beloved *Italian* Symphony of what they were missing under the Nazi regime.

THE WAR TAKES ITS TOLL

But Pfitzner's triumph with the Symphony in C was transitory. In the summer of 1942, his old friend Paul Cossmann, living in retirement in a suburb of Munich, was dispossessed by the Nazis and taken to the concentration camp at Theresienstadt (Terezin), where he died of dysentery, probably aggravated by the weakness from his heart disease, on the following October 19. After the war, when the Jewish conductor Bruno Walter solicitously asked Pfitzner whatever became of Cossmann, the bitter and cynical composer replied that his lifelong friend had "died peacefully in a concentration camp."[60] Angry ironic tone often does not transfer well to paper, but it appears that Pfitzner was trying to say that Cossmann had died of natural causes rather than extermination because Theresienstadt was not a camp used for systematic annihilation.

The Saalbau in Frankfurt, where Pfitzner's Symphony in C had its premiere, was totally destroyed by bombs in 1944. The 1880 Opera House, where Pfitzner's and Cossmann's fathers had played and where Meissner's cycle of five Pfitzner operas had taken place, was left a burned-out shell, reputedly with unexploded bombs still in its basement. It defied reconstruction for three decades, reopening as the Alte Oper, a concert hall, only in 1981.

With Germany's economy on the decline as World War II raged on, Pfitzner became something of a recluse in his Munich home until Allied bombs destroyed it in 1943. He and his wife Mali moved from place to place, first to Rodaun, a suburb of Vienna, then to Garmisch, in order to flee the advancing Russians (only to find themselves in a refugee camp uncomfortably close to Richard Strauss's residence). In 1946 they moved back to Munich (two rooms in a retirement community), and in 1948, when Pfitzner was exonerated of war crimes, the Vienna Philharmonic provided the couple with an apartment in the gardener's wing of the Belvedere (where Anton Bruckner had lived in the 1890s). After moving there in 1949, they stopped at Salzburg on their way to a birthday concert in Frankfurt. Here, in the city of Mozart's birth, Pfitzner (already frail and nearly blind) suffered a stroke and died on May 22. He was buried in a grave of honor[61] near Beethoven, Schubert, and Brahms in Vienna's Zentralfriedhof [Central cemetery].[62]

FRIENDS IN HISTORY

Possibly Pfitzner had been misguided, misanthropic, and misunderstood, but, like his friend Paul Cossmann, he remained in Germany when people of greater political sensibilities were fleeing Hitler's regime. However "peacefully" the journalist Cossmann perished, but the composer Pfitzner lived and, in his Symphony in C from 1940, used Mendelssohn's rhythmic motive to thumb his nose in protest against the Nazis and the inhumanity that he witnessed in their world.[63]

NOTES

1. Personal experience as the result of living in Frankfurt, Germany, in the U.S. Army from 1970 to 1972; extensive working visits to Vienna, Austria, every year from 1996 to the present as well as a side trip to Weimar, Germany, in June 2019. Most music lovers in America (except for those who enjoy German art song) have never heard

of Pfitzner at all outside of lists of composers active between the two World Wars.

2. The standard encyclopedia articles in English are Helmut Wirth, "Pfitzner, Hans," in *New Grove Dictionary of Music and Musicians* (ed. Stanley Sadie; 20 vols.; London: Macmillan, 1980), XIV, 612–15; and Peter Franklin, "Pfitzner, Hans," in *New Grove Dictionary of Music and Musicians* (2nd ed.; ed. Stanley Sadie; 29 vols.; London: Macmillan, 2001), XIX, 540–43. Their counterparts in German are Wilhelm Mohr, "Pfitzner, Hans," in *Die Musik in Geschichte und Gegenwart* (ed. Friedrich Blume; 17 vols.; Kassel: Bärenreiter, 1949–89), IX, cols. 1170–80 and table 74; and, most extensively of all, Hans Rectanus, "Pfitzner, Hans," in *Die Musik in Geschichte und Gegenwart* (2nd ed.; ed. Ludwig Finscher; 29 vols.; Kassel: Bärenreiter, 1994–2008), Personenteil, XIII (2005), cols. 466–94.

3. Johann Sebastian Bach (1685–1750), Wolfgang Amadeus Mozart (1756–1791), and Ludwig van Beethoven (1770–1827). Other popular composers are also allowed.

4. Joseph Joachim (1831–1907) was a Hungarian-born virtuoso violinist often associated historically with the composer Johannes Brahms (1833–1897), who began life as a Hamburger and ended it as a Wiener.

5. Karl Alexander von Müller, "Cossmann, Paul Nikolaus," in *Neue Deutsche Biographie* (ed. Bayerische Akademie der Wissenschaften; 26 vols.; Berlin: Duncker und Humblot, 1953–2021, projected); III (1957), 374–75.

6. Hans Pfitzner, "Eindrücke und Bilder meines Lebens," in *Reden, Schriften, Briefe* (ed. Walter Abendroth; Berlin-Frohnau: Hermann Luchterhand, 1955), 196–97 and 330. At one time, Pfitzner cynically called his old friend a bigot in this respect.

7. Peter Cahn, *Das Hoch'sche Konservatorium in Frankfurt am Main, 1878–1978* (Frankfurt: Waldemar Kramer, 1979), 145–46 and 158; quoted in Wolfgang Osthoff, "Pfitzner und das Hoch'sche Konservatorium," *Mitteilungen der Hans Pfitzner-Gesellschaft* 41 (April 1980): 64.

    The meaning of most of the poem is clear. Engelbert Humperdinck (1854–1921), composer of the opera *Hänsel und Gretel* (1893), was one of the professors at the Frankfurt Conservatory. Hänsel and Hänschen are both familial diminutives of the name Hans. The final line means "So what kind of people are these!"

8. For a photo of Cossmann in ca. 1925, see Johann Peter Vogel, *Pfitzner: Leben, Werke, Dokumente* (Zürich: Atlantis Musikbuch-Verlag, 1999), 122.

9. Müller, "Cossmann," 374–75.

10. In fact, Palestrina composed that particular mass well before the Council considered any reforms in music. Even then, the Council essentially sought to remove secular influences from liturgical music (masses utilizing popular tunes, for instance) and to affirm that in all musical settings the religious texts would be heard clearly.

11. During the last part of Pfitzner's tenure in Strassburg, his assistant and frequent substitute was Otto Klemperer (1885–1973), whose experiences are recounted in Peter Heyworth, *Conversations with Klemperer* (London: Victor Golancz, 1973), 45–54;

as well as his *Otto Klemperer: His Life and Times* (Cambridge: Cambridge University Press, 1983), I, 87–119.

12. Franklin, "Pfitzner," 542, effectively summarizes the cantata's significance. A good account is found in John Williamson's extensive program note for the 1992 CD reissue of the 1965 recording: Pfitzner, *Von deutscher Seele*, Soloists, Bavarian Radio Orchestra and Chorus, conducted by Joseph Keilberth (Deutsche Grammophon CD 437 033-2), booklet, 6–18; and John Williamson, *The Music of Hans Pfitzner* (Oxford: Clarendon Press, 1992).

13. Bernhard Adamy, *Hans Pfitzner: Literatur, Philosophie, und Zeitgeschehen in seinem Weltbild und Werk* (Tutzing: Hans Schneider, 1980), 310. Adamy is often preferable to other sources because his own citations are clearer.

14. Kurt Levin, "Erinnerungen," in *Festschrift Hans Pfitzner* (ed. Walter Abendroth and Karl Robert Danler; Munich: Peter Winkler, 1969), 64.

15. Adamy, *Pfitzner*, 310–11.

16. Interestingly, the two antagonists had met in February 1924, when Hitler, then a minor agitator, had visited the hospital where Pfitzner just happened to be recovering from a hernia operation. After a brief flurry of pleasantries, little else seems to have developed from the acquaintance. See Adamy, *Pfitzner*, 300–301.

17. Pfitzner hated France and the French from World War I and its aftermath, and he did not care for the English. At least three members of his family had come to the United States: cousin Max (who seems to have worked in the New York area), cousin Walther (b. 1882, who taught music and conducted choirs at Bethany College in Lindsborg, Kansas, from 1915, and later at Dakota Normal School in Spearfish, South Dakota), and brother Heinrich (who, sometime after 1900, brought his boorish American wife to visit the Pfitzners' Berlin home). See Pfitzner, "Eindrücke," 180–83, 218–19, and 248–49; and Cesar Searchinger, ed., *International Who's Who in Music and Musical Gazetteer* (New York: Current Literature, 1918), 489; and *Grove's Dictionary of Music and Musicians: American Supplement* (ed. Waldo Selden Pratt; Philadelphia: Theodore Presser, 1920), 104. The *American Supplement* was printed, virtually unaltered, as vol. 6 of *Grove's* second (1920) through fourth editions (1940).

18. When Archbishop Hieronymus Colloredo angrily dismissed Mozart from his service on June 25, 1781, his steward Count Arco reportedly kicked the composer in the backside as he exited the room. Adamy, *Pfitzner*, 322–25; Pfitzner, *Reden, Schriften, Briefe*, 313.

19. Adamy, *Pfitzner*, 325–27.

20. For further details, see Bernhard Adamy, "Hans Pfitzner als Goethe-Preisträger der Stadt Frankfurt," *Mitteilungen der Hans Pfitzner-Gesellschaft* 45 (February 1983): 56–63.

21. Even so, Felix never lost his personal identification with his Jewish roots, the main premise of Eric Werner, *Mendelssohn: A New Image of the Composer and His Age* (trans. Dika Newlin; New York: Free Press of Glencoe, 1963). Newlin (1923–2006)

was my advisor at North Texas State University, 1967–1973. Customarily positive and generous, she reported that dealing with the irascible, opinionated, Viennese-born Werner (1901–1988) was sometimes difficult, but that the insights were well worth it.

22. There have been many recordings of Mendelssohn's complete Overture and incidental music to *A Midsummer Night's Dream*, but none better than the Boston Symphony Orchestra and Chorus, conducted by Erich Leinsdorf, with Inga Swenson, narrator (in English), recorded in 1962, but still available on CD as RCA/BMG 7816-2-RV.

23. In addition to the singing societies, there were parallel gymnastic societies [*Turnvereine*], marksmanship societies [*Schützenvereine*], and similar organizations to provide social outlets among the grassroots *Volk* of Germany and wherever Germans settled, including the United States. Even today, Omaha has a German-American Society with its *Sängerchor* [a mixed chorus combined from the former Omaha *Musik-Verein* male chorus and the Concordia Ladies Singing Society], the *Singenden Wanderer* [men's chorus for German folk songs], *Heimat Tänzer* [folk dance groups for children and adults], and a *Schützenverein* [using air pellet rifles]. And what about the origins of Omaha's Turner Park? For such organizations in America that developed without any appreciable contact with or influence by choruses elsewhere in the United States, see Theodore Albrecht, "German Singing Societies in Texas" (Ph.D. diss., North Texas State University, 1975).

24. Franz Josef Ewens, *Das deutsche Sängerbuch: Wesen und Wirken des Deutschen Sängerbundes* (Berlin: Deutsche Buchvertriebsstelle, 1930), 52–57. The exact same large format book appeared as *Deutsches Lied und deutscher sang: Wesen und Wirken des Deutschen Sängerbundes* (Karlsruhe: W. Schille, 1930) with different colored covers.

25. Werner, *Mendelssohn*, 355, characterized it thus: "For good or ill, a landmark for the German male chorus, since it has been imitated *ad nauseam* by every Tom, Dick, and Harry."

26. A good representative performance is by the *Männerchor* [Men's chorus] of the Berlin Radio Choruses, conducted by Dietrich Knothe, *Berühmte Männerchöre*; Capriccio CD 10 422 (1992).

27. There are many fine recordings of Mendelssohn's *Elijah* in both German and English.

28. Within Mendelssohn's works, *Der Jäger Abschied* is No. 2 of a collection of unaccompanied choral songs, Op. 50, and "Lift Thine Eyes" is an unaccompanied trio of angels (often sung by chorus) from his oratorio *Elijah*.

29. Adamy, *Pfitzner*, 309, 318–19, and 421. Although written during the Renaissance, Shakespeare's plays were considered highly romantic. Most producers and directors made cuts to suit their casts, means, and purposes. For an instance of this practice in English, merely compare the texts of *Henry V* as filmed by Sir Laurence Olivier (1944) and Kenneth Branagh (1989).

30. Ibid., 312–13, 316, and 330.

31. Ibid., 315. As Adamy noted, the Nazis' musical expectations could be met by third-rate composers, and thus they were not interested in a composer of Pfitzner's stature. Pfitzner often envied Richard Strauss's seemingly more secure and rewarding governmental position, but the fragility of even that relationship became all too evident when Strauss insisted upon collaborating artistically with Stefan Zweig, a Jew.

32. Relatively recent CD issues of Pfitzner's conducting include Beethoven, Symphonies Nos. 1 and 6 (Naxos Historical, 8.110927); Beethoven, Symphonies Nos. 1 and 4 (Preiser 90220); Beethoven, Symphony No. 4 (Naxos Historical, 8.110919); Beethoven, Symphonies Nos. 3 and 8 (Naxos Historical, 8.110910); Beethoven, Symphony No. 3 (Preiser 90201); and Beethoven, Symphonies Nos. 6 and 8 (Preiser 90221). Pfitzner's five Beethoven Symphonies, all recorded with Berlin orchestras between 1928 and 1933, were part of a projected Beethoven cycle, also conducted by other notable conductors, including Erich Kleiber and Richard Strauss.

33. Levin, "Erinnerungen," 64–65; Adamy, *Pfitzner*, 310–11.

34. Turnau came to New York City in 1939 and, after the war, taught at Hunter College.

35. Americans will recognize him immediately as William Steinberg (1899–1978), who was the successful music director of the Pittsburgh Symphony Orchestra from 1952 to 1976. He made numerous recordings with this ensemble, but a good example, available in multiple formats for over five decades, is Johannes Brahms, Symphony No. 4, originally recorded by Everest Records on February 13–16, 1960, and available in the CD era as Everest/Omega/Vanguard EVC 9016 (1995) and Everest/Criterion EVER CD 006 (2008).

36. Horst Reber and Heinrich Heym, *Das Frankfurter Opernhaus: 1880 bis 1944* (Frankfurt: Kettenhof, 1969), 46–48. A photograph of the young William Steinberg appears on p. 35.

37. Ibid., 48–52. A further concern was the antisemitic Nazi *Gauleiter* Jakob Sprenger (1884–1945), responsible for seeing that party directives were carried out.

38. In the photo taken at the event, Pfitzner stands on the steps of the Goethe House with seven other people, including Hans Meissner and Mayor Krebs. Walter Abendroth, *Hans Pfitzner: Sein Leben in Bildern* (Leipzig: Bibliographisches Institut, 1941), plate 79, shows the entire group; while Joseph Müller-Blattau, *Hans Pfitzner: Lebensweg und Schaffensernte* (Frankfurt: Waldemar Kramer, 1969), table 11, facing p. 96, provides another shot, with the three figures in uniform, including Krebs, cropped and edited out. Meissner, however, remains.

39. Adamy, "Pfitzner als Goethe-Preisträger," 56–63.

40. Müller-Blattau, 110; Adamy, *Pfitzner*, 331 and 427.

41. Like Pfitzner's *Palestrina*, Hindemith's opera, *Mathis der Maler*, loosely deals with historical events in which an artist finds himself at odds with society. In this case it was the painter Mathias Grünewald (1470–1528) and the pressures on him during

the Peasants' War of 1524–1525. When he completed the opera in 1935, Hindemith could not get it performed, but a "symphony" that he made from three excerpts was performed by the Berlin Philharmonic under Wilhelm Furtwängler in 1938. The regime criticized the conductor for championing Hindemith's work, and he even wrote an essay defending his actions. In many ways, this paved the way for Furtwängler's performances of Pfitzner's Symphony in C in 1940 and beyond.

42. Similar honors and titles were conferred upon the much more recognizable composer Richard Strauss (1864–1949), and they should be kept in a similar perspective when we remember that his literary collaborators included the Jewish writers Hugo von Hofmannsthal (1874–1929), six librettos [1909–1933], including *Der Rosenkavalier* [1911]; and Stefan Zweig (1881–1942), including *Die schweigsame Frau* [1935]. It almost seems that, in his mature years, Strauss sought out Jewish writers for his operatic librettists.

43. Although Hitler and Mussolini had actually met earlier, their first official meeting was in Rome on May 3, 1938. The Germans brought five hundred staff members and journalists to Rome in three trains. The incident is hilariously depicted, with several details changed, in Charlie Chaplin's inspiring satire *The Great Dictator* (1940).

44. Pfitzner, *Reden, Schriften, Briefe*, 155.

45. *Schädel* means "skull." Pfitzner, *Reden, Schriften, Briefe*, 155; also Walter Abendroth, *Ich warne Neugierige* (Munich: List-Verlag, 1966); quoted in his "Pfitzner der Unzeitsgemässe," *Mitteilungen der Hans Pfitzner-Gesellschaft* 16 (May 1983): 16.

46. Adamy, *Pfitzner*, 330–31. Munich had also been planning a large-scale public celebration but had to cancel it in favor of a single program over the radio.

47. Frankfurt's *Theater Almanac*, its stage prospectus for the 1939–1940 season, provided a look at the pressures that Meissner faced: Its red cover depicted the Opera House and three other venues for dramatic productions. Inside, the first illustration was a sculpture of the Führer himself, lending a tone of Teutonic seriousness rather than joy to the season. Then came a series of portraits of cultural and governmental leaders from *Reichsminister* Joseph Goebbels, to *Gauleiter* Sprenger, to the scarred and shaven Mayor Krebs. The eighth portrait is Hans Meissner, who, with his long wavy hair, looked like a woolly radical or a true artist next to his ghoulish Nazi superiors.

48. Albert Richard Mohr, *Die Frankfurter Oper, 1924–1944* (Frankfurt: Waldemar Kramer, 1971), 334; quoted in Adamy, *Pfitzner*, 427; Erich Valentin, *Hans Pfitzner: Werk und Gestalt eines Deutschen* (Regensburg: Gustav Bosse, 1939), 68; and Cahn, *Das Hoch'sche Konservatorium*, quoted in Osthoff, "Pfitzner und das Hoch'sche Konservatorium," 63.

     As early as 1934, the Conservatory, led by Bertil Wetzelsberger, had attempted to engage the controversial former Frankfurt residents Pfitzner and Paul Hindemith as guest faculty, but with no luck.

49. Adamy, *Pfitzner*, 422.

50. Ibid., 317.

51. Ironically, the Buchenwald Concentration Camp was only six miles northwest of Weimar.

52. Goethe's poem (in a prose English translation) reads: "Over every hilltop is peace. In every treetop you feel hardly a breeze. The little birds are silent in the forest. Just wait, soon you too shall be at peace."

Pfitzner's sarcastic parody similarly reads: "Over every square foot is noise. Everywhere chatter and loud revelry from 'Strength Through Joy' groups and Hitler Youth. The birds are silent all around; they think it's stupid, too—God protect us!"

Among other details, Pfitzner changed Goethe's opening "Über alle Gipfeln ist Ruh" to "Auf allen Plätzen is Lärm," but in his German parody he kept some semblance of Goethe's rhythm and rhyme. See Pfitzner, *Reden, Schriften, Briefe*, 315.

53. Pfitzner, *Reden, Schriften, Briefe*, 315; Joseph Wulf, *Musik im Dritten Reich* (Gütersloh: S. Mohn, 1963), 310; quoted in Adamy, *Pfitzner*, 302–3.

54. Pfitzner, *Reden, Schriften, Briefe*, 315–16.

55. Peter Muck, ed., *Einhundert Jahre Berliner Philharmonisches Orchester: Darstellung in Dokumenten* (3 vols.; Tutzing: Hans Schneider, 1982); quoted in Wolfgang Osthoff, "Pfitzner und die Berliner Philharmoniker," *Mitteilungen der Hans Pfitzner-Gesellschaft* 45 (February 1983): 53. The score and parts had already been printed by Adolf Fürstner in Berlin-Grunewald on September 21, 1940.

56. Among CD issues are Pfitzner's own recordings of the Symphony in C (Preiser 90029) and the three Preludes to *Palestrina* (EMI, Composers in Person, CDC 5 55225 2), coupled with other works conducted or played by the composer. Furtwängler's 1949 performances of both the Symphony in C and *Palestrina* Preludes (AS-disc, AS370) are of solid historical interest. Gerard Schwarz's recording of the Symphony in C with the Seattle Symphony, from April 1996 (Naxos, 8.572770), offers a fine interpretation with modern sound.

57. An account of that performance, meant to interest other conductors in the work, was Theodore Albrecht, "A Gentle Protest: Hans Pfitzner's Symphony in C, Op. 46 (1940)," *Journal of the Conductors Guild* 6:2 (Spring 1985): 34–44. The principal hornist was Shelley Marshall, principal trumpeter Phil Schaefer, and English horn soloist Carol Padgham Albrecht.

58. Rolf Tybout, "An die Freunde. Die Widmung von Hans Pfitzners Sinfonie op. 46," *Acta Musicologica* 74:2 (2002): 195–218. Tybout, a professor of ancient history at the University of Leyden, is also interested in Pfitzner and believes that the dedication is a reference to a poem ("An die Freunde") by Eichendorff, as well as to the composer's friends in Munich and Frankfurt in general. As we have seen, Pfitzner was fond of Eichendorff's poetry and had frequently set it to music, in solo songs and especially in the cantata *Von deutscher Seele*. As we have also seen, the composer's wordplays

often have multiple meanings, easily allowing for the validity of Tybout's thesis in addition to the one presented here. Indeed, it might even be an allusion to Moses Mendelssohn's final essay, *An die Freunde Lessings* [To Lessing's friends].

59. Pfitzner, *Reden, Schriften, Briefe*, 315–16.

60. Peter Heyworth, *Conversations with Klemperer* (London: Victor Golancz, 1973), 50. Otto Klemperer (1885–1973) had been one of Pfitzner's assistant conductors during the Strassburg years. Bruno Walter (birth name Schlesinger, 1876–1962) had remained friends with Pfitzner since he conducted the premiere of *Palestrina* in Munich in 1917. Walter told Klemperer about the letter, and he related it to Heyworth.

61. Vogel, *Pfitzner: Leben, Werke, Dokumente*, 174–83.

62. To find Pfitzner's grave in Group 14C, face Beethoven's grave, turn half right, and walk (as walkways allow) around Brahms's grave, past Johann Strauss's family, to parallel rows of graves where Pfitzner and Arnold Schoenberg are buried, perhaps a hundred feet from each other. Schoenberg has a crazily tilted stone on his grave, and Pfitzner's features a three-dimensional face of the composer, scowling out, as in life, to greet the visitor.

63. The music lover who is politically numbed by even the encyclopedia articles mentioned in the introduction to this essay might try the CD of Pfitzner's three *Palestrina* Preludes and other orchestral excerpts with the Orchestra of the German Opera Berlin, conducted by Christian Thielemann; Deutsche Grammophon 449 571-2 (1996). The hypnotic first Prelude will provide welcome comfort at the end of a hard day.

NOT SO SILENT

Jewish Religious and Cultural Life in Kiev, 1945–1970s

VICTORIA KHITERER

LIE WIESEL VISITED the Soviet Union in fall 1965 during the Jewish High Holidays. Due to Soviet censorship, Jews in Western countries knew very little about the life of Jews in the Soviet Union. Wiesel wrote, "I went to Russia drawn by the silence of its Jews. I brought back their cry."[1] Wiesel described his visit to the Soviet Union in his book, *The Jews of Silence*.[2] He wrote about Antisemitism and the suppression of Jewish life in the Soviet Union. Jewish scholarly, educational, and cultural organizations were closed by the Soviet authorities in the second half of the 1930s–1940s. However, in spite all the efforts of the authorities, Jewish religious life was never completely suppressed in the Soviet Union.

Official Soviet reports show that a significant percentage of Kievan Jews continued to attend synagogue or clandestine minyanim after the Second World War and celebrated Jewish religious holidays. So, the Kiev synagogue became a place of dissent and spiritual resistance against the Soviet state Antisemitism and assimilation policy. The authorities understood this well and attempted to break Jewish resistance by discrediting and attacking Judaism and Jewish religious life.

REVIVAL OF JEWISH RELIGIOUS LIFE IN KIEV AFTER THE SHOAH

Before World War II, Kiev had the second largest Jewish urban population in the Soviet Union after Moscow. In 1939, 224,236 Jews lived in Kiev out of 847,000 inhabitants (26.5 percent). The Jewish population of Moscow in 1939 was 250,181. By January 1, 1947, Jews constituted 18.8 percent of the Kiev population: 132,467 of 704,609 city inhabitants. Thus the Jewish population of Kiev had decreased from 1939 to 1947 by 91,769 people.[3] Most of these Jews were either killed by the Nazis in Babi Yar or perished on the front during the war.

Despite their great losses, Kievan Jews attempted to restore their cultural and religious life after the war. The last Jewish scholarly, cultural institutions and public organizations were closed in the Soviet Union in the late 1940s during the anti-cosmopolitan campaign. However, Jewish religious life was never completely suppressed in the country. There are several reasons for this. The Soviet Union officially had a policy of freedom of conscience. But unofficially the authorities put considerable pressure on believers of all denominations. Most churches, mosques, and synagogues were closed in the Soviet Union in the 1920s and 1930s. Before the February 1917 revolution, Kiev had four synagogues and sixteen prayer houses, but they all were closed by the Soviet authorities in the late 1920s and early 1930s.[4] However, in spite of the closure of the synagogues and the anti-religious propaganda, a significant part of the Jewish population in Kiev and the Soviet Union remained observant.

After World War II, the Soviet authorities returned the synagogue at 29 Shchekavitskaia Street in the Podol district (where most Kievan Jews lived) to the Kiev Jewish Community. It was the first synagogue built in Kiev in 1895, financed by the merchant Gessel Markovich Rosenberg. The Moorish-style building was designed by the architect Nikolai Gardenin. The synagogue was closed by the Soviet authorities in 1929 and turned into the Club of Jewish Artisans. During the occupation of Kiev, the Nazis used the synagogue as a stable.[5]

During and immediately after World War II the Soviets decreased their pressure on religious institutions. Josef Stalin even sought support from the Russian Orthodox Church to raise patriotism among the population. Religion helped people overcome the psychological trauma of losing family members, friends, and relatives during the war. Religious Jews, who returned from the front and evacuation to Kiev, petitioned the authorities to return to them the synagogue at 29 Shchekavitskaia Street and their request was fulfilled in 1945.[6]

In the 1950s–1970s many Kievan Jews attended the only operating Kiev synagogue. According to official reports in 1951 and in 1956–1958, about thirty thousand Jews (approximately one fifth of the Jewish population) attended the synagogue on Yom Kippur holidays: "Shchekavitskaia Street, where the Kiev synagogue is located, was so crowded on Yom Kippur in 1958 that no transportation could move on the street. On the adjoining streets the crowds of Jews moved continuously."[7] Four cantors participated in the religious service in the synagogue during the religious holidays.[8]

One synagogue obviously could not satisfy the religious needs of the Kievan Jewish population. Religious Jews repeatedly appealed to the authorities to allow the opening of a second synagogue in Kiev after World War II; however, all requests were rejected.[9] Furthermore, two Kiev rabbis were dismissed by the Soviet authorities. Kiev Rabbi

Itsko Gershkovich Shekhtman (in office 1945–1952) was deprived of his accreditation at the end of 1952 for unauthorized fundraising for repair of the synagogue. He was reported to have publicly requested in the synagogue that "every Jew should support the only synagogue in the city Kiev."[10] The report also stated: "Furthermore, an illegal 'Jewish mutual help cashbox' was found in the Kiev synagogue. Itsyk Goifman was in charge of this cashbox, in which up to 12,000 rubles was detected."[11]

In addition to "financial crimes," the commissioner of the Council for the Affairs of Religious Cults (CARC) of the Ukrainian SSR accused Rabbi Shekhtman of trying to turn the synagogue into a "'kahal' [i.e., to give to the prayer house a specifically national character], and to save by any means the 'only' synagogue as the 'only' place of 'Jewish organization.'"[12] In other words, Rabbi Shekhtman was accused of trying to re-create the pre-Soviet Jewish community structures in Kiev. The commissioner of the CARC reported the lively Jewish religious activity in Kiev under the leadership of Rabbi Shekhtman. This ran counter to the official policy of the ultimate suppression of religious life in the Soviet Union. So, Rabbi Shekhtman was dismissed, and he died a few months later in April 1953.[13]

Avrum Al'terovich Panich became the new Kiev Rabbi (in office 1953–January 1958). However, Rabbi Panich was deprived of his accreditation in January 1958 by the CARC for the similar crime of "fundraising [for the synagogue] in private apartments and in offices."[14] Of course the rabbis had to raise money because neither they nor the synagogue had any other revenue. The Soviet authorities certainly understood this, but they used the accusation of illegal financial activities to deprive Kiev religious Jews of their rabbi. From January 1958 until 1987, Kiev Jews did not have a rabbi at all.[15] The Kiev synagogue remained open but was under strict observation by the KGB. People who attended the synagogue were also under KGB observation, and some of them had problems at their work or even were fired from prestigious positions. In the absence of a rabbi, the synagogue was operated by the board of the Kiev religious community, members of which were preselected and approved by the CARC. Of course the members of the board, which depended on the CARC, were generally obedient to the Soviet authorities.

Elie Wiesel visited the Kiev synagogue on the second day of Sukkot in 1965. He recalled:

The Jews I found in the synagogue differed from those in other cities. Their fear is more solid, more compact, and perhaps more justified. Their own leaders terrorize them . . . you can feel it in your bones. Nowhere else in Russia did I see such hatred on the part of Jews toward their own leaders. . . .

The *gabbai*[16] of the synagogue was a clumsy and vulgar Jew by the name of Jonah Gandelman [Gendelman]. His eyes were permanently enraged, his voice continually shouting. He had the domineering character of a military commander and seemed to hold a whip over the congregation. One look from him, and the object of his wrath was cowed into obedience.[17]

The authorities, who under Nikita Khrushchev launched a new anti-religious campaign, hoped that without a rabbi the number of religious Jews would decrease in Kiev. The authorities at least partially achieved their goal: the number of observant Jews who attended the synagogue significantly dropped. In 1978, twenty years after Rabbi Panich was removed, 600 Jews attended the synagogue on the first day of Pesach on April 22, and 950 Jews attended the synagogue on the last day of Pesach. On the other days of Pesach, the attendance at the synagogue was 100–150 per day.[18]

However, Jewish religious life in Kiev was not limited to the synagogue. There were also numerous minyanim. According to the report of the CARC commissioner P. Vil'khovyi, for the last quarter of 1952 about 100 illegal minyanim operated in Kiev:

> The authorities took measures to stop the operation of the minyanim in known loca-
> tions, however some of them probably continue their activity underground. These
> minyanim gathered in average from 40 to 60 people. For example, on Kreshchatik
> Street #58 in a private apartment, there was a special minyan for Jewish intelligen-
> tsia (medical doctors and other professionals). Not less than 100 people partici-
> pated in this minyan.[19]

In 1952 the Jewish religious community in Kiev included five thousand people who were officially registered as members of the single synagogue. About five thousand Jews participated in minyanim. So, there were at least ten thousand observant Jews in Kiev in the last year of Stalin's rule. In 1973 the chairman of the Kiev Jewish religious community, I. B. Zhydovetskii, reported that the synagogue produced and sold sixty-two tons of matzah before Pesach that year. Eighty-two hundred Jews from Kiev and its suburbs submitted orders for matzah. The customers purchased on the average five to six kilograms (ten to twelve pounds) of matzah.[20] So, considering the number of orders for matzah, the number of religious Jews had not decreased signifi-cantly in Kiev from 1952 to 1973, in spite of all the efforts of the Soviet authorities to suppress Jewish religious life in the city.

According to Zhydovetskii, "if 40 illegal minyanim were not operating in different districts of the city, the [Kiev] synagogue would always be overcrowded."[21] Thus, the CARC commissioner M. Gladarevskii, who reported a conversation with Zhydovetskii on May 15, 1973, concluded that "obviously the increased activity of the Jewish religious community makes it necessary to more thoroughly control" its activity.[22] Control over the synagogue was reinforced, but it did not help much. Five years later, on Pesach in

1978, the Kiev synagogue produced and sold over sixty-one tons of matzah.[23] This was almost the same amount as in 1973, which means that the number of observant Jews had remained about the same.

The CARC commissioners explained their failure to suppress ongoing Jewish religious life in Kiev by the stubbornness of observant Jews. The CARC commissioners complained that Jewish religious fanatics often broke work discipline and Soviet law by refusing to work on Jewish holidays. For example, according to the report of the CARC commissioner, on Yom Kippur in 1951 many stores were closed in Kiev: "There were 34 stores closed on Yom Kippur in Podol district alone; all salesmen of these stores were in the synagogue on this day."[24]

My great-grandfather, Yankel' Berkovich Khiterer, was one of these "stubborn" observant Jews about whom the CARC commissioners complained. In Stalin's time, when the workweek was six days and the only weekend day was Sunday, he refused to work on Saturdays. He said that God did not allow him to work on Saturday. A command from God was apparently persuasive for Stalin's authorities because my great-grandfather was allowed to work five days per week. Perhaps it also helped that my great-grandfather worked in modest positions. Before the war he sold magazines and newspapers in a booth; after the war he worked at the post office.

The CARC commissioners also accused observant Kievan Jews of a lack of Soviet patriotism. For example, the CARC commissioner A. Oleinikov wrote in his report of April 7, 1953, about the inappropriate behavior of Kievan Jews on the day of Stalin's funeral, on March 9, 1953:

> On March 9 of this year, on Monday, a day unusual for religious service, an unusually large number of Jews visited the Jewish synagogue in Kiev. Over five thousand Jews came to the synagogue, among whom the majority were unbelievers or those who seldom come to the synagogue (only on Yom Kippur).
>
> Exactly on this Monday, on March 9 this year, the funeral of I.V. Stalin took place. Due to this, a huge number of Soviet people gathered to listen to the radio broadcast [of Stalin's funeral] on Kreshchatik and other large squares of Kiev.
>
> Why did a significant part of Jews not come to Kreshchatik to be with all the people there, but instead concentrated at the synagogue?
>
> I assume that this happened (the concentration of Jews at the synagogue on that day) because the synagogue is the center for all Jews, not only the prayer house for observant Jews. Synagogues are really the place of concentration and gathering of almost all the local Jewish population.
>
> The above listed facts show that "behind the shoulders and backs" of the registered Jewish communities and their synagogues, hide some dark forces and possible

nationalists, who use Judaism as a curtain for some specific purposes. I hope that our state security [i.e., KGB] will pay attention to this.[25]

Perhaps many Kievan observant and nonobservant Jews concentrated in the synagogue on the day of Stalin's funeral because they were afraid of a new pogrom in the city. The memories of the Jewish pogrom in Kiev on September 7, 1945, were still fresh. During this pogrom sixteen Jews were killed and over a hundred were seriously injured.[26]

The situation in Kiev was quite explosive. Stalin died during the "Doctor's Plot" campaign, when a significant part of the local gentile population believed that "the Jewish doctor-wreckers" had poisoned Soviet leaders. During the campaign local Antisemites called in their leaflets for the killing or the expulsion of all Jews from the city. So Kievan Jews used the proven tactic of survival during a pogrom: to concentrate in large numbers in one place and prepare to defend themselves in case of danger.

Although the number of religious Jews who attended the synagogue significantly dropped after removal of the rabbi, the synagogue and its vicinity remained the place of Jewish gathering and the center of Jewish national life in Kiev. The chairman of the Kiev Jewish Community, Gendelman, reported to the authorities in 1966 that a thousand religious Jews attended the synagogue on Yom Kippur and that "the rest of the twenty thousand, which created the crowd near the synagogue, were not observant, but they considered that it was their duty to show Jewish national unity in this day."[27]

The representative of the CARC, A. Sharandak, wrote in his secret report "About Hostile Activities Under Coverage of the Synagogue" to the chairman of the CARC, A. A. Puzin, on November 15, 1962: "The nationalist elements consider the [Kiev] synagogue as the only place of Jewish communication and the center of Jewish unity in the surrounding hostile environment."[28] Sharandak reported that ninety-six foreign tourists, including twenty Israeli citizens, visited the Kiev synagogue in 1962. He stated that Israeli Ambassador to the Soviet Union Yosef Tekoah,[29] along with the attaché officer and his wife, attended the Kiev synagogue on Yom Kippur, on October 8, 1962, and stayed there from 10 a.m. to 7 p.m. They came out several times and communicated with the Jews, who gathered in large numbers on the street near the synagogue. Sharandak claimed that these diplomats "provided nationalist propaganda and invited Jews to immigrate to Israel, distributed Zionist and nationalist illustrated brochures and Zionist badges."[30] Sharandak wrote that the Israeli diplomats provoked "anti-Soviet activities among some Jews, who came to the synagogue. Some people screamed from the crowd that the Soviet authorities didn't give freedom to Jews, discriminated against them in the right to work and education, and wanted to repeat the fascist Babi Yar. The screamers from the crowd addressed their statements to the Israeli diplomats and asked them for protection."[31]

Sharandak reported that the Israeli diplomat Karmel and the entire Israeli volley-
ball team attended the Kiev synagogue on the Jewish holiday of Sukkot, on October
20–21, 1962, and distributed there "Israeli nationalist literature in Russian, English
and Hebrew."[32]

Sharandak wrote that the Kiev City Council was considering closing the synagogue, "which is not the place of satisfaction of religious needs of the observant Jews,
but a center for connection with the agents of the foreign intelligence services, a site
of the instigation of Jewish bourgeois nationalism, a stronghold of the Israeli Embassy
in the USSR for spreading of undermining Zionist activity, and a black stock market
for various dealers, businessmen and crooks."[33]

However, the Kiev synagogue was not closed, and visits of foreign tourists there
continued in the 1960s–1970s. Nine musicians of the Cleveland Symphony Orchestra
attended the synagogue on the last day of Passover on April 24, 1965. They distributed
their religious literature and talliths (prayer shawls).[34] As noted earlier, Elie Wiesel
attended the synagogue on the second day of Sukkot in 1965.

During Sukkot on September 28, 1966, three young Jews came to the synagogue
during the religious service and demanded that the religious board announce to the Jews
that there was a memorial meeting in Babi Yar at 5 p.m. on September 29. The meeting
was devoted to the twenty-fifth anniversary of the Holocaust of Kiev Jews in Babi Yar.
The chairman of the Kiev Religious Community, Gendelman, spoke to the congregation in the synagogue on September 29, 1966. He said that the authorities did not
allow any meeting in Babi Yar and that rumors about the such a meeting were a prov-
ocation. Gendelman called upon the congregation to not go to Babi Yar.

The next day, September 30, a group of Jews came to the synagogue and blamed
Gendelman for intentionally misinforming them. There had in fact been a meeting in
Babi Yar on September 29—unsanctioned by the authorities—where writer Victor
Nekrasov, dissident Ivan Dziuba, and others presented their speeches, and Kiev cine-
matographers shot a documentary. On September 30 V. Sukhonin (his position is not
mentioned in the source) reported to the secretary of the Kiev City Committee of
the Communist Party of Ukraine, A. P. Botvin, about the unsanctioned meeting in
Babi Yar: "Gendelman told the Jews that the synagogue should not participate in such
events because the observant Jews should commemorate the dead according to the religious ritual in the synagogue, but not in a meeting. In response to Gendelman, Panakh
called the leaders of the Jewish religious community the enemies of Jewish people."[35]

Thus, despite all efforts by the authorities to keep the Kiev synagogue under control,
it became a center of Jewish national life and a place of both spiritual and physical resistance to the state and popular Antisemitism and the assimilation policy of the Soviet
authorities. The authorities and local Antisemites understood this well and attempted
to break Jewish resistance by attacking Judaism.

ANTI-RELIGIOUS CAMPAIGN AND PUBLICATIONS IN KIEV

In 1958 the Central Committee of the Communist Party began a new anti-religious campaign. Although it affected all religious denominations, "the most violent and vicious attacks were directed against the Jewish religion."[36] Benjamin Pinkus wrote that in the 1960s that "between 15 and 20% of all the anti-religious articles in the Soviet press were directed at the Jewish religion, and not at the main religions in the country.... In this period, fifty four books were published against the Jewish religion in Russian alone."[37] However, none of these books received such "worldwide publicity and evoked [such] sharp reactions in the West" as *Iudaism bez prikras* [Judaism Without Embellishment] by Trofim Kichko. Published in 1963 by the Ukrainian Academy of Sciences, with 12,000 copies printed in Ukrainian, it was addressed to a Ukrainian audience. The book was openly antisemitic, asserting that hypocrisy and bribery were "admissible in Judaism, as are 'contempt and even hatred' for non-Jews."[38] Kichko wrote that "Jewish capital opened for Hitler the road to power and Jewish bankers received from Hitler titles as 'honorary Aryans,' which protected them from persecution."[39] The book was illustrated by crude cartoons, which depicted Jews in the Nazi *Der Stürmer* style.[40]

Kichko's book was not coincidentally reminiscent of Nazi antisemitic publications, because Kichko was a Nazi collaborator during the war. An article about his collaboration with the Nazis had appeared on February 10, 1953, in one of the main Soviet newspapers, *Literaturnaia gazeta*. The article said that Kichko, who represented himself as a Soviet partisan, was really a Nazi collaborator during the war in the Ukrainian city of Vinnitsa. He was expelled from the Communist Party in 1948 due to the accusation of collaboration with the Nazis but was readmitted to the party in 1954.[41] So Kichko's collaboration was well known; nevertheless, the Ukrainian Academy of Sciences published his book. If such an openly antisemitic book had been published in Moscow or Leningrad, it would have provoked the protest of all the liberal intelligentsia. But in Kiev, due to the strong popular Antisemitism, every attack on Jews (physical or verbal) was received with pleasure by much of the population.

However, considerable protest came from abroad. On February 24, 1964, Morris Berthold Abram, the president of the American Jewish Committee, supported by a United States representative to the United Nations Commission on Human Rights, brought Kichko's work to worldwide attention by criticizing it during a press conference. He called the book a "disgusting example of the religious hatred and antisemitic literature" that was reminiscent of Hitler, Goebbels, and Nazi propaganda.[42] The work was condemned in the United States and many European countries. Under intense international pressure, the Soviets denounced the book and withdrew it from circulation.

On April 4, 1964, the newspaper *Pravda* published the report of the Ideological Commission of the Central Committee of the Communist Party of the Soviet Union about Kichko's book, which stated:

> The author of the book and the authors of the preface wrongly interpreted some questions concerning the emergence and development of this religion. . . . A number of mistaken propositions and illustrations could insult the feelings of believers and might even be interpreted in the spirit of Antisemitism.

It is difficult to say whether Ukrainian Antisemites accidentally exceeded the allowed limits of attacks upon Jews and Judaism, or, more likely, they intentionally tried to expand the limits. A few years later, in 1968, Trofim Kichko published a new anti-semitic book, *Iudaizm i Sionism* [Judaism and Zionism], by the *Znannia* [Knowledge] publishing house.[43] The book was published in Ukrainian and designed for a wide audience. On January 20, 1968, the newspaper *Pravda Ukrainy* reported that "Kichko was being rewarded by the Presidium of the Supreme Council of Ukraine with an honorary diploma for his services to atheist propaganda." This shows clearly that Kichko's publications received support from the Ukrainian Soviet authorities.

Certainly, there were many other publications against Judaism and Zionism in Kiev and Ukraine, but Kichko's works attracted the attention of the world for their rabid Nazi-style Antisemitism.

JEWISH CULTURAL LIFE IN KIEV

I think that the most amazing thing about Jewish cultural life in Kiev is that it continued to survive under the conditions of strong popular and state Antisemitism. All Jewish performances were forbidden in the Soviet Union in the last years of Stalin's regime; however, during Khrushchev's Thaw some Jewish concerts and performances were again allowed.

In 1959, the hundredth anniversary of the birth of the Yiddish writer Sholom Aleichem was celebrated in the Soviet Union. The authorities permitted in that year "a relatively large number of Yiddish concerts."[44] Soviet Yiddish singer Nehama Lifshitz came with her concerts to Kiev in December 1959.[45] Historian Yaacov Ro'i wrote that Nehama Lifshitz's concerts "were not only cultural events, but 'happenings' of great national significance."[46] Yiddish writer Itsik Kipnis, the poetess Riva Balasnaia, and the widow of David Hofshtein, Feige, came to Lifshitz's concert in Kiev in December 1959. Nehama came with her Jewish concerts to Kiev, Odessa, Kharkov, and other Ukrainian cities several times in the 1960s before her immigration to Israel in 1969.

But the strongest impression was made by her first performance in Kiev in December
1959. Ro'i wrote:

> Jewish cultural events were very rare in the Ukrainian capital. The large hall was so
> packed that there was no standing room at all. Nehama concluded her concert with
> the "Lullaby to Babii Iar" by a Jewish poet from Kiev, Shayke Driz, set to music by Riva
> Boiarskaia (also of Kiev). Nehama usually sang this particular song last, as she found
> it difficult to continue singing after it. But to sing about Babii Iar in Kiev was not like
> singing about it elsewhere. Here no one applauded. The hall seemed to be electrified.
> The entire audience rose to its feet like one man and stood in absolute silence, in the
> atmosphere of fear that characterized the Jews of Kiev. In Nehama's words, this was
> a "curtain of tears." As she left the hall people stood outside, still silently weeping, in
> order to touch her hand or sleeve as though she were some holy person.[47]

In addition to rare Jewish performances, Kievan Jews enjoyed reading books by
Jewish and Russian-Jewish writers Sholom Aleichem, Babel, Ilia Ehrenburg, Itsik
Kipnis, Grigorii Polianker, and others. Their works were published in Russian in the
Soviet Union in 1950s–1970s.

Yiddish poet and writer Itsik Kipnis was expelled from the Ukrainian Writers
Union and arrested in 1949 for "bourgeois nationalism." He was imprisoned in concentration camps until 1954.[48] After his liberation he did not receive permission to live in
Kiev until 1958. He settled in the Kiev suburb of Boiarka. His apartments in Boiarka
and later in Kiev were the unofficial "center of Jewish culture. Many Kievan Jews came
to the Kipnis apartment to look at Jewish books, receive advice about how to learn
Hebrew, to listen to Kipnis's observations about Jewish literature, which became an
important part of their spiritual life."[49]

As a "clerical language," Hebrew was forbidden in the Soviet Union from the
1920s. But illegal Hebrew courses [*ulpanim*] functioned in Kiev, the first of which
were opened in 1969. The first two teachers, Evgeniia Bukhina and Anatolii Gerenrot,
were "young people who had previously learned Hebrew from older Zionists in Kiev
itself."[50] Nobody published Hebrew literature in the Soviet Union. But Hebrew books
arrived from Israel to the Kiev synagogue and private individuals. According to Vera
Yedidya, the owner of an illegal secondhand bookstore sold Hebrew books from private
collections. "His store even became a meeting place for Jews seeking an opportunity
to talk Hebrew."[51]

In the 1970s the Jewish *samizdat* [clandestine] journal *Evrei v SSSR* [Jews in the
USSR] circulated in Kiev as well as in Moscow, Leningrad, Minsk, Khar'kov, Riga,
and Baku in tens of copies. One of the journal's publishers, Alexander Voronel, wrote:

"It was our intention to provide Soviet Jews with cultural material to compensate for their dearth of national self-consciousness that was the result of the total silence of the Soviet publications on Jewish history and culture."[52] By 1980, twenty volumes of *Evrei v SSSR* had been published. "Altogether more than five thousand pages were published in *Evrei v SSSR* by more than one hundred authors. The 'Jews of silence' showed that they were not altogether silent."[53]

Kievan Jewish artists Zinovii Tolkachev (1903–1977) and Mikhail Turovsky (b. 1933) devoted many of their works to Jewish themes, particularly to the Holocaust. During the war Tolkachev served in the Soviet Army, with which he came to the Nazi death camps Majdanek and Auschwitz. He later depicted the horror of the camps in his albums *Majdanek* (1944–1945) and *Flowers of Auschwitz* (1945). Many of Tolkachev's paintings were made in the camps immediately after their liberation. At some point he ran out of paper and, while rummaging through one of the Nazi offices in Auschwitz, found paper with the letterhead "Commandant of Concentration Camp Auschwitz," which he used for his paintings. So this letterhead became part of his works, showing the creator of this horror.[54]

Tolkachev's two albums, published in Warsaw in 1945–1946, were in the name of the Polish government sent to the leaders of the Soviet Union, United States, Great Britain, and France. During the anti-cosmopolitan campaign, the newspaper *Pravda Ukrainy* accused Tolkachev of creating paintings with "Zionist-religious content," and the artist was denounced as a "bourgeois nationalist and rootless cosmopolitan."[55]

In his later years Tolkachev worked as a book illustrator, and he also made a series of portraits of Ukrainian and Jewish writers. In the 1960s he returned to Jewish and Holocaust themes and made two series of paintings, *Auschwitz* and *Shtetl*. *Auschwitz* was published as an album of twenty-six paintings in Kiev in 1965, with an introduction by the Ukrainian Jewish writer Leonid Pervomaiskii. An expanded version of the album with eighty paintings was published in Moscow with an introduction by the Russian writer Aleksander Borshchagovskii.

The Kievan artist Mikhail Turovsky immigrated to the United States in 1979. Before his emigration, he was already recognized as a prominent artist with the title People's Artist of Ukraine. He was also a member of Academy of Arts of Ukraine. However, Turovsky left Ukraine in search of artistic and personal freedom. In America, Turovsky created his series of works, *Holocaust*, in which he devoted many paintings to the Babi Yar massacre.[56]

The Holocaust and Babi Yar massacre themes were dominant in the works of Kievan Jewish artists and writers in the postwar period because they were the most traumatic experiences in their lives. The Babi Yar massacre changed the atmosphere of the entire city. Not only Jews but many gentiles were traumatized by the massacre.

THE EMIGRATION
MOVEMENT

The main reasons for the emigration of Jews from Kiev were the same as from the rest of the Soviet Union: state and popular Antisemitism, the suppression of Jewish national and religious institutions, and low living standards. So, Jews who searched for a better and more "meaningful Jewish life" tried to emigrate from the USSR.[57]

State discrimination continued in the Soviet Union until the late 1980s. Kievan Jews were not hired for prestigious positions nor accepted into prestigious universities. They were considered by the authorities to be a fifth column that could leave the country at any time and take with them precious knowledge and state secrets.

But Jews suffered even more from popular Antisemitism in Kiev. Antisemites often insulted and sometimes beat Jews on the streets, in stores, markets, and schools, and on public transportation. Many Jewish graves were vandalized in Kiev cemeteries, and antisemitic signs and leaflets often appeared in different parts of the city. Sociological research conducted by Ludmila Tsigelman found that 74 percent of Jews who emigrated from the Soviet Union to Israel reported that they had experienced Antisemitism in their childhood.[58]

Many Kievan Jews wanted to emigrate from the Soviet Union. However, Jewish emigration was severely restricted by the Soviet authorities. Jewish *refusniks* [people refused permission to leave the Soviet Union] organized unsanctioned meetings at the synagogue and in Babi Yar, where they demanded that they be allowed to leave the country and to commemorate the victims of the Holocaust. Many of these Jewish activists were arrested. But in spite of all of this persecution, the authorities never succeeded in completely suppressing the Jewish national movement in Kiev.

The Six-Day War raised the national self-esteem of Soviet Jews. Jewish youth dreamt about emigration to Israel. Tsigelman wrote that in many Jewish families, the youth initiated the emigration from the Soviet Union in the late 1960s and early 1970s. In some cases, when their parents refused to leave the country, the young people emigrated alone. According to Tsigelman, "Of twenty-four youth who finished one of the Kiev mathematical schools in 1971, fifteen had already been living in Israel for several years by 1980. Those youths decided on repatriation independently, as in the cases of Mark Lutsker and Iakov Vinaver, who left despite their parents' objections, after having served three-year prison terms for their refusal to serve in the Soviet army."[59]

Soviet Ukrainian authorities reported the growth of a Zionist mood among the Jewish population of Ukraine. They explained this phenomenon by the influence of Zionist propaganda from the radio station Voice of Israel. Thus, a secretary of the Central Committee of the Communist Party of Ukraine, F. Ovcharenko, wrote in his secret report to the Central Committee of the Communist Party of the Soviet Union (TsK KPSS), on April 22, 1971:

> According to the information of the local communist organization, a significant part of the Jewish population of Chernovtsy, Odessa, Kiev, Vinnitsa, and some other cities of Ukraine listen to programs of the "Voice of Israel," especially in Russian....
>
> Considering this circumstance, we ask TsK KPSS to take measures to jam the programs of the radio station "Voice of Israel" by the radio station *Maiak* [Beacon], or by the programs of the Ukrainian radio station *Promin'* [Beam], especially in the cities of Chernovtsy, Odessa, Kiev, Vinnitsa, and others, where a significant Jewish population lives.[60]

However, despite the struggle of the Soviet authorities against Zionism and "enemy voices," thousands of Kievan Jews left for Israel and the United States in the 1970s.

CONCLUSION

The Soviet authorities never succeeded in completely assimilating the Jews or suppressing the Jewish national movement. From 1945 through the 1970s, Jewish national life continued in Kiev: religious Jews (about 20 percent of the Jewish population) attended the only open synagogue or prayed in minyanim in private homes. Hundreds of Jews attended unsanctioned memorial meetings in Babi Yar on September 29 (the day when the Jewish massacre began there). They, together with Russian and Ukrainian liberal intelligentsia, ultimately forced the Soviet authorities to build a monument in Babi Yar in 1976. Kievan Jews enjoyed Jewish cultural life, sanctioned or unsanctioned: rare Jewish public performances and often unofficial gatherings in private homes, where they discussed Jewish literature and *samizdat*, as well as talked about the newly created State of Israel and its conflict with the Arab countries. Many discussed the possibility of emigrating from the country and studied Hebrew.

In his essay *Babi Yar*, composed on the third anniversary of the massacre on September 29, 1944, Itsik Kipnis wrote that nobody could exterminate all Jewish people. "A people half and three-quarters of which has been annihilated, is like a glob of mercury. Wrench half of it away, and the other half will become rounded and whole again."[61] To echo the words of Kipnis, I can say that it was impossible to deprive Jews of their national identity or completely suppress their religious and cultural life. All of the official pressure on Jews to assimilate into the Russian Empire and the Soviet Union brought about the opposite results: the rise of Jewish national consciousness and the emigration of Jews from the country. State and popular Antisemitism just accelerated these processes and never silenced the Jews.

NOTES

1. Elie Wiesel, *The Jews of Silence: A Personal Report on Soviet Jewry* (New York: Schocken Books, 2011), xi.

2. Ibid.

3. Mordechai Altshuler, *Soviet Jewry on the Eve of the Holocaust: A Social and Demographic Profile* (Jerusalem: The Center for Research of East European Jewry of the Hebrew University of Jerusalem, Yad Vashem, 1998), 277; Antony Polonsky, *The Jews in Poland and Russia, Volume III, 1914 to 2008* (Oxford, Portland: The Littman Library of Jewish Civilization, 2012), 275; A. V. Kudryts'kyi, ed., *Kiev. Entsyklopedychnyi Dovidnyk,* (Kiev: Golovna redaktsia Ukrains'koi Radians'koi Entsyklopedii, 1981), 22; The Central State Archive of Public Organizations of Ukraine (TsDAGO U), f. 1, op. 23, d. 4913, ll. 2–3.

4. Mikhail Kalnitsky, *Sinagoga Kievskoi iudeiskoi obshchiny 5656–5756. Istoricheskii ocherk* (Kiev: Institut Iudaiki, 1996), 18–19.

5. Ibid., 14–19.

6. Ibid.

7. Mikhail Mitsel', *Obshchiny iudeiskogo ispovedaniia v Ukraine (Kiev, L'vov: 1945–1981 gody)* (Kiev: Biblioteka Instituta Iudaiki, 1998), 62.

8. The Central State Archives of Supreme Bodies of Power and Government of Ukraine (TsDAVOU), f. 1, op. 24, d. 1572, ll. 314–16.

9. The Central Archives for the History of the Jewish People (CAHJP), RU 1996.

10. CAHJP, RU 2004, l. 64.

11. Ibid.

12. Ibid.

13. Mitsel', *Obshchiny iudeiskogo ispovedaniia v Ukraine,* 144.

14. Ibid., 97–98.

15. Kalnitsky, *Sinagoga Kievskoi iudeiskoi obshchiny 5656–5756,* 20–21.

16. *Gabbai* or *shamash*, a person who assists in the running of synagogue services. The official position of Jonah Gendelman was the Chairman of Kiev Religious Community. (Mitsel', *Obshchiny iudeiskogo ispovedaniia v Ukraine,* 122).

17. Wiesel, *The Jews of Silence,* 31–32.

18. Mitsel', *Obshchiny iudeiskogo ispovedaniia v Ukraine,* 141.

19. CAHJP, RU 2004, l. 64.

20. Mitsel', *Obshchiny iudeiskogo ispovedaniia v Ukraine,* 138–39.

21. Ibid., 140.

22. Ibid.

23. Ibid., 142.

24. CAHJP, RU 2003, l. 98.

25. Mitsel', *Obshchiny iudeiskogo ispovedaniia v Ukraine*, 77–78.

26. Victoria Khiterer, "We Did Not Recognize Our Country: The Rise of Anti-semitism in Ukraine before and after World War II (1937–1947)," *Polin: Studies in Polish Jewry* 26 (2014): 370–71.

27. Mitsel', *Obshchiny iudeiskogo ispovedaniia v Ukraine*, 125.

28. Ibid., 112.

29. Yosef Tekoah (Tukaczynski) was the Israeli Ambassador to the Soviet Union (1962–1965). His last name is misspelled in the report as Gekoah.

30. Mitsel', *Obshchiny iudeiskogo ispovedaniia v Ukraine*, 111.

31. Ibid.

32. Ibid.

33. Ibid, 112.

34. TsDAVOU, f. 4648, op. 2, d. 451, l. 25.

35. Mitsel', *Obshchiny iudeiskogo ispovedaniia v Ukraine*, 122–23.

36. Benjamin Pinkus, *The Jews of the Soviet Union: The History of the National Minority* (Cambridge and New York: Cambridge University Press, 1988), 287.

37. Ibid.

38. Zvi Gitelman, *A Century of Ambivalence: The Jews of Russia and the Soviet Union, 1881 to the Present* (Bloomington and Indianapolis: Indiana University Press, 2001), 165.

39. Trofim Kichko, *Iudaism bez prikras*, http://mognovse.ru/qt-iudaizm-bez-prikras.html.

40. Pinkus, *The Jews of the Soviet Union*, 287.

41. Ibid.; Leonid Vladimirov, *Rossia bez prikras i umolchanii*, http://www.urantia-s.com/library/vladimirov/rossiya_bez_prikras/13; Trofim Kichko, *Iudaizm bez prikras* [comments to the book], http://mognovse.ru/qt-iudaizm-bez-prikras.html.

42. Kichko, *Iudaizm bez prikras* [comments to the book], http://mognovse.ru/qt-iudaizm-bez-prikras.html.

43. T. K. Kichko, *Iudaizm i Sionism* (Kiev: Znannia, 1968).

44. Yacoov Ro'i, "Nehama Lifshitz: Symbol of the Jewish National Awakening," in *Jewish Culture and Identity in the Soviet Union* (ed. Yaacov Roi and Avi Beker; New York and London, New York University Press), 172.

45. Ibid.

46. Ibid., 173.

47. Ibid., 179.

48. Mordechai Altshuler, "Itsik Kipnis: The 'White Crow' of Soviet Yiddish Literature: The MGB File of 1949," *Jews in Russia and Eastern Europe* 2:53 (Winter 2004): 68–167.

49. "Kipnis, Itsik," *Electronnaia evreiskaia entsiklopedia*, http://www.eleven.co.il/article /12082.

50. Vera Yedidya, "The Struggle for the Study of Hebrew," in *Jewish Culture and Identity in the Soviet Union*, 156–57.

51. Ibid., 143.

52. Alexander Voronel', "Jewish Samizdat," in *Jewish Culture and Identity in the Soviet Union*, 257.

53. Ibid., 259.

54. Elena Shapiro, "Letopis' Osventsima i Maidaneka," *Evreiskii obozrevate* 1 (265), January 2015, http://jew-observer.com/pamyat/letopis-osvencima-i-majdaneka/.

55. "Tolkachev Zinovii," *Elektronnaia evreiskaia entsiklopediia*, http://www.eleven.co.il /article/14124.

56. "*In Confidence: Holocaust History Told by Those Who Lived It*; Installation to Open at the Museum of Jewish Heritage—A Living Memorial to the Holocaust," https:// d3k74ww17vqc8e.cloudfront.net/app/uploads/2018/09/24225648/In-Confidence -press-release_final.pdf

57. Zvi Gitelman, "The Evolution of Jewish Culture and Identity," in *Jewish Culture and Identity in the Soviet Union*, 15.

58. Liudmila Tsigelman, "The Impact of Ideological Changes," in *Jewish Culture and Identity in the Soviet Union*, 69.

59. Ibid., 59.

60. CAHJP, RU 1616, l. [without number].

61. Nora Levin, *The Jews in the Soviet Union since 1917: Paradox of Survival* (New York and London: New York University Press, 1987), vol. I, 469.

WHEN AUTHORITY WAS A FORM OF DISSENT

Postwar Guides to Reform Practice

JOAN S. FRIEDMAN

HIS ESSAY ANALYZES two guides to Reform observance, *A Guide for Reform Jews* (1957) and *Liberal Judaism at Home* (1967),[1] published by individual members of the Central Conference of American Rabbis (CCAR), the Reform rabbinic organization. While the former attempted to define and mandate norms of observance for Reform Jews, the latter sought to persuade them to become more observant. Despite their differences, however, they constituted an important stage in the evolution of Reform Judaism's relationship to ritual observance.

A GUIDE FOR REFORM PRACTICE?

That the traditional 613 mitzvot fell into two essential categories—eternal ethical laws revealed or inspired by God and mutable "ceremonies" created by human beings—was a fundamental premise of Reform Judaism in its first century of existence. The perpetual dilemma for Reform rabbis, therefore, was whether to offer any guidance, or set any standards, for ritual observance, and if so how and on what basis. This was particularly true in the United States, a haven for nineteenth century Reformers too radical for the European context. Almost all Reform rabbis agreed with Kaufmann Kohler, the dominant voice of classical Reform, that some ritual was essential to religion because it had an edificatory purpose: "Judaism is a system of religious and moral truths, the ceremonies being only the means to higher ends not ends in themselves. . . . In order to have a positive religious value and significance, ceremonies must either directly or symbolically express thoughts and feelings that appeal to us while elevating, hallowing and enriching our lives."² But who decided which "ceremonies" were to be retained, which ones eliminated, which innovations encouraged? For this question there was no agreed-upon answer.

Already early in the twentieth century some rabbis and laypeople were calling for guidance in ritual matters and for the reintroduction of discarded ritual observances. This call gathered momentum in the interwar years as the Reform rabbinate and Reform congregations filled up with Jews of East European origin. While the 1937 Statement of Principles (the "Columbus Platform") affirmed the importance of ritual, it continued to view it from a utilitarian perspective. The innovative element in its attitude toward ritual was that rational "edification" was no longer the sole acceptable criterion for what made a ritual worth observing.³ After the CCAR adopted the "Columbus Platform," it joined forces with the Union of American Hebrew Congregations (UAHC, the movement's powerful congregational organization) to establish a Joint Commission on Ceremonies to "revive old rituals, introduce new ones, and experiment with original ceremonial materials."⁴

Nevertheless, encouraging Jews to light Shabbat candles and hold Passover Seders was a far cry from publishing anything that might appear to tell them that there was a correct way to do so or that they must do so, which was what a vocal minority was demanding. In 1941, therefore, the older and more classically oriented leadership invited the widely respected Solomon B. Freehof to deliver a paper at the rabbinical convention explaining why any code of Reform practice was an impossibility. Arguing that Reform could not legislate matters of praxis without becoming another version of Orthodoxy, Freehof allowed only that one could offer limited, de facto guidance by describing the few areas of Jewish practice where Reform had evolved a more or less standard pattern and explaining the reasoning behind their departures from traditional norms.⁵ Several years later he proceeded to do precisely this in *Reform Jewish Practice and Its Rabbinic Background*.

The book's purpose, Freehof explained, was "to describe present-day Reform Jewish practices and the traditional rabbinic laws from which they are derived."⁶ It had only four chapters: "Public Worship," "Marriage and Divorce," "Naming of Children and Circumcision," and "Burial and Mourning" — in other words, it "guided" only life cycle rituals and some aspects of public worship. Each chapter was divided encyclopedia-style into a number of entries. Each entry usually addressed one ritual or category of observance where Reform practice differed from the traditional norm. Freehof first briefly stated the Reform practice and then described the traditional practice and explained why Reformers had decided to alter it. In no way could it be construed as a complete guide to Jewish practice.

Freehof went a bit further in recognizing the importance of ritual and his colleagues' desire for more guidance when he next addressed the subject, in 1946. He acknowledged the "sense of the increased validity of the ritual practices within Judaism," though he could not explain this beyond the vague affirmation that "they are not quite law but they do have a certain authority." Still, he stood utterly opposed to a Reform guide, much less a code. He insisted that it was far too early to begin any process of codification because the laypeople were completely unprepared to hear that Reform expected them to observe anything. The rabbis had to "change the mood of the people. Otherwise our listing of Mitzvoth will seem meaningless and even ludicrous to them."[7] Most of the responses to his lecture criticized his temporizing and demanded some sort of guide or code of practice to set standards of observance for Reform Jews.[8]

The issue of a guide to Reform practice and the nature of its authority continued to roil Reform rabbis and laity for the next decade, as evidenced by a flurry of committees, convention papers, roundtables, and journal articles, but with Freehof's considerable influence mitigating against it, advocates for a guide still faced an uphill battle. Exacerbating tensions, and adding to the sense of urgency, was the phenomenal growth of the Reform movement in those years, fueled by an influx of second-generation East Europeans, who often expected a more traditional aesthetic in their new congregations.[9] In 1952–1953 the National Federation of Temple Brotherhoods (NFTB), in conjunction with the CCAR's Committee on Reform Jewish Practice, surveyed the religious practices of Reform congregants "to help determine whether there should be a code or a guide of Reform practices to aid UAHC congregations and their memberships."[10]

A series of articles in *American Judaism*, the magazine sent to every household affiliated with a UAHC member congregation, shared highlights of the results in 1953–1954. These articles revealed information such as this:

> Bar Mitzvah, the traditional rite of inducting a boy of thirteen into the congregation, is practiced in varying degrees in 92 per cent of the Reform temples, and 77 per cent of the Reform laymen answering the poll endorse this practice. While the survey showed that 45 per cent of the laymen would prefer that their sons wear a talis [sic] at the Bar Mitzvah ceremony, only 21 per cent would want a hat to be worn during the ceremony.[11]

But they also assured their readers that there was no danger of Reform going "too far" toward observance:

> The answers to the questionnaire clearly refute the contentions of those who predicted the survey would indicate that Reform Judaism was going Orthodox.
> On the Sabbath, the vast majority of Reform Jews keep their businesses open, 88 per cent; work, 90 per cent; ride, 99 per cent; and smoke, 82 per cent.

Seventy-four per cent have a Seder in their homes on Passover eve; 93 per cent eat matso [sic] during Passover, but 59 per cent also report that they eat bread.[12]

Among the critics of Freehof's resistance were Frederic A. Doppelt[13] and David Polish.[14] Both men also disapproved of what they saw as the movement's superficial approach to ritual. Polish derided the NFTB-CCAR survey as Reform ritual practice by plebiscite and observed acerbically that something was not right when Reform Jews were equally "enthusiastic" about Christmas and bar mitzvah. The growing enthusiasm for performing rituals, he opined, was disconnected from any genuine spiritual content: "Surely custom and ceremony were to be judged by their capacity to elicit deeper religious commitment and conduct. Are we unwittingly saying to our people that the essence of Judaism can be captured by a rite? Do we truly believe that the first stage on the path of Jewish revival is the lighting of Shabbos candles?"[15] Meanwhile, Doppelt, who was among Freehof's critics in 1946, was arguing at the 1954 rabbinical convention that neither aesthetic appeal, national survival, nor ethical concerns were appropriate criteria for determining Reform practice; rather, the mitzvot themselves had to be the starting point. (The paper he delivered there would become the basis for the essay "The Authority of the Mitzva" in the *Guide*.[16])

COVENANT THEOLOGY AND THE
GUIDE FOR REFORM JEWS

In 1957, Doppelt and Polish privately published a small, slim volume titled *A Guide for Reform Jews*.[17] Although it was quickly republished the same year by Bloch, and again by Ktav in 1973, it is largely forgotten today. The *Guide* offered its readers three essays where the authors expounded—at length—their reasoning and then seventeen short chapters, each chapter opening with a bolded paragraph beginning, "It is a Mitzva [commandment, sic] to . . ." Each "It is a Mitzva" declaration included a scriptural basis. After each declaration, numbered paragraphs in regular type offered the specific procedures (which the authors labeled *Halachot* [laws]) for fulfilling the defined mitzvah. After the *Halachot*, an italicized list presented what the authors labeled "*Minhaggim*" [customs]—generally descriptions of uniquely Reform ways of practicing.

The two authors aimed at nothing less than a complete redefinition of the entire debate about the significance of ritual in a Reform context by completely rejecting the classic Reform distinction between ethics and ritual. This was a direct challenge to the position taken by Freehof, the movement's dominant voice in the postwar decades on all matters relating to Jewish practice. They mounted their challenge by rooting themselves in the new postwar theology that would become known as covenant theology.

In the postwar years, conversation among American rabbis and Jewish intellectuals took a theological turn, not only in response to the war but also in response to what they perceived as the shallowness and emptiness of most synagogue life.[18] Influenced primarily by Martin Buber and Franz Rosenzweig, they self-consciously attempted to create a new Jewish theology. "The tradition needed to be confronted on its own terms, they declared, rather than surrendered to categories imposed from the outside—as had been the case in the previous generation."[19] As the *Guide* explained it: "In the preparation of a Guide for Reform Jewish Practice, it is imperative that one turn to the historic ways in which Judaism has expressed itself whenever it came to the issue of religious observance."[20] Among the new theologians there was a consensus that one of these external categories, alien to Judaism, was the distinction between binding ethical laws and utilitarian ceremonies that had been central to Reform thought. Thus, from the beginning among Reform rabbis, the new theological discourse centered on what mitzvah meant for Reform Jews.[21]

A small group of Conservative and Reform rabbis, including Emil Fackenheim and Eugene B. Borowitz, began gathering in the early 1950s with the goal of creating a new theology. W. Gunther Plaut, also a participant, later recalled that the group reached a consensus that "the covenant between God and Israel had to be emphasized as the single most important element in our spiritual existence."[22] Borowitz, who would eventually become its greatest expositor, first used the term "covenant theology" in 1961[23] to articulate a reaffirmation of the centrality of the covenant relationship between God and Israel established at Sinai, understood in existential terms. Covenant theology, he explained, defines Jewish existence as

> a way of living one's life based on a relationship with God . . . in which the whole self is involved. . . . Under the Covenant the Jews . . . have pledged themselves to live by [God's] law. Here the new theologians emphasize the *mitzvah*, for it is through this service, individually and communally, that Israel testifies to God's reality, nature, and existence all through history. . . . The central task of modern Judaism, according to this theology, is to win the conscious, willed loyalty of the modern Jew to the Covenant. . . . Each Commandment becomes a way not only to personal improvement and fulfillment, but also helps to satisfy his responsibility to God and to mankind.[24]

David Polish was a participant in this group[25] and shared its desire to bring a deeper spirituality to synagogue life.[26] In the *Guide*, he and his collaborator sought to bring this deeper spirituality to Reform Judaism by offering a radically different paradigm for Jewish life.

The *Guide* opens with the disclaimer that the book is not intended to "legislate conduct and observance, but rather to make available a guide for those who feel the need for it," but the authors immediately add that "once a Jew takes the assumptions and the discipline of a guide seriously, and seeks to live by them, he thereby makes them authoritative in his life. Authority in Jewish life can no longer be binding without the consent of those involved; yet this does not absolve us from striving to find that way of religious living to which they may consent."[27]

Before readers reach page 51 and find actual guidance, however, they must wade through three dense essays. In "Why a Guide?" the authors advance several arguments in support of a guide to Reform practice. First, they argue, somewhat disingenuously, that Reform Judaism was never as opposed to ritual observance as people suppose. In any case, if that was true in the past, it is no longer: "In Jewish theology, it is being emphasized once more that in Judaism . . . the 'deed' leads to the 'creed,' that the way of 'doing' leads to the way of 'believing.'"[28] Second, thoughtful Reform Jews realize that they cannot just leave this up to everyone's personal preference because (using an argument that would certainly have resonated with a readership that lived through the Depression) "it has . . . become evident that unbridled individualism in religion can be as destructive to spirituality as laissez-faire individualism has been to democracy."[29] Third, this is not being imposed from above. Rather, it will "help bring a greater degree of observance, self-disciplining commitment, and spirituality into our religious life, because it is essentially a response to many who have long been seeking guidance."[30] Finally, it cannot possibly lead back to Orthodoxy because Reform Jews know that we always have the ability to change our practices as needed.

"Criteria for Reform Jewish Observance" offers a lengthy and florid exposition of covenant theology, with a twist. The authors anticipated the lay reader's skepticism: for a traditional believer, the covenant is real because God actually revealed Torah at Sinai. For existentialist and covenant theologians it is sufficient to say, as the authors do, that "the historicity of the events . . . is of less moment than Israel's acknowledgement of their historicity."[31] But what about the modern Jew who does not believe in divine revelation and does not yet find existentialist arguments compelling because she is not predisposed to have a spiritual turn of mind? The authors needed a way to convince their readers that a spiritual approach to their Jewishness was essential. They did this by offering the best, most compelling, rational, "scientific" proof from an expert.

To bolster their theological argument the authors cite no less a figure than William F. Albright, the (Christian) dean of biblical archaeologists, asserting that nineteenth century Protestant critics were completely wrong when they insisted that the Patriarchal narratives and the Exodus story were fiction.[32] By grouping the biblical narratives of Abraham's journey and the Exodus from Egypt with later, unquestioned historical events—the Maccabean revolt, the destruction of both Temples, the European genocide, and the rebirth of the State of Israel—Doppelt and Polish create a seamless whole:

all are "salient . . . moments in our history" that are "informed with crucial experiences affecting the people's dual relationship to its God and to the world."[33]

Furthermore, they hurriedly continue: "Interwoven with this historical sense are two additional values without which Jewish observance can have no real meaning. They are *kedusha* [holiness] and *mitzva*."[34] In other words, if the best modern scholarship proves that Abraham, Moses, and the Exodus were real, then the average Jew can't simply dismiss the Torah as a myth and will therefore have to take it seriously. And that means acknowledging and accepting that from its earliest moments, Jewish history has been about the relationship between the Jewish people and God. The implication is clear: a secular or nonobservant lifestyle is not an authentic Jewish lifestyle.

"The Authority of the Mitzva" explains how covenant theology answers all the questions about observance that have long troubled Reform Judaism: Who decides what should be practiced? What is the nature of the observances that we do include, i.e., are all of equal religious significance? And why should these practices be perpetuated? What is their meaning and purpose? Is any particular practice to be determined "by Divine commandment, by ecclesiastical authority, or by popular vote?"[35]

The authors use those three terms to denote what they call the tripartite "river of Jewish observance." A *Mitzva* is a "Divine commandment," deriving from some "spiritual [moment] in Jewish history when the Jewish people came upon God."[36] A *Mitzva* is an act that is such an essential element of an authentic Jewish spiritual life that in its absence the covenantal relationship is broken. Therefore, they note pointedly, we "should [never] ask for a popular show of hands" about which *Mitzvot* should be included in a code of Jewish practice.[37] "Ecclesiastical authority" means the *Halachot*—"the accepted ways in which one should proceed to do the *Mitzvot*." While "Jewish history" is the "basic authority" for *Mitzvot*, the *Halachot* derive their authority from the rabbis. They have the right to make them, and to change them as conditions demand.[38] "Popular vote" refers to the *Minhaggim* [sic], the "customs and folkways" originating in the people's own creativity, and not in any organized body. Since the people created them, they simply fall away when the people stop doing them.[39]

Doppelt and Polish assert that a Reform Jew must observe certain mitzvot because each is the result of some historical moment of spiritual encounter between God and Israel.[40] Their list of mitzvot bears no relation to the traditional enumeration of 613 commandments. Some are broad categories of observance that include dozens of traditional commandments (e.g., the Mitzva to observe the three festivals); others they defined themselves (e.g., the Mitzva to establish and maintain a synagogue). Still others correspond to a traditional commandment but are not linked to the verse from which the rabbis traditionally derived them. The Mitzva to educate one's children, for example, is not linked to Deuteronomy 6:7 (*ve-shinantam le-vanekha*, "teach them to your sons") but to a verse in Isaiah that refers to the covenant.[41] In several places the authors felt free to invent new blessings for recitation at moments they apparently regarded as insufficiently spiritualized by existing practices. Thus the bride and groom, standing at the "altar" before the wedding ceremony begins, are to "[clasp] hands and in awareness of the sanctity of the moment" recite the new blessing, "Who has sanctified us by His Mitzvot and commanded us to sanctify life through the marriage covenant."[42]

The seventeen chapters of the *Guide* mandate the following *Mitzvot*:

1. *Birth:* "It is a Mitzva ... to bring children into the household of Israel, in fulfillment of the promise our fathers received. ... [It is] doubly incumbent upon us in these times because of the decimation of our people." [Gen 17:7]

2. *Circumcision (Mila):* "to submit every male child to Circumcision, to bring him into the Covenant" with Abraham [Gen 17:11]

3. *Naming:* "to name our children in the midst of a Congregation, to commit them to God as did our fathers" [Gen 17:19]

4. *Education of children:* "to educate our children in the heritage of Israel [to fulfill] the spiritual destiny of the Jewish people" [Isa 59:21]

5. *Confirmation:* "to be confirmed in the Faith of Israel in order to relive the experience of the Covenant which God made with Israel at Sinai through the giving of the Torah" [Deut 29:13–14]

6. *Adult Jewish learning:* "to engage in the study of Torah throughout life in keeping with the intellectual and spiritual discipline of our people throughout its history" [Josh 1:8]

7. *Marriage:* "to marry in accordance with the traditions of our Torah and to establish a Jewish home" [Gen 24:67]

8. *Illness and death:* "to accept every personal life-crisis, even the approach of death, with trust and hope in God's justice and mercy, as did our fathers in every trial and tribulation" [Ps 130:7]

9. *Burial:* "to bury our dead in accordance with the sancta of our tradition which regards it as a Chesed shel Emet" [Gen 49:29]

10. *Mourning:* "to mourn our beloved deceased and to keep alive their memory out of reverence for their life" [Gen 23:2]

11. *Kaddish:* "to keep alive the memory of our beloved deceased, as did our father Jacob" [Gen 48:7]

12. *The Jewish home:* "to endow our homes with the spirit of our faith, the symbols of our way of life, the spiritual and cultural treasures of our people, and the living practices of our heritage" [Deut 6:9]

13. *The Synagogue:* "to establish and support a Synagogue in every community, so that we might be united in prayer, study, and spiritual fellowship, and that the Divine command may be fulfilled" [Exod 25:8]

14. *Shabbat:* "to observe the Shabbat, as a sign of Israel's continuous relationship with God, both in our personal lives and in the historical experiences of our people" [Exod 31:16–17]

15. *The High Holy Days:* "to observe the Yamim Noraim [Days of Awe] as a period of intense self-searching, earnest communion with God, and sincere reconciliation with our fellow man" [Lev 23:1, 24, 27, 32]

16. *The Three Festivals:* "to observe the three Festivals (Sukkot, Pesach, Shavuot) as reminders of the spiritual truths proclaimed through our people's historic experiences, and to relive those experiences as meaningful and recurrent for every generation" [Lev 23:2]

17. *Minor holidays and special days:*
    - *Chanukah:* "to observe Chanukah in order to renew the spiritual experience of our people's victory over tyranny, and the rededication of the temple, thereby reliving our age-old struggle for religious freedom" [I Macc 4]
    - *Purim:* "to celebrate Purim in order to relive Israel's historic experience of deliverance from enemies bent on our destruction, as our Torah states" [Est 9:20–23]
    - *Israel Independence Day:* "to observe the fifth of Iyar, the anniversary of the re-establishment of the State of Israel as a special holiday, commemorating a redemptive moment in the life of the Jewish people." [Jer 31:10–11]
    - *Memorial Day for Martyrs of Nazism:* "to observe the tenth of Tevet as a memorial for the millions of our people who perished at the hands of the tyrant" [Lam 3:19–21][43]

The most significant aspect of this idiosyncratic mix is that Doppelt and Polish did what Freehof said could not be done: they offer a theological basis for Reform Jews' obligation to perform actions and behaviors whose meaning—irrespective of any ethical import—is the expression of a unique Jewish religiosity by virtue of their performance. A Jew who lives them is a faithful Jew; a Jew who neglects them is a faithless Jew. Reform Judaism expects its adherents to be faithful Jews; Reform Judaism can say therefore that a Jew must do these things.

The *Guide* received widely differing reviews from Reform rabbis. Before the book appeared, the *CCAR Journal* published the text of the sections on practice; editor Abraham J. Klausner introduced it with an editorial titled "Reform 'Guide-d' toward Authoritarianism."

A code or a guide . . . reflects the growing desire for conformity or authoritarianism
in religious living. This desire is reflected in our political and cultural enterprises and
is at the core of the present struggle between Conservatism and Liberalism. . . . [The
discussion of this guide will] reflect on the one hand, the strength of our true liberal
spirit in a refusal to take from man his freedom and with it his responsibility for
working out his religious convictions, and on the other hand, our tendency to conservatism or authoritarianism in a readiness to permit the Jew "to lay his freedom
humbly at our feet" in exchange for a guide—a way of life the clergy has arbitrarily
tailored for him.[44]

While Klausner objected to the work's aspiration to be a code, a later reviewer objected
to a code that set such a very low bar. He dismissed the *Guide* as just "a prosaic,
down-to-earth outline of standards of Jewish observance that are in effect in many
congregations labeled 'Reform' or 'Conservative.' The religious guidance . . . reads like
a manual of instruction of some fraternal organization." In his view it did no more
than reflect the status quo: "We all know that this is the usual range of Jewish observance in the average congregation, but the authors did not have to give it the stamp of
'scholarly approval.'"[45] Both men criticized the *Guide* for its inconsistencies, its arbi-
trariness, and its failure to include references to the traditional literature to explain or
justify its pronouncements.

    Those were valid criticisms. But while Doppelt and Polish were trying to establish
a minimum and consistent standard for Reform Jewish practice, in propounding that
standard they were also staking their position in the postwar process of creating an
American Jewish identity. The *Guide* also needs to be seen as a template for American
Jewish life on the new suburban frontier.

WHY THESE MITZVOT?

Between 1945 and 1965, American Jews moved to the suburbs in droves, where they
built and joined Conservative and Reform synagogues in record numbers. But, as we
saw earlier, this massive institutionalization of religion appeared hollow to thoughtful observers. Acculturated Jews loved being American and appeared far too willing
to bend, redefine, or simply dispense with much of their Judaism in order to be fully
American. The *Guide*'s list of Jewish practices makes perfect sense if one reads it as
a protest against the sort of Jewish life so memorably studied by Herbert Gans and
Marshall Sklare.[46] Its authors were at least as much concerned with resisting acculturation as with launching a Jewish spiritual revival or overcoming Solomon Freehof's
resistance to a guide for Reform practice.

They tried to insist that Jews must live a religiously, culturally, and socially Jewish life, even while making themselves at home in America. Jews must have homes that are identifiably and appropriately Jewish; Jews must be active and involved members of synagogues, attending services as well as cultural and social programs; Jews must observe all Jewish holy days; Jewish children must receive a religiously based Jewish education; Jews must feel and express a connection to their people by commemorating the recent tragic European past and celebrating their newly reestablished sovereign homeland. Wherever they go in America's increasingly open society, Jews must not neglect to bring their Judaism with them. A Halachah even directed college students, for example, to "identify [themselves] actively with organized Jewish life on the campus and help advance the study of Torah there," to socialize with Jews, and to take Jewish studies courses if any were offered.[47]

Consider, for example, chapter 12, "The Home." The authors write: "It is a Mitzva to endow our homes with the spirit of our faith, the symbols of our way of life, the spiritual and cultural treasures of our people, and the living practices of our heritage, as our Torah states: 'Write them upon the door-posts of your house.' (Deut 6:9)."

The individual *Halachot* in chapter 12, "The Home," are as follows:[48]

1. To conduct a "special service of thanksgiving and dedication" upon moving into a home. The reader is referred to the appropriate service in the *Union Home Prayer Book*.
2. "A mezuza should be affixed to the doorpost of the entrance of the home."
3. "Symbols and sancta of the Shabbat and Festivals should be kept as decorations and adornments in plain view."
4. "Every home should have a collection of books, periodicals, art objects and recordings pertaining to Judaism."
5. The "blessing for food (Hamotzi)" should be recited before each meal (provided in transliteration in the appendix), and grace after each meal (a single blessing excerpted from the traditional Grace After Meals, also in the appendix).
6. "The family should recite appropriate prayers upon retiring at night and upon awakening."
7. "Prayers on special occasions in the life of the individual or of the family should be recited at home."
8. "Time should be set aside for the family reading of Biblical and other Jewish selections, particularly on Shabbat."
9. "Holidays which are alien to the spirit and practice of Judaism should not be observed in the home, in any manner whatsoever. Holy symbols and images of other faiths should not be displayed in the home."
10. "Although Reform Judaism does not adhere to the traditional dietary laws, many

Reform Jews still abstain from eating the meat of the pig. This is based on historical associations, since the pig was often used as an instrument of persecution of
our people who were tormented by their enemies into eating it."

In other words, your new, tastefully decorated suburban home must be identifiably
Jewish. Don't store the candlesticks and Chanukah menorah out of sight on the bottom
shelf of the new china cabinet; add some Jewish LPs to the collection you play on your
new hi-fi; supplement your Book of the Month Club fare with some Jewish books. Pray
daily as a family. Don't put up a Christmas tree or stockings for the kids. Remember
how your ancestors suffered and don't eat pork. And join a synagogue.

Concerning the synagogue, the *Guide* mandates: "It is a Mitzva to establish and
support a Synagogue in every community, so that we might be united in prayer, study,
and spiritual fellowship, and that the Divine command may be fulfilled, as the Torah
states, 'They shall make for Me a sanctuary that I may dwell among them (Exod
25:8).'"[49] In fact, the chapter on the synagogue was one of the two longest chapters in
the *Guide*—six pages, the same length as the chapter addressing engagement, marriage,
and divorce. It began with the statement that the synagogue was a "House of God, and
the source from which Torah emanates." No activity that was not consistent with that
purpose could take place there: "Any activity tending to degrade the spiritual character of a Synagogue is sacrilegious and should not be countenanced."[50] That included
gambling, card playing, and performances not in good taste.[51]

Being a synagogue member was more than a matter of paying dues: "Membership
involves attendance at services, participation in the adult education program, cooperation with the religious school, generous support of the Synagogue's financial requirements, and participation in some phase of the Congregation's organizational life."[52]
This list of expectations mirrors the Statement of Principles that congregants adopted
when they formed Beth Emet in 1950, with the conscious intent of creating an ideal
synagogue.[53] The *Halachot* in this chapter dwell in great detail on qualifications for
synagogue membership, qualifications for synagogue office, relationships among rabbi,
board, and congregants, and other matters that obviously grew out of the distinctive
Beth Emet environment.

It is doubtful that many Reform laypeople actually made their way through the turgid
prose of the *Guide's* three introductory essays and impossible to know how many people
actually used it. Two retired rabbis who responded to my inquiries about its use had
negative reactions. One "looked at it but decided not to give it to congregants"; the other
tried giving it to new converts, but they found it difficult to follow.[54] At the Hebrew
Union College-Jewish Institute of Religion it did not figure into the curriculum.[55]

But the demand for guidance continued to grow. In the 1940s Freehof had insisted
that a guide to Reform practice was an impossibility: one could only describe what

consensus had been reached and otherwise submit individual questions to the CCAR Responsa Committee. As its chair, he responded to hundreds of inquiries, many of which stated that they were writing after finding no guidance in his *Reform Jewish Practice*. By the 1960s, however, generational change brought enough voices to positions of influence within the CCAR to change the terms of the debate. In 1968 a special CCAR Committee on the Sabbath, headed by W. Gunther Plaut, reported its plan for a published guide that would include standards for Shabbat observance. In 1906 the rabbis had rejected a committee proposal to include guidance on life cycle rituals in the forthcoming rabbis' manual; nearly seventy years later they reached a milestone with the publication of *A Shabbat Manual*.[56] As Michael A. Meyer has pointed out, however, acceptance by the rabbinic body required "painful compromise" that resulted in the elimination of language that might hint at any notion of obligation, resulting in only an inoffensive manual for teaching Reform Jews how to make Shabbat at home.[57]

REFORM JUDAISM AND NOSTALGIA FOR *YIDDISHKAYT*

In 1958, Leon Uris's potboiler *Exodus* hit the best seller list; the 1960 film version was a smash at the box office. In 1964, Broadway's biggest hits were *Funny Girl* and *Fiddler on the Roof*. All of these popular culture offerings reflected the extent to which Jews and Jewishness were visible and acceptable, even cool; but they also pointed to how Jews themselves were being swept away both by nostalgia for the *shtetl*, the lost locus of "authentic" Jewish existence, and pride in the State of Israel, the new locus of "authentic" Jewish existence.[58] Not surprisingly, therefore, in 1967, when another Reform rabbi, Morrison David Bial,[59] produced a guide to Jewish practice for his congregation in the comfortable suburb of Summit, New Jersey, it was light on theology but heavy on cloying descriptions of how Jews lived in the *shtetl* and how you too can create a warm and attractive Jewish home that will ensure that your children grow up to love Judaism.

Bial's goal was to encourage Reform Jews to lead a life in which Jewish ritual played a more significant role. The book's first chapter, "The Criteria of Reform Jewish Practice," informs the reader that while Liberal Jews will never be bound by a code of practice, nevertheless there is a need "to help establish ... correct, thoughtful, efficacious Reform Jewish practice." Every Reform Jew has to be informed and make their own decisions. But how does one decide, if one does not believe the commandments are divinely revealed? All Bial offers is a vague appeal to a "meaningful" life: "The answer must be a sense of *k'dusha*, of holiness, of that which will help him sanctify his life, to make it truly meaningful. By this he must live, and it will help give his life that inner meaning by which we seek fulfillment."[60] The language of meaning and holiness may be reminiscent of covenant theology, but the key element of covenant theology—"You must"—is absent. This is essentially the older Reform theology in which ritual has only utilitarian value, merely expressed in contemporary language: "Do it because it will make you feel good."

In 1967 most Reform Jews still didn't want mitzvah, but they did want *Yiddishkayt*. They wanted the aesthetics and the warmth of "tradition." Bial gave them what they wanted and tried to push them to go a little deeper into the meaning of what they were doing, drawing his readers in with passages that read like something out of *Life Is with People*. Consider the following example:

> Every people has its lullabies; the Jewish cradle songs were unique in their emphasis on piety and the love of wisdom. *Die beste schora ist das Torah.* "The best merchandise is the Torah," sang the mother to her baby. So from his earliest days was the Jewish child bent to know our path of life.
>
> A lovely old custom was to weigh a child on each birthday and donate a sum proportionate to his gain in weight to charity, especially a fund for scholars.
>
> As the child grew he was immersed in a Jewish atmosphere that was more real in determining the direction of his life than even his rigorous schooling. He savored the flavor of Judaism, the peace of Sabbath serenity, the festive spirit of the holidays. Enraptured, he listened to *Kiddush* and *Havdalah*, and early learned to respond with hearty amen—and received his own tiny sip of wine. He looked with glistening eyes at the Chanukah candles, fondled his store of nuts, twirled his dreidel, and was happy for eight consecutive nights. Passover with its *sedarim* was exciting even though he fell asleep over his thimble of wine long before the *Haggadah* was finished. . . .
>
> An aura of Jewishness is as important today as it ever was for our forebears. The Reform Jewish home should provide the early start that makes our children conscious of the beauties of their religion even before they are ready for school. . . .
>
> The Sabbath and the holidays provide the obvious time to practice Judaism's customs and ceremonies with our children.[61]

Very carefully, Bial attempted to steer his readers toward observance through judicious use of language: "No Sabbath is truly observed unless we join in communal Sabbath worship." "Certainly, Liberal Jews should include many of these [ritual items, books, and pictures of Jewish content] in their homes." "Liberal Jews differ among themselves on fasting. . . . Therefore, no hard and fast rule can be drawn for Reform Jews. However, fasting should not lightly be dispensed with for it has been an integral, meaningful aspect of Yom Kippur for millennia."[62]

Liberal Judaism at Home turned out to be the right book at the right time. While the rabbinical organization dithered, the Union of American Hebrew Congregations, the powerful congregational arm of North American Reform Judaism, made its own decision to publish Bial's book. Between 1971 and 1976 it went through five printings.

CONCLUSION

In 1979, the CCAR finally published *Gates of Mitzvah: A Guide to the Jewish Life Cycle*, followed in 1983 by a companion volume dedicated to the holy days.[63] The Reform movement had at last dared to state that there were standards of practice, even if, as Michael A. Meyer observed, "they represented [only] an ideal."[64] In its explicit use of the word "mitzvah" in the title, in its introduction of observances with the phrase "The mitzvah of . . . ," and in its manual format, it followed the path laid out by Doppelt and Polish, while diverging from their model in two significant ways. First, it abandoned their idiosyncratic and incoherent list of mitzvot, generally limiting the use of the term to biblically or rabbinically sanctioned acts. Second, it redefined the link between theology and deed. In place of Doppelt and Polish's covenant theology, *Gates of Mitzvah* offered four essays (one by David Polish), each offering a different theology of mitzvah. Thus the dissent of 1957 had become the norm.

NOTES

1. Frederic A. Doppelt and David Polish, *A Guide for Reform Jews* (Jenny Loundy Memorial Fund, 1957); Morrison David Bial, *Liberal Judaism at Home: The Practices of Modern Reform Judaism* (Summit: Temple Sinai, 1967).

2. Kaufmann Kohler, "The History and Functions of Ceremonies in Judaism," *Central Conference of American Rabbis Yearbook* 17 (1907): 206, 222.

3. See Michael A. Meyer, *Response to Modernity: A History of the Reform Movement in Judaism* (New York: Oxford University Press, 1988), 319–20; and Joan S. Friedman, *"Guidance, Not Governance": Rabbi Solomon B. Freehof and Reform Responsa* (Cincinnati: Hebrew Union College Press, 2013), 27–28.

4. Meyer, *Response to Modernity*, 323.

5. Solomon B. Freehof, "A Code of Ceremonial and Ritual Practice," *Central Conference of American Rabbis Yearbook* 51 (1941): 289–97.

6. Solomon B. Freehof, *Reform Jewish Practice and Its Rabbinic Background* (New York: Union of American Hebrew Congregations, 1944), 15.

7. Solomon B. Freehof, "Reform Judaism and the Halacha," *Central Conference of American Rabbis Yearbook* 56 (1946): 290.

8. "Discussion," *Central Conference of American Rabbis Yearbook* 56 (1946): 307.

9. See Friedman, *"Guidance, Not Governance,"* ch. 8.

10. "National Federation of Temple Brotherhoods," in *Proceedings of the Union of American Hebrew Congregations* 15 (1956): 412–13. I am grateful to Rabbi Ben Gurin for tracking down this and other references for me.

11. "How Much Religious Education Do You Want for Your Children?," *American Judaism* 3:1 (September 1953): 23.

12. "Ceremonies Reform Jews Observe at Home, on Marriage, Birth, and Death," *American Judaism* 3:4 (March 1954): 22.

13. Frederic Doppelt (1906–1973) was born into a Chasidic family that immigrated to the U.S. from Poland in 1920 and settled in Chicago. He studied at the Hebrew Theological College and then at the University of Chicago, where his studies shattered his traditional worldview. He entered the Hebrew Union College in 1928, where he became an advocate for modern Hebrew; he was ordained in 1931 and served a congregation in Ft. Wayne, Indiana, until 1969. (American Jewish Archives, near-print biography.)

14. David Polish (1910–1995) was born in Cleveland to East European immigrants and was ordained at Hebrew Union College in 1934. He was serving a Chicago congregation with an anti-Zionist board and senior rabbi when Stephen Wise died in 1949; Polish eulogized him from the pulpit and was locked out of the building when he tried to enter it the following week. With a loyal following of congregants, he broke away and established Beth Emet — The Free Synagogue in Evanston, Illinois, a few weeks later, where he remained until his retirement in 1980. (American Jewish Archives MS-631 3/1.)

15. David A. Polish, "A Critique on Some Ceremonies," *Central Conference of American Rabbis Journal* 5 (April 1954): 43.

16. William B. Silverman, "Changes in Reform Jewish Practice," *Central Conference of American Rabbis Yearbook* 64 (1954): 126. No copy of Doppelt's paper survives aside from the session report. According to Silverman, Eugene B. Borowitz observed with approval that Reform Judaism had entered a new stage in its development, deeply dissatisfied with formerly agreed upon praxis and desirous of more traditional practices, but noted the need to reconcile the desire for guidance with the commitment to freedom. Alvin Rubin argued that a code would contradict Reform's basic tenets; Alfred L. Friedman countered that the absence of a code or guide was the reason for the current "ritualistic anarchy." Doppelt's paper, positing that a life of mitzvot, including what others called "rituals" or "ceremonies," was a sine qua non of an authentic Jewish life, "elicited the most controversy."

17. Doppelt and Polish, *Guide*.

18. Will Herberg targeted this phenomenon in his *Protestant, Catholic, Jew: An Essay in American Religious Sociology* (Garden City: Doubleday and Co., 1955). The literature

on this subject is voluminous. For overviews see Jonathan D. Sarna, *American Judaism: A History* (New Haven: Yale University Press, 2004), 274ff; Hasia R. Diner, *The Jews of the United States* (Berkeley: University of California Press, 2004), 288ff; and Riv-Ellen Prell, "Triumph, Accommodation, and Resistance: American Jewish Life from the End of World War II to the Six-Day War," in *The Columbia History of Jews and Judaism in America* (ed. Marc Lee Raphael; New York: Columbia University Press, 2008), 114–41. A classic study of the tension between religious and secular expressions of Jewishness is Herbert G. Gans, "The Origin and Growth of a Jewish Community in the Suburbs: A Study of the Jews of Park Forest," in *The Jews: Social Patterns of an American Group* (ed. Marshall Sklare; Glencoe: Free Press, 1958), 205–48. See Norman E. Frimer, "The A-Theological Judaism of the American Community," *Judaism* 11:2 (Spring 1962): 144–54, for a skeptical view of whether it was possible to reawaken Jews' spirituality.

19. Arnold M. Eisen, *The Chosen People in America: A Study in Jewish Religious Ideology* (Bloomington: Indiana University Press, 1982), 127. See also Robert G. Goldy, *The Emergence of Jewish Theology in America* (Bloomington: Indiana University Press, 1990), 23ff; and Meyer, *Response to Modernity*, 360ff.

20. Doppelt and Polish, *Guide*, 33.

21. Eugene B. Borowitz, "Theological Conference: Cincinnati, 1950," *Commentary* 10 (January 1, 1950): 567–72.

22. W. Gunther Plaut, *Unfinished Business: An Autobiography* (Toronto: Lester & Orpen Dennys, 1981), 181.

23. Borowitz went on to become its most articulate expositor in *Renewing the Covenant: A Theology for the Post-Modern Jew* (Philadelphia: Jewish Publication Society, 1991).

24. Eugene B. Borowitz, "Crisis Theology and the Jewish Community," *Commentary* 32:1 (July 1, 1961): 40.

25. Plaut, *Unfinished Business*, 181.

26. David A. Polish, "Evaluation of the UAHC Biennial," *Central Conference of American Rabbis Journal* 5 (April 1955): 45–46.

27. Doppelt and Polish, *Guide*, v.

28. Doppelt and Polish, *Guide*, 4–5. Freehof himself used the trope "deed, not creed" in the introduction to *Reform Jewish Practice and Its Rabbinic Background*, from which the authors quote. But he did not intend it as a repudiation of the classical Reform insistence on the doctrine of ethical monotheism and the primacy of the ethical law over mere ceremonies. On the use of this expression in the context of Reform observance, see Joan S. Friedman, "The Writing of *Reform Jewish Practice and Its Rabbinic Background*," *Central Conference of American Rabbis Journal* 51:3 (Summer 2004): 52–53.

29. Doppelt and Polish, *Guide*, 8.

30. Ibid., 9.

31. Ibid., 12.

32. They cite William F. Albright, *The Archaeology of Palestine*, originally published in 1949. By the 1950s the Albright school dominated the field of biblical archaeology; its application to biblical criticism meant that Jewish scholars no longer viewed the latter as "the higher anti-Semitism," as Solomon Schechter had so pithily phrased it. Reform Jews in the 1950s might well have read any of several books by Albright or even more likely a slim volume by one of their own, Rabbi Bernard Bamberger, *The Bible: A Modern Jewish Approach* (New York: Schocken Books, 1955). See Alan T. Levenson, *The Making of the Modern Jewish Bible* (New York: Rowman & Littlefield, 2011), 155ff.

33. Doppelt and Polish, *Guide*, 13.

34. Ibid., 18.

35. Ibid., 30.

36. Ibid., 41.

37. Ibid., 41.

38. Ibid., 43.

39. Ibid., 44.

40. Ibid., passim.

41. "And this shall be My covenant with them, said the LORD: My spirit which is upon you, and the words which I have placed in your mouth, shall not be absent from your mouth, nor from the mouth of your children, nor from the mouth of your children's children—said the LORD—from now on, for all time (Isa 59:21)."

42. Doppelt and Polish, *Guide*, 72.

43. Ibid., passim. At the very end of this final section they instruct the reader that "it is not a Mitzva to observe Tu B'Shvat and Lag Ba-Omer, but the Halakha tells us to mark them as special days in our homes" and that we should also refrain from holding weddings on Tisha B'Av "in deference to those who still observe this day of mourning for the destruction of the Temple, even though the State of Israel has been re-established."

44. Abraham J. Klausner, "Editor's Comments: Reform 'Guide-d' toward Authoritarianism," *Central Conference of American Rabbis Journal* 14 (June 1956): n.p.

45. Israel Harburg, "An Evaluation of 'A Guide for Reform Jews,'" *Central Conference of American Rabbis Journal* 8:2 (January 1960): 35–36.

46. See n. 18.

47. Doppelt and Polish, *Guide*, 67.

48. Unless otherwise noted, all references here are to Doppelt and Polish, *Guide*, 89–90.

49. Ibid., 89, 91.

50. Ibid., 91.

51. These *Halachot* closely resemble several of Freehof's responsa. Gambling for syna-gogue fundraising was a sensitive issue in the Reform movement, implicitly touch-ing on issues of class and acculturation. For a thorough discussion of this issue, see Friedman, *"Guidance, Not Governance,"* 179ff.

52. Doppelt and Polish, *Guide*, 93.

53. The Statement of Principles is available on the synagogue's website: "Beth Emet the Free Synagogue Statement of Principles," accessed July 5, 2020, https://bethemet.org/images/Statement_of_Principles.pdf.

54. Emails to the author from Rabbi Ralph Mecklenburger, July 21, 2017, and Rabbi Stuart Geller, October 5, 2017.

55. This assertion rests on the author's personal recollection and anecdotal evidence from colleagues.

56. W. Gunther Plaut, ed., *Tadrikh le-Shabbat: A Shabbat Manual* (New York: Central Conference of American Rabbis, 1972).

57. Meyer, *Response to Modernity*, 377.

58. This phenomenon has been addressed in many recent scholarly studies from a variety of perspectives. See, for example, David E. Kaufman, *Jewhooing the Sixties: American Celebrity and Jewish Identity* (Waltham: Brandeis University Press, 2012); Markus Krah, *American Jewry and the Re-invention of the East European Jewish Past* (Boston: De Gruyter, 2017); Rachel Kranson, *Ambivalent Embrace: Jewish Upward Mobility in Postwar America* (Chapel Hill: University of North Carolina Press, 2017); Antony Polonsky, ed., *Polin: Studies in Polish Jewry: Volume 17: The Shtetl: Myth and Reality* (Oxford; Portland, Oregon: Liverpool University Press, 2004), http://www.jstor.org/stable/j.ctv4cbg9j; and Alisa Solomon, *Wonder of Wonders: A Cultural History of Fiddler on the Roof* (New York: Metropolitan Books, 2012).

59. Morrison David Bial (1917–2004), born in New York City to East European immi-grant parents, received a B.A. from Brooklyn College and was ordained at the Jewish Institute of Religion in 1945. As a delegate to the May 1942 Biltmore conference, he introduced the motion that the resolution calling for a Jewish state be published in Hebrew. After serving several congregations in and around New York City, in 1953 he became the first rabbi of Temple Sinai in the upscale suburb of Summit, New Jersey. (American Jewish Archives, nearprint biography.)

60. Bial, *Liberal Judaism at Home*, 1–2, 6.

61. Ibid., 16.

62. Ibid., 101, 53, 113.

63. Simeon J. Maslin, ed., *Gates of Mitzvah: A Guide to the Jewish Life Cycle* (New York: CCAR, 1979); and Peter S. Knobel, ed., *Gates of the Seasons: A Guide to the Jewish Year* (New York: CCAR, 1983).

64. Meyer, *Response to Modernity*, 377.

"DISPUTE FOR THE SAKE OF HEAVEN"

Dissent and Multiplicity in Rav Shagar's Thought

EITAN ABRAMOVITCH

S HIMON GERSHON ROSENBERG (1949–2007), known as Rav Shagar, was one of the most unique and original thinkers in Modern Orthodoxy of our time.[1] His thought—spread through his books and articles, through his teaching in various institutions, and by his influential students—has had a deep influence on religious discourse in Israel. He majorly influenced the Religious Zionist community to which he belonged, but his influence is also felt in the realm of Jewish studies in Israeli universities and in the margins of the Haredi community. In 2017 a selection of his essays was translated into English for the first time and published in the United States, followed by vibrant discussion in various forums.[2]

Rav Shagar is known for his ability to incorporate in his thinking Chasidic and mystical ideas on the one hand and existential and postmodern philosophy on the other. In this essay I use the term "dispute for the sake of heaven" [*machloket leshem shamayim*, Mishna *Avot* 5:17] to present an example for such an encounter. Rav Shagar's discussions about harmony and dispute, unity and multiplicity, can lead us to some of the central innovations of his thought and at the same time help us situate his teachings in the context of the Religious Zionist community in Israel and the dramatic transitions that it has undergone in recent decades.[3]

ETERNAL DISPUTE

The Mishna in *Avot* 5:17 states that "a dispute for the sake of heaven is destined to endure," and the example it brings for such a dispute is the one between Hillel and Shammai. But what value can there be for a dispute to endure? Why not strive for a conclusion, for a halachic ruling, or maybe turn to an authority that will settle the argument one way or another? This question is related to a more general and fundamental question: how does a monotheistic religion deal with multiplicity, with conflicts and differences that cannot be settled, both in the philosophical and in the political domains?[4]

Rav Shagar thoroughly explores these questions in his writings, but to better understand his discussion, it should be seen in relation to the philosophy of Rav Abraham Isaac Kook. Rav Kook's philosophy has had a defining influence on the Religious Zionist community in Israel, and it is one of the central influences on Rav Shagar's thought. Moreover, Rav Shagar explicitly presents his approach as a reaction to Rav Kook and as an alternative to the way Rav Kook's understanding has shaped the Religious Zionist community in Israel. Therefore, a brief analysis of Rav Kook's attitude toward this discussion is needed before we discuss Rav Shagar's point of view.

RAV KOOK'S HARMONIOUS "SUPREME HOLINESS"

A core tenant of Rav Kook's thought is that he strives for harmony and synthesis between different opinions and worldviews.[5] The primary example of this can be seen in his attitude toward the struggles between Orthodox Judaism and modern secular movements such as Zionism and Socialism, struggles that nearly tore the Jewish people apart in his time. Rav Kook saw these struggles as taking part in a dialectic process, one that is destined to lead to a higher level of faith and Jewish self-understanding. In one of his essays he describes the three major ideologies that were clashing in the Jewish society in his time—liberalism, nationalism, and Orthodoxy—and suggests that the truth lies in the synthesis of all three of them in a point of view that he calls "the supreme holiness" [HaKodesh HaElion].[6]

The structure of this argument is characteristic of Rav Kook's attitude toward the questions posed in the previous section: profound conflicts are meant to lead to a higher perspective, one that will allow for a harmonious synthesis of the underlying contradictions. This Hegelian understanding of history sees every dispute as an intermediary phase leading to its resolution. The dispute might be "for the sake of heaven," as the Mishna quoted in the previous section suggests, but only if it is resolved and does not endure.

For the purpose of this discussion it is important to note that, according to Rav Kook, this "supreme holiness," the higher perspective that unites all differences, is not identical to the Orthodox worldview that he identifies with; nevertheless, in this text and others, Rav Kook is speaking as an Orthodox rabbi taking part in the struggles he is describing, while at the same time looking at this struggle from above, pointing at a synthesis that is destined to be different than the particular trend he is fighting for.

Appreciating the effects of this point of view is crucial to understanding Rav Kook's influence on the Religious Zionist community. The struggle to hold on to the higher synthesis creates an ongoing inner tension in this community's self-understanding. On the one hand, it is a religious Orthodox community, and therefore it exists as a particular sector, a minority group, in the Israeli society; on the other hand, it tends to see itself as representing a full synthesis between the worldviews of all other sectors, and therefore it strives to a leading role that will allow it to give every sector its appropriate place. It is a sector that wishes to be more than a sector, a part that wants to be a whole.

A typical example for this tension can be seen in the name that Rav Kook gave to the yeshiva he founded in Jerusalem: The Central Universal Yeshiva [*HaYeshiva HaMerkazit HaOlamit*]. It is a yeshiva, a traditional Orthodox institution like many others; but at the same time it wishes to play a "central" and even "universal" role by incorporating the different worldviews and aspirations of the Jewish people, thus adopting the point of view of the "supreme holiness" that Rav Kook wrote about.

Over the last few years, this tension is also manifested in the political party representing the Religious Zionist sector—the Jewish Home [*HaBait HaYehudi*, formerly *HaMafdal*]. Since 2012, under the leadership of Naftali Bennett, the Jewish Home began aspiring to be more than a representation of its sector; it saw itself fitting to lead the entire Israeli society. In order to do so, the party leaders were willing to include secular and even non-Jewish representatives, and on many occasions they left the political struggles on religious issues to the Haredi parties. In 2019 the inner tension described here was manifested in a splitting of the party: the Jewish Home restored its focus on representing the Religious Zionist sector, and Bennett formed a new party, the New Right [*HaYamin HaHadash*], no longer representing the Religious Zionist sector and instead aspiring to attract a wider audience.

RAV SHAGAR'S PROPOSAL:
THREE TRANSITIONS

This brief look at Rav Kook's influence will allow us to understand the context in which Rav Shagar is situated and also to highlight the innovation of his philosophy. As we shall see, although Rav Shagar sees himself as a successor of Rav Kook,[7] he consciously turned to different and even opposite directions.

In one of his essays, written in 1996, Rav Shagar outlines the transitions that he believes the Religious Zionist community should go through, in accordance with his understanding of the spirit of the time:

For Religious Zionism to renew itself, and to leave the straits in which it finds itself, it must change its path significantly. It must give up on its ideology and its quest for harmony. In this sense it is postmodernism, ostensibly so dangerous to it, that can open up new, exciting, paths for it. . . .

Religious Zionism got its path and its drive for harmony from its great teacher, Rav Kook. In truth, he was well aware of the contradictions and gaps torn in the modern world. . . . However, Rav Kook believed that we could mend the tears. . . .

Rav Kook spoke in many places about the ideal of unity and harmony. Even when he describes pluralism, he deals with it in a non-pluralistic manner. He believes that you can find a higher perspective in which everything unites. . . . This position matches the philosophy and social science of Rav Kook's era. The former believed in the all-encompassing unifying narrative of a single cognitive truth obligating all people. The latter believed it could derive, from the complexity of reality, universal rules that would apply to any society. However, the science and philosophy of today no longer believe this. Today, Rav Kook's harmonious statements fall prey to a lack of faith; they do not fit with what people call "the spirit of the time," in the world writ large but also even within our little community. We have lost our faith in unity and metanarratives.[8]

Rav Shagar identifies Rav Kook's strive for harmony, and the Religious Zionist ideology influenced by it, with the context of the modern search for a unifying metanarrative that will explain everything. Following Jean-François Lyotard and other postmodern philosophers, who defined the postmodern era through the loss of faith in metanarratives, Rav Shagar claims that this kind of thinking has become outdated. Harmonious metanarratives do not hold anymore, not only in the domain of science but also in the Religious Zionist community. Rav Shagar's conclusion is that this community must go through a deep and even revolutionary transition, which he describes in the following paragraphs. Here we can see how the concept of dispute takes its place in his discussion, following Rav Naḥman of Bratslav:

This postmodern, split mindset sharply raises the question of whether or not Religious Zionism can find a new guiding light: Rebbe Naḥman of Bratslav. Not only did Rebbe Naḥman not believe in mending tears, he even sought them out. Rebbe Naḥman sought out dispute [*machloket*]. As he says in one of his teachings, dispute creates the empty space [*halal hapanui*], the only atmosphere in which he could act, and through which he could express his uniqueness that was so important to him. He did not exist in a harmonious world, and he did not believe it was possible to unify opposites. On the contrary, he drew spiritual strength from harmony-less dissonance.

Living as religious people in a modern secular world creates contradictions. Against these contradictions, Rebbe Naḥman did not suggest harmonization like Rav Kook's school did, which as we have seen can lead to inflexible coercion of contradictory poles. Instead, he proposed the spiritual capacity to live in many worlds simultaneously.... The divine infinite can be realized in this world as life lived in multiple worlds.... This, to my mind, is the meaning of religious Post-Zionism.[9]

In these foundational paragraphs, Rav Shagar proposes three simultaneous transitions: from Rav Kook to Rav Nahman, from harmony to multiplicity, and from unity to infinity. According to Rav Shagar, these transitions will turn Religious Zionism to Religious Post-Zionism, a term that points to their political implications.

In order to better understand Rav Shagar's proposal, we dedicate the following paragraphs to a thorough discussion of these transitions, concluding with their implications in the social and political domains. First, we will take a deeper look at the role of the term "the divine infinite" [*HaEinsof HaEloki*] in this text. As we shall see, it will also lead us to the transition from harmony to multiplicity.

THE DIVINE INFINITE AND THE POSTMODERN RELIGIOUS EXPERIENCE

Rav Shagar's use of the term "infinity" plays a central role in the way he incorporates postmodern philosophy in his thought. We can see this in another essay, where he uses the term to distinguish between the way modern Jewish philosophers dealt with conflicting ideologies and the postmodern way that he proposes:

After all, any system can ultimately be perceived as being directed by a divine hand; any system—even if it is heretical, like Marxism—presupposes an underlying, logical structure to reality, and any order ultimately points to guidance from above. It is at this point that the believer enters, "translates" the logic into the invisible hand of God, and finds his place in the Torah. What is our problem today? Nowadays we discover that there is neither method nor system, so this "translation" cannot take place. The world that we struggle with has no narrative.

Yet even in our own fragmented and relativistic world, "sparks" can be found. Moreover—and here I approach a rather sensitive, profound point—it is precisely the postmodern world that can cultivate an even deeper faith, one of mysticism and concealment. Why is this? When we are in any system or given framework, we are constrained within the finite, and cannot access the infinite directly.... Only when the laws of science are broken and a checkered board of many options opens—it is then that we can see infinite-ness in our existence. We come to understand that that which exists is the result of one outcome out of millions of possibilities contained in the Infinite, Blessed Be He. Thus relativism leads to a kind of faith on a mystic level: at this level, mysticism is not a game or a pretense, but an expression of the myriad possibilities that are inherent in the Divine. The crisis of postmodernity can thus break idols and statues—for nothing is absolute but God himself—and bring us closer to an unmediated encounter with God.[10]

These paragraphs portray the transition that Rav Shagar proposes as a shift in the religious sensibility, one that is based on a different theological attitude revolving around the term "infinite." According to Rav Shagar, modern Jewish philosophy is constantly looking for synthesis because it is based on a religious experience of unity. Its underlying image of God is that of the invisible guiding hand, the one that ensures that in the end all contradictions will lead to a harmonious unity. The alternative religious sensitivity that Rav Shagar proposes is based on an opposite attitude: its image of God is that of the divine infinite, and therefore it encounters it in the experience of multiplicity, dispute, and conflict.

A modern believer like Rav Kook is struggling to find the point of view from which he can identify the unity, the logic, the invisible hand that operates behind the conflicts he encounters. The postmodern believer that Rav Shagar describes, however, prefers the experience of multiplicity, the inability to reach a final explanation, or to arrive to the point of view of the "supreme holiness" that Rav Kook strived to achieve. This kind of believer does not see the world as a unified, harmonious system, but as an open space in which different and conflicting worldviews exist, and none of them can take precedence over the others. For the postmodern believer, the effort to develop a finite worldview that will incorporate all differences is like building an idol. In his view, the highest religious experience is that of multiplicity, not unity.

FROM RAV KOOK TO RAV NAHMAN: A DISSONANT MELODY

The transition from unity to infinity and from harmony to multiplicity expresses a deep shift in the existential disposition of the believer. From the paragraphs quoted in the previous section we can derive that in Rav Shagar's view, these transitions are not just a way to preserve faith in changing times but also a path to a deeper faith, which he describes as mystical.[11] As we have seen, Rav Shagar identifies this alternative disposition with Rav Nahman of Bratslav and proposes him as a "new guiding light" for the Religious Zionist community, an alternative for Rav Kook.

Rav Nahman's affinity for conflicts and disputes can be seen in various aspects of his life and writing, and it has also been a central theme in the research about him.[12] This affinity is specifically manifested in his use of the term "dispute for the sake of heaven" in his book *Likutei Moharan*: "There is a type of dispute that is for the sake of heaven, and that is a very great way of thinking [*da'at*], greater than the peaceful way of thinking, because this dispute is itself great love and peace."[13]

Rav Nahman prefers dispute over peace and sees it as a way of achieving a higher religious understanding. In one of his essays, Rav Shagar describes this attitude as the fundamental contribution of Rav Nahman's torah for the Religious Zionist community:

> More than anything else, I learned from Rebbe Naḥman that sometimes contradiction and dispute are truer than a harmonious depiction of reality. Rav Kook's philosophy, which influences us greatly, encourages our tendency to unify and harmonize different ideas, ideologies, positions, and streams. However, Rebbe Naḥman's Torah enables us to understand that this is indeed a lofty spiritual ideal, but not one that is always achievable. In actual reality, it seems more important to know how to learn to live with contradiction, which is certainly truer than false, forced, or violent harmony. This harmony requires stretching or shortening the opposites in order to make them fit into the Sodomite bed of supposed harmony. Our challenge is not to create harmony between conflicting sides or even to decide between them, but rather the ability to live by combining contradictory elements, which persist in their contradiction and disagreement. This combination creates a sort of melody which is composed of dissonances, but which is also exciting, deep, and infinite.[14]

This paragraph portrays the transition from Rav Kook to Rav Nahman in a similar way to the shift in religious sensibility described above, while also adding a musical metaphor. According to Rav Shagar, Rav Nahman teaches the Religious Zionist believer to enjoy a dissonant melody, to see the contradictions a believer in postmodern times faces as a necessary religious experience, not as obstacles in the way of harmony.

Furthermore, this text also adds another aspect to the discussion, one that takes a crucial place in Rav Shagar's critique of Rav Kook's influence on the Religious Zionist community: the demand for sincerity. In his actual life, Rav Shagar claims, the modern believer faces contradictions that cannot be solved, and she might never reach the harmonious arrangement that will settle all conflicts. Striving for harmony, like Rav Kook taught, often leads to a denial and repression of external and internal contradictions and might foster insincerity or even false consciousness.[15] Rav Shagar claims that instead of forming a community that will be a living synthesis between Jewish tradition and modern secular ideas, like Religious Zionism aspired to do, their ideology

created a community that is stuck in the middle, unable to fully identify with the tradition it inherited and not fully able to understand the secular ideas it wishes to adopt.

While describing Rav Kook's harmonious aspirations as "a lofty spiritual ideal," Rav
Shagar maintains that Rav Nahman's ability to live with contradictions is more suited
for the actual situation of the Religious Zionist community. Rav Shagar demands that
the believer acknowledge his schizophrenic situation and avoid insincere syntheses.
Since such syntheses form the basic structure of the Religious Zionist identity, Rav
Shagar's proposal to postpone them and instead learn to live with the contradictions is
far from easy to adopt. We will see that as we move to examining the social and political implications of Rav Shagar's worldview—the transition to Religious Post-Zionism.

RELIGIOUS POST-ZIONISM?

Following our discussion of the theological and existential alternative that Rav Shagar
proposes for the Religious Zionist community, we can now turn to its social and political implications.

If we go back to the complicated self-understanding of the Religious Zionist
community described earlier, we can now begin to understand what Rav Shagar means
when he proposes a shift toward a Religious Post-Zionism. We discussed the inner
tension between this community's basic identification with the Orthodox worldview
and the aspiration to reach a higher point of view that incorporates all other conflicting worldviews. In accordance with what he sees as the spirit of the time, Rav Shagar
proposes that Religious Zionism let go, or at least postpone, its universal and harmonious aspirations. Instead, he proposes to adopt a different complex: living in multiple
worlds without seeking synthesis between them. In another part of the essay quoted in
the previous section, he is pointing to the implications of this attitude for some of the
central conflicts between the State of Israel and the Orthodox community:

> We can maintain multiple worlds side by side within ourselves, unbothered by
> the fact that we cannot unify them. We can enact this type of existence not just on
> the personal-cultural level, but also on the social-institutional level. For example, in
> regard to the state: The solution to the troubling problems of dealing with Reform
> Jews, civil marriages, etc., lies in separating the political realm, where principles of
> freedom and equality should reign, from the society and community that need to
> be more Jewish and halachic. The obvious conclusion is that we must separate reli-
> gion and state, to some degree. In this way we can bridge the gap between specific
> ethical values and halachah, a gap that we cannot resolve in the present situation.

Does this necessarily mean that the state is not the realization of the prophets' dream? No, quite the contrary! To my mind, this can, in some sense, actually strengthen this faith. . . . Creating this separation can enable a religious person to realize certain values that he believes in (such as feminism) within the context of the state, while recognizing that they cannot be fully realized in the religious world without upending halachah's very existence.[16]

There are areas where we cannot apply Religious Zionism's harmonistic approach. For example, some ethical problems cannot be resolved sincerely and without apologetics within today's religious framework. This is the case with our relationship to non-Jews and the status of women. However, as I claimed, we do not need to resolve them. We must know how to separate our lives as citizens of the state, which exists in a universal and egalitarian world, from the religious, halachic world with the hierarchical and patriarchal conceptions that underlie it.[17]

To fully understand the implications of the transition that Rav Shagar is proposing in these paragraphs, we should bear in mind what the connection between religion and state means for the Religious Zionist community. From the point of view of this community's mainstream ideology, the State of Israel was founded only in order to be a Jewish state, one that will unite the religious and national aspirations of the Jewish people. As we have seen, Rav Kook strove to create a synthesis between religion, nationalism, and liberalism; in his view, and in the eyes of his successors, the Jewish state is destined to form the dialectic unity of these conflicting worldviews, a unity that is of a messianic value, "a realization of the prophets' dream."

This is the context in which Rav Shagar is discussing the connection between religion and state, a context that explains the careful yet determined tone he is using. The conflict between Orthodox halachah and egalitarian worldviews, manifested in the ongoing debates in the Religious Zionist community about the status of women and of other Jewish denominations, serves in this quote as an example of a conflict that cannot be solved in the present situation without "stretching or shortening the opposites." Therefore, postponing the dream of harmonious unity and acquiring the ability to live with contradictions, as Rav Shagar proposes, is expressed in accepting a separation of religion and state, at least "to some degree."

It is important to note that the conflict that Rav Shagar is relating to exists inside the Religious Zionist community and even inside its religious worldview. According to Rav Shagar, modern values like freedom and equality have gained religious meaning in the Religious Zionist worldview, although they sometimes contradict the "hierarchical and patriarchal conceptions" of Orthodox halachah. Therefore, the separation of religion and state is the political expression of the schizophrenic situation of this

community and also a way to live with the contradiction. Rav Shagar is proposing that
the Religious Zionist community should restrain its immediate identification with
the state and strengthen its Orthodox identity, while at the time relying on the secular state institutions to represent the modern values that are also part of its religious
worldview. Paradoxically, Rav Shagar claims, the separation of religion and state will
bring it closer to a "realization of the prophets' dream," since it will allow for a simultaneous existence of the conflicting worldviews struggling inside the Religious Zionist
community. In the end, Rav Shagar is not so far from Rav Kook's influence: he also
sees the State of Israel as a vehicle of redemptive reconciliation, although in a much
more moderate and complicated manner.

An excerpt from another essay, originally a sermon for Israeli Independence Day
[*Yom HaAtzmaut*], will allow for a deeper look at the context and motivation for Rav
Shagar's discussion of these issues:

> The mystical believer does not see democracy's multicultural discourse as simply
> a tool for balancing society's extremes. For him, this discourse will be accompa-
> nied by the wondrous recognition that "all statements are received from Heaven"
> (Rebbe Naḥman, *Lekutei Moharan* I 56:9). . . . The world becomes more flexible as
> it approaches multicultural and multi-national democracy; this is revealed as a possi-
> bility for elevating the religious world itself.[18]

In this text we can see what drives Rav Shagar's discussion on the separation of
religion and state. Unlike other adherents of this idea, he is not driven only by liberal
ideology or pragmatic understanding of the contemporary situation. His discourse
takes place on a whole other level. The state structure that he promotes is the political
equivalent of the religious sensitivity he advocates. For Rav Shagar, the political realm,
precisely because it is divided beyond any synthesis, allows for the religious experience
of the encounter with the divine infinite. Rather than representing the dialectic unity
of all conflicts, like Rav Kook aspired to, the Jewish state that Rav Shagar describes
is a domain for the dispute for the sake of heaven, an institution that represents the
infinite and colorful multiplicity of the Israeli society.

Furthermore, the political implications of this attitude go beyond the question
of religion and state. Later in that sermon, Rav Shagar is relating also to the ongoing conflict between the Israelis and the Palestinians and proposes to see it also as a
dispute for the sake of heaven:

> The fact that the Arab, the Palestinian, lives here and sees this land as his beloved
> homeland (and it really is his beloved homeland), need not impinge upon my
> belonging to this land. His existence cannot harm my connection to this stretch of

land itself as my homeland. This is the miraculous land of Israel, wherein "all statements are received from Heaven." This way of thinking can perhaps enable us to reach
a sense of kinship, not through abstraction or reducing different people, cultures, or
faiths to one-dimensionally similar things. This is the kinship between those who
are different, or even opposed.[19]

In this text, the transition from modernism to postmodernism, from Zionism to
Post-Zionism, leads to a different perception of the land of Israel. Like the state, the
land could also be a domain of multiplicity, a homeland for both nations; and again,
this solution is also not considered as a pragmatic compromise, but as a way to arrive at
a higher religious awareness, even a mystical achievement. The peace that Rav Shagar
speaks about is not just a political arrangement. It is a religious peace, based on the
complex awareness that he believes that the postmodern era permits.

CONCLUSION

This utopian vision, not yet realized, leads us to our conclusion.

The concept of dispute for the sake of heaven has led us to the fundamental and
unique aspects of Rav Shagar's philosophy. As we have seen, Rav Shagar deals with the
conflict between monotheism and multiplicity that this concept implies by providing a complicated theological vocabulary accompanied by a corresponding religious
sensitivity, both aimed at creating a new kind of believer.

We discussed Rav Shagar's project in light of the context in which it was formed:
the fundamental influence of Rav Kook's philosophy on the shaping of the Religious
Zionist identity. We have seen how Rav Shagar incorporated concepts and tenden-
cies inspired by postmodern philosophy in his critique of Rav Kook's worldview and
used them to offer an alternative identity for the Religious Zionist community. In
order for this community to become Religious Post-Zionism, Rav Shagar proposed a
transition from Rav Kook to Rav Nahman, from harmony to multiplicity, and from
unity to infinity. These transitions are intended to create a different kind of religious
sensitivity, one that enjoys Rav Nahman's dissonant melody instead of striving for Rav
Kook's harmonious "supreme holiness."

At the same time, the theological and existential changes that Rav Shagar proposes
lead to dramatic social and political implications, ones that affect the foundations of
the Jewish state. The transition from Religious Zionism to Religious Post-Zionism is
manifested in Rav Shagar's careful adherence to the separation of religion and state
and to turning the State of Israel into a multinational state that will serve also as the
Palestinian homeland.

These dramatic implications emphasize the distance between Rav Shagar's proposal and the actual social and political situation in the State of Israel nowadays. Nevertheless, as Shaul Magid pointed out, the theological and existential transitions that Rav Shagar spoke about are already taking place in parts of the Religious Zionist community.[20] Therefore we can conclude by saying that at least in the community that he addressed, Rav Shagar's ideas have gained a notable influence, one that might develop in the future.

NOTES

1. For a biography of Rav Shagar and a short presentation of his philosophy, see Zohar Maor's introduction to the volume of Rav Shagar's essays translated into English: Rabbi Shagar, *Faith Shattered and Restored* (Jerusalem: Magid books, 2017), xi–xxiv. The academic research on Rav Shagar's philosophy has now only begun. See Miriam Feldmann Kaye, *Jewish Theology for a Postmodern Age* (Liverpool: Littman Library of Jewish Civilization, 2019); Avichai Zur, "Holy Deconstruction" (M.A. diss., The Hebrew University in Jerusalem, 2008); Ohad Zechraia, "The Nothingness in Rav Shagar's Thought" (M.A. diss., Bar-Ilan University, 2015).

2. Rabbi Shagar, *Faith Shattered and Restored*. See Marc Dworkin (August 6, 2018), *Notes on the Conversation surrounding Faith Shattered and Restored/Post-Modern Orthodoxy*, https://www.thelehrhaus.com, for a summary of the discussion on this volume. See also Shaul Magid (September 19, 2017), *The Settler Nakba and the Rise of Post-Modern Post-Zionist Religious Ideology on the West Bank*, https://www.tabletmag .com; Julian Sinclair (November 15, 2017), *The Orthodox Rabbi Who Set Out to Turn Postmodernism to Jewish Gain*, https://mosaicmagazine.com; Zach Truboff (July 3, 2017), *The Earth-Shattering Faith of Rav Shagar*, https://www.thelehrhaus.com; Miriam Feldmann Kaye (December 11, 2017), *The New Jewish Philosophy of Rav Shagar*, https://www.thelehrhaus.com; William Kolbrener, "Faith Shattered and Restored: Book Review," *Tradition* 51:2 (2019): 122–34.

3. See Hanan Moses, "From Religious Zionism to Post-Modern Religious: Directions and Developments in Religious Zionism Since the Assassination of Yitzhak Rabin" (Ph.D. diss., Bar Ilan University, 2009).

4. On this subject, see Avi Sagi, *The Open Canon: On the Meaning of Halakhic Discourse* (New York: Continuum, 2007).

5. See Avinoam Rosenak, *Cracks: Unity of Opposites, the Political and Rabbi Kook's Disciples* (Tel Aviv: Resling, 2013); Yoel Bin-Nun, *The Double Source of Human Inspiration and Authority in the Philosophy of Rav A.I.H. Kook* (Bnei Brak: Hakibutz Hameuhad, 2014).

6. Abraham Isaac HaKohen Kook, *Orot* (Jerusalem: Mosad Harav Kook, 1993), 70–72.

7. Rav Shagar (August 14, 2015), *The Rav as a Father Figure*, https://musaf-shabbat.com.

8. Rav Shagar, *Tablets and Broken Tablets: Jewish Thought in the Age of Postmodernism* (trans. Levi Morrow; Tel Aviv: Miskal, 2013), 152–54.

9. Ibid., 155–56.

10. Ibid., 401–2. Translated by Dalia Wolfson.

11. Rav Shagar's use of the term "mystical" is idiomatic and deserves its own discussion.

12. See for example the first part of Weiss's classic research, dedicated to "Rav Nahman's life and the dispute against him": Joseph G. Weiss, *Studies in Braslav Hassidism* (Jerusalem: the Bialik Institute, 1974), 5–87.

13. Rav Nahman of Bratslav, *Likutei Moharan* I, 56:8.

14. Rav Shagar, *Lectures on Likutei Moharan II* (trans. Levi Morrow; Alon Shvut: The Institute for the Advancement of Rav Shagar's Writings, 2015), 470.

15. See also Rav Shagar, *Tablets and Broken Tablets*, 184–93.

16. Ibid., 157–58.

17. Ibid., 161–62.

18. Rav Shagar, *On that Day: Sermons and Essays for Iyar Festivals* (Alon Shvut: Institute for the Advancement of Rav Shagar's Writings, 2012), 185–86.

19. Ibid., 186–87.

20. Magid, *The Settler Nakba.*

LIMITING THE AUTHORITY OF THE COUNTRY

Disobedience in the IDF

SHLOMO ABRAMOVICH

INTRODUCTION

DISOBEDIENCE AND THE military are two opposites, as discipline and obedience to the commanders' orders are the basis of the military structure. However, every army faces cases of disobedience of soldiers, and each army has its own ways of dealing with these situations as well as avoiding them.

The case discussed in this essay is the disobedience of Israeli soldiers during the summer 2005 evacuation of the settlements in the Gaza Strip. The Israeli government decided to evacuate the settlements in a unilateral act, not as part of a peace agreement with the Palestinians. This decision was extremely controversial in Israeli society and triggered severe demonstrations by settlers and their supporters all over the country. The involvement of the army in the execution of the evacuation aroused the fear of massive disobedience by soldiers who would refuse to participate in this controversial act.

The reality was far from these predications, and the main topic of this essay is the reasons for the lack of massive disobedience, despite the predictions of such. The focus is on religious Zionist soldiers and their participation in the evacuation of the settlements. The reason for focusing on this group is that they strongly identified with the settlers and therefore were more likely to refuse to take part in their evacuation. Eventually, even the religious Zionist soldiers did not disobey for the most part, and various explanations for it will be presented.

Another reason for focusing on religious Zionists is that this case presented a few of the core questions and conflicts of this group. The obedience to the army in this case was presented in religious Zionism as a question of contradicting authorities—between the military and religion, the commanders against the rabbis—and therefore it turned into a vital ideological issue. The different reasons for the lack of disobedience present different approaches in religious Zionism regarding its core values, which adds to the importance of this discussion.

DISOBEDIENCE AND REFUSALS IN THE IDF

The history of disobedience in the IDF (Israel Defense Forces) starts from its very first days. One of the famous first cases was the story of ship *Altalena*, when the few pilots of the new Israeli air force and artillery soldiers refused to bomb the cargo ship, which carried weapons and members of the Irgun, an underground paramilitary organization. Another famous symbol for refusals in the early days of Israel was Natan Hofshi, one of the leaders of an organization called Brit Shalom, who promoted pacifism and the refusal to serve in the Israeli army.[1]

The first Lebanon War in 1982 and the First Intifada in 1987 were important turning points in the history of refusals in the IDF. The reason for that was the unique circumstances of these events, which stimulated the spreading of refusals to serve in the army over wider groups in society.

Ruth Linn presents two main reasons that can lead a soldier to refuse to follow orders:

In times of war, an individual may "refuse to play the patriot" either because he thinks his country has no right to go to war [*jus ad bellum*] or because he thinks the country may fail to maintain justice in the war [*jus in bello*] or both.[2]

In the eyes of many, these reasons appeared in the First Lebanon War and the First Intifada. The First Lebanon War was the first war to be considered by many as a war of choice and not as a defensive war, and therefore not as a justified war. In addition, the suffering of the people in Lebanon and of the Palestinians in the First Intifada brought some people to claim that Israel lost its justification to fight due to its actions.

There might be other reasons for the rise of refusals in the IDF since the 1990s. The constant decline in the status of nationality in Israeli society, the emergence of strong individualism, and the weakening of the ethos of the army in Israel are among the social reasons for the appearance of more cases of refusal in the IDF.

Linn describes two types of disobedience in the army: an absolute objection to any type of military service and a selective conscientious objection.[3] While pacifistic approaches still exist and there are some cases of absolute objections, selective conscientious objection has become more common in the past few decades.

The absolute objection is typically based on general pacifism, which leads to a refusal to be part of the military framework. However, in some cases, an objection to a specific policy of the military might lead some to refuse to take part in the army at all. The selective objection is usually motivated by the refusal of the soldier to take part in a specific act to which he objects. It might also be used as a tool to pressure the government to change its policy regarding specific controversial decisions.

Typically, there are two main reasons for a selective objection in Israel. On the left side of Israeli politics, the main reason is the objection to the settlements, which leads to a refusal to serve in the West Bank. On the right, the main reason is the refusal to participate in the evacuation of settlements. The focus of this article is on the latter.

FEARS AND REALITY IN THE EVACUATION OF THE GAZA STRIP

The plan to evacuate the settlements in the Gaza Strip aroused great tension between the government and the settlers. The latter and their supporters branded Prime Minister Ariel Sharon as a traitor, since he was actively involved in establishing many of the settlements and now was pushing to evacuate them. On the other hand, Sharon harshly criticized the reactions of the settlers and described their plan to resist the army during the evacuation as a revolt that should be treated as such, with force.[4]

The Israeli leadership was concerned not only about the reactions of the settlers but also of the soldiers. The fear of massive disobedience of soldiers who supported the settlers or disagreed with the morality of this plan was widely presented in the media and became a major threat to the success of the evacuation. The army was the main source of manpower for the evacuation. Without the full cooperation of its soldiers, the plan to evacuate the settlements could not be accomplished. This fear was used by the settlers to pressure the government to call off its plan by stating that the army would not have the ability to carry out this mission due to the massive disobedience of soldiers. Sharon's response was clear: he would not accept any threats, and any soldier who would refuse to carry out his orders would be harshly punished.[5]

The public discussion focused mostly on the religious Zionist soldiers. Their identification with the settlers, most of whom were religious Zionists, made them main suspects for refusal. In addition, the dilemma of these soldiers was also presented as a question of their dual loyalty. Prominent religious Zionist rabbis called on the soldiers to refuse to take part in the evacuation, describing this act as against the Jewish laws. The religious soldiers were described as standing in a situation where they needed to choose between their rabbis and their commanders, to follow their religious commitment or their military obligation.[6]

This is an example of the tension between religion and the military, which finds its expression in many other cases in Israel, among them the debate over the military service of Haredi [ultra-Orthodox] yeshiva students, and the conflict between the service of female soldiers and religious male soldiers. Stuart Cohen[7] and Elisheva Rosman-Stollman[8] describe this tension by using Lewis Coser's term "greedy institutions," as both religion and the army demand exclusive and undivided loyalty and do not accept competing authorities. The clash of two institutions of this type creates a serious conflict.

This was not the first time that religious soldiers were suspected of dual loyalty.[9] However, in this case, the test for their loyalty was easy to determine: whether the religious soldiers would follow the orders of their commanders, or not. The results in this case were clear and undoubted.

Despite the predictions, very few soldiers refused to participate, and the evacuation of the settlements in the Gaza Strip was executed as planned with no serious problems. The chief of staff of the IDF, Dan Halutz, reported in the Knesset that 63 soldiers refused, and the military prosecution reported about 163 cases of refusals. This is very far from what was predicted by both the government and the settlers. The question that will be discussed now is the reason for that sharp difference between the predications and the reality, especially regarding the religious Zionist soldiers.

PRACTICAL EXPLANATIONS

The main focus will be on the social explanations for this phenomenon, as the lack of disobedience points to several social structures that exist in religious Zionism. However, before getting to the more complex and hidden explanations, there are some practical reasons that might explain why most of the religious Zionist soldiers followed the orders of the army and not the orders of their rabbis.[10] The different explanations do not contradict each other, as a complex social phenomenon has more than one reason for its occurrence.

The first possible reason for the fact that the soldiers followed the orders is that the army was ready and prepared for this mission. The fear of massive disobedience led the army commanders to take the mission of motivating the soldiers to follow the orders very seriously, as part of the larger mission to carry out the evacuation itself. The army was aware that without the full cooperation of the soldiers it would not be able to accomplish its mission, and therefore plans were made to avoid the predicted disobedience.

First, the army developed a well-designed program of preparing the soldiers who were assigned to take part in the evacuation of the settlements. Commanders and soldiers participated in special training sessions, where among other issues they discussed the ethical and psychological aspects of the planned mission and the importance of discipline and order in the army in a democratic country.[11] The goal was to prepare the young soldiers for the pressure they would experience during the evacuation from the settlers and their supporters and to strengthen their commitment to the army. These preparation programs were severely criticized by the settlers and were described by them as "brain-washing" of the soldiers, allegedly to make them act "like robots."[12] In the eyes of the army, however, these programs succeeded in their primary goal as very few soldiers disobeyed.

Second, the army chose carefully which units would participate in this mission. Units with a high percentage of religious soldiers, who were suspected of supporting the settlers—for instance the infantry brigade Golani—did not take part in the actual evacuation.[13] Instead, the army picked units whose soldiers had more to lose from the consequences of their disobedience, such as cadets in commanders' and officers' courses or soldiers in permanent service.[14] These soldiers would not want to risk their career in the military and therefore were less likely to refuse.

In addition, despite public declarations to the contrary, in practice the army was sensitive and open to personal requests from soldiers who asked not to participate in the evacuation. Soldiers who lived in the settlements in the Gaza Strip, had family or friends there, or were strongly opposed to this act and went quietly to their commanders and asked not to participate in many cases received favorable responses.[15] In that way, the number of refusals was very low, since many of the soldiers who might have refused got permission not to participate.

The preparation of the army is one explanation for why there was no massive disobedience among the religious soldiers. Another is the claim that the fearful predications were exaggerated.

Cohen presents in detail the great distance between the image of religious Zionists portrayed in the media and academia and reality as he finds it in his studies. He illustrates various ways the false image of this group is created. Sometimes small extreme subgroups are presented as representing the entire group through the use of vague statistics to blur the actual numbers of these subgroups. Sometimes superficial understanding of religious terminology creates wrong understanding of statements and actions of religious Zionists.[16] Cohen shows from various studies the types of subgroups that exist in religious Zionism and presents the power of liberal groups that do not fit into the extreme image of religious Zionism often being presented in the media and academia.[17] According to his view, the fear of massive disobedience was a result of the false extreme image of religious Zionists, and therefore its absence should not be surprising.

However, despite these practical explanations, the question remains: why did almost none of the religious soldiers follow the orders of their rabbis? Even if the predications of massive disobedience were exaggerated and the army was well prepared, the extremely low number of refusals among religious Zionists soldiers requires more explanation. Many prominent religious Zionist rabbis, some of them from the mainstream of religious Zionism, called upon their followers to refuse to take part in the evacuation, and yet most of them chose to follow the orders of their commanders. In this conflict between the rabbis and the army, the rabbis lost, and that requires more explanation.

This question will serve as a test case to present some of the main social structures that exist in religious Zionism. The different explanations represent different religious Zionist subgroups. Each has a different view of the core values of religious Zionism, but all of them eventually followed the army's orders in the evacuation of the Gaza Strip, even if for different reasons.

SOCIAL EXPLANATIONS

The first two explanations are based on the studies of Eliezer Don-Yehiya and Charles Liebman, who present different responses of traditional religion to modernization and secularization.[18] The conflict in the discussed situation, between obedience to the rabbis and obedience to the military, is an expression of this tension, and therefore the social structures developed by Don-Yehiya and Libman can assist in explaining the discussed case.

One of the responses of traditional religion to modernization and secularization, as presented by Don-Yehiya and Libman, is "rejection and segregation." According to this response, the solution for the conflict is the separation of areas of authority. Religion keeps its total authority in some areas of life, but other areas are beyond its limits of responsibility. The rabbis' opinion, according to this view, is irrelevant in certain areas.

In most cases this is not an ideological approach, but it is a practical solution used by many. It seems that many rabbis and religious leaders do not accept this view, as the exclusiveness and absolutism of religion are widely accepted concepts, but as a way of life it is a very common solution among many modern religious people.

One of the main implications of this view is the lack of the observance of halachah in certain areas of life. The segregation of religion into limited spheres of life eliminates the relevancy of halachah in other aspects of life. Therefore, some people might be very strict in following the Jewish laws in what is considered in their eyes as belonging to their religious identity, but at the same time they might be more lenient regarding other parts of their life, which they consider to be beyond the limits of religion.

An example for this can be found in the studies of Mordechai Bar Lev about the religious practices of religious Zionists. Bar Lev surveyed the norms and habits in religious Zionism, particularly among high school yeshivot graduates in varied areas of life. One of his main conclusions was that religious Zionists live in separated spheres: areas that are considered as part of their religious life are controlled by Jewish laws, but in other spheres, like culture for instance, they do not follow the strict rules of halachah. For example, he shows that a high percentage of high-school yeshivot graduates keep the laws of kashrut and Shabbat, but at the same time 58 percent of them swim at mixed-gender beaches and swimming pools, even though it is halachically forbidden.[19]

According to this view, the reason that the religious soldiers did not follow their rabbis but their commanders is that in their eyes this situation was not considered as part of their religious life. These soldiers did not accept the attempt of the rabbis who opposed the evacuation to describe it in religious terminology and compared the participation in the evacuation to other forbidden sins. Therefore they chose to follow the orders of their commanders, the primary authority in this area of life. According this view, there was no real conflict between the rabbis and the commanders, as they rule over different spheres of life.

Another response to modernity presented by Don-Yehiya and Liebman is "expansion and domination." This response is the opposite of rejection and segregation: instead of isolating religion in specific spheres, this response expands the territory ruled by religion and gives it control over the entire spectrum of life. In the conflict between religion and modernity, the latter receives a religious meaning and becomes part of the religious world. Secular terms, ideas, or institutions receive a religious connotation and as a result gain importance in the eyes of the religious believers.

Don-Yehiya describes this approach as religious fundamentalism, as everything is under the authority of religion, the only existing source of authority. Nothing is left behind.[20] In the religious Zionist thought, this approach is presented in the idea that there is no separation between religion and Zionism, since Zionism is also part of religion.[21] One of the main implications of this perspective is the attitude toward the State of Israel and its institutions. According to this approach, often called *mamlachtiut* or royalism,[22] the State of Israel, its leaders, and also the army receive a fundamental religious importance and are even considered, in the eyes of some thinkers, as holy.

This approach presents a unique explanation for the discussed case: the soldiers followed the orders of the commanders because, in their eyes, these orders had a religious meaning and fulfilling them was a religious obligatory. The conflict between the rabbis who called for disobedience and the army is not a conflict between religion and an external source of authority, since everything is included in the realm of religion. The conflict still exists, but it has a different connotation as an internal dispute within the religious world. This approach creates conflicts and paradoxes that are hard to resolve. For example, what should a soldier do if his commander orders him to act against the Jewish laws—for instance, to break the laws of Shabbat? How can the holy army act against the source of its holiness, the Torah? These cases often happen in reality, and they require creative explanations from the followers of this approach.

The evacuation of the settlements in the Gaza Strip caused a major crisis among the followers of this approach. The aggressive act of the government against the settlers and the feelings that the country betrayed them led to doubts regarding the holiness of the State of Israel. For some, the indisputable loyalism to the country turned into skepticism and cynicism. In some cases those feelings were expressed in ceasing to say the prayer for the sake of the country in the synagogue,[23] and in others it led to refusal to serve in the army.[24]

A main representative of this approach—expansion and domination—with regard to the discussed case is Rav Shlomo Aviner, a prominent religious Zionist rabbi who opposed the rabbis who called for disobedience. He explained his view about the importance of following the army's orders by using religious terminology and said that the holiness of the country and the army does not allow the soldiers to disobey its orders in this case.[25]

Rav Aviner is a follower of Rav Zvi Yehuda Kook, whose followers are the main representatives of this approach. As mentioned, the different approaches represent different subgroups in religious Zionism. While the approach of expansion and domination represents some of Rav Zvi Yehuda Kook's followers—a religiously strict observant subgroup—the approach of rejection and segregation is identified with subgroups who are more lenient with the observance of halachah. However, these opposing social groups arrived at the same conclusion and chose to follow the orders of the army, even if for different reasons.

The third explanation for the lack of disobedience among the religious Zionist soldiers is not identified with a distinct subgroup of religious Zionism but rather derives from the essence of the group as a whole. The claim is that disobedience and opposition to the larger society and its main leadership is against the DNA of religious Zionism.[26]

Asher Cohen claims that an unconditional patriotism exists as the basis of the religious Zionist's perspective and that this type of patriotism will allow a person to accept even extremely controversial decisions made by the government.[27] His positive attitude toward this unconditional patriotism can be compared to Linn's criticism of what she described as "blind patriotism." Linn prefers the "critical patriot" who, despite "his positive evaluation of the group," in extreme problematic situations might "let conscientious concerns take over regardless of the personal consequences."[28]

This unconditional patriotism is rooted in religious Zionism from its very beginning. Religious Zionists often compare themselves to the Haredim (ultra-Orthodox), particularly in cases of disagreements with the government. A common saying after the evacuation was that if the settlers were Haredim, it would not have happened due to their aggressive resistance.[29] Religious Zionists often feel that the Haredim know better how to fight for their rights, how to protest and demand, and so they are more likely to receive what they want. The conclusion of this thought is that they, the religious Zionists, should learn how to be more like the Haredim. However, it is more than a matter of behavior, how to act in certain situations. The difference between these two Israeli religious groups in their way of struggle with the government is an expression of a deeper difference between the leading narratives of these groups.

The Haredi society was formed as a minority who fight for their rights and survival against the strong majority. This was the ethos of Orthodoxy, which was reinforced in ultra-Orthodoxy in the historical battles against various modern movements such as the Reform movement and secular Judaism. This ethos is expressed in the separation of the Haredim from the larger society, as presented for instance in their unique clothes and their closed communities. Religious Zionism, on the other hand, was formed with an opposite ethos. The first religious Zionist political movement was called the Mizrachi, a Hebrew acronym for Merkaz Ruchani—a spiritual center—founded in 1902, and its goal was to inspire and influence the Zionist movement. This was the basis for one of the main values of this group: its involvement in the larger society. This is the reason religious Zionists choose to get involved in their surrounding culture and to serve in the army with the rest of society as part of this ideology.

Therefore, fighting with the government or refusing to follow the army's orders is against the nature of the average religious Zionist. Despite the conflict with of some of his rabbis, the religious Zionist soldier obeyed the orders of his commanders because he was raised to be part of, not to separate himself from, the larger society. It is not a matter of ideology, like the other explanations presented above, but it is a result of the basic religious Zionist subconscious, which appears to be stronger than any conflicting religious ideological statements.

Several studies point to different times of change, when religious Zionists tend to adopt a more Haredi attitude of separation from Israeli society. Gideon Aran claims that during the first years of the State of Israel, the fear of the strong secular nature of the new country caused a movement toward rejection and separation, as expressed in the establishment of religious Zionist yeshivot.[30] Others point to the evacuation itself as a turning point in religious Zionism, when the deep disappointment with the actions of the government caused religious Zionists to change their attitude toward the State of Israel and to limit their involvement in Israeli society, as expressed in a decline in the motivation to serve in the army.[31]

In practice, these changes happened only among distinct small groups in religious Zionism. A fear of the secularism of Israeli society, among other things, created the group Hardal - Haredi religious Zionists, who adopted some of the Haredi characteristics and separated themselves from the larger society in more aspects of their lives. However, the mainstream of religious Zionism has remained loyal to its original value of involvement in the larger society and accepted the rules of democracy, even when those rules contradict their ideology. Therefore, it seems that future mass refusals of religious Zionist soldiers are not predicted.

SUMMARY

Conflicts between the authority of the country and religious authorities create situations that force religious soldiers to choose a side and to show to whom their commitment is stronger. The evacuation of the settlements in the Gaza Strip was one of these cases, as religious Zionist rabbis called on their followers to refuse take part in it. In practice, very few soldiers refused, and in this case the authority of the country and the army overcame the authority of religion and the rabbis.

In addition to a few practical explanations for this result, several factors in religious Zionism were presented to explain the obedience of the religious Zionist soldiers. An approach of separating the authorities and limiting religion to specific areas of life made this case irrelevant to the religious authorities. The same result comes from an opposite approach, which extends religion to all areas of life and gives the State of Israel and the army a religious status. Therefore, there is no contradiction between religion and State, since everything is part of religion, and following the orders of the army is also part of the religious commitment of the religious Zionist soldier. Finally, resisting the army and the government is against the nature of religious Zionism, as involvement and cooperation with the larger society are at the heart of the ideology of this group.

Similar cases happen all the time, and pressure from rabbinic figures on religious soldiers to refuse continues. Every once in a while, when a new plan for a peace agreement with the Palestinians appears and includes evacuation of settlements in the West Bank, the discussion about refusals arises again. In addition, the fear of massive refusals if the army is asked to evacuate settlements still exists among the army leaders.[32]

Recently the Supreme Court acquitted two rabbis who were prosecuted for offering money to soldiers to refuse to evacuate settlements.[33] The reason for the decision to acquit was that these rabbis have the right of freedom of expression, but also the Court estimated that there is little likelihood that soldiers will comply with the rabbis' wishes.

Future studies might show whether this Supreme Court decision is still accurate. The changes and developments in religious Zionism, and particularly in the complex relationship with the State and its institutions, might weaken the unconditional patriotism of this group and make refusals more likely among religious Zionist soldiers. If that becomes the reality, it means that a fundamental change has happened in religious Zionism, as some if its core values, the DNA of this group, has changed.

NOTES

1. Yaron Unger, *The Limits of Discipline and Disobedience to the Military Order* [Hebrew] (Jerusalem: Knesset Research and Information Center, 2010), 4. This research paper contains a brief but detailed summary of the history of refusals in the IDF.

2. Ruth Linn, "When the Individual Soldier Says 'No' to War: A Look at Selective Refusal during the Intifada," *Journal of Peace Research* 33:4 (November 1996): 421.

3. Ibid.

4. "We Will Break the Settlers' Bones" [Hebrew], *INN*, January 7, 2005, www.inn.co.il /News/News.aspx/99741, accessed July 3, 2019.

5. "Israeli Soldiers May Refuse Orders," *CBS News*, January 4, 2005, www.cbsnews.com /news/israeli-soldiers-may-refuse-orders.

6. For example, a former chief rabbi of Israel, Avraham Shapira, compared the participation in the evacuation to eating nonkosher food. See Efrat Weiss, "Rabbi Shapira: Evacuating a Settlement—Like Eating Pork" [Hebrew], *Ynet*, January 16, 2005, www .ynet.co.il/Ext/Comp/ArticleLayout/CdaArticlePrintPreview/1,2506,L-3033422,00 .html, accessed July 18, 2019.

7. Stuart Cohen, "The Hesder Yeshivot in Israel: A Church-State Military Arrangement," *Journal of Church and State* 35:1 (1993): 113.

8. Elisheva Rosman-Stollman, "Religion and the Military as Greedy Frameworks: Religious Zionism and the Israel Defense Forces" [Hebrew] (Ph.D. diss., Bar Ilan University, 2005), 172–99.

9. For example, Eliash presents the fear of the leaders of the *Mahctarot* [paramilitary units] about the involvement of rabbis in religious units, which can cause conflict with authorities (Yechiel Eliash, *Ma'ase Ha'Ba Be'Chazon* [Hebrew] [Jerusalem: Merkaz Elitzur, 1983], 62).

10. It is true that not all the rabbis called for disobedience, as will be presented later in this essay, but a large group of prominent religious Zionist rabbis did call for it—enough to anticipate a larger number of refusals.

11. Efrat Weis, "Good Morning, I Came to Evacuate You" [Hebrew], *Ynet* (June 14, 2005), https://www.ynet.co.il/articles/0,7340,L-3096808,00.html, accessed August 7, 2019. The writer interviews a commander in the IDF who participated in some of those programs.

12. Gadi Eshel, *The Mental Preparation for the Disengagement and Its Aftermath in the IDF*, June 2008, www.mentalpreparation.org/BRPortal/br/P102.jsp?arc=17534, accessed August 7, 2019.

13. "Golani Soldiers Will Not Participate in the Evacuation" [Hebrew], *Walla*, June 16, 2005, https://news.walla.co.il/item/732159, accessed August 8, 2019; Unger, "The Limits of Discipline and Disobedience," 10.

14. Hanan Greenberg, "The IDF Is Preparing for the Evacuation" [Hebrew], *Ynet*, August 14, 2005, https://www.ynet.co.il/articles/0,7340,L-3126753,00.html, accessed June 25, 2020.

15. Unger, "The Limits of Discipline and Disobedience," 10.

16. Asher Cohen, "The Yarmulke and the Barret—Image and Reality," in *The Yarmulke and the Barret* [Hebrew] (ed. Moshe Rehimi; Ikana and Rehovot: Orot College, 2010), 92–94, 106.

17. Ibid., 100–103.

18. Charles S. Liebman and Eliezer Don-Yehiya, *Civil Religion in Israel* (Berkeley: University of California, 1983), 185–86. Later in their book they discuss how these options appear in different religious groups in Israel.

19. Mordechai Bar Lev, "The Graduates of the Yeshiva High School in Eretz-Yisrael: Between Tradition and Innovation" [Hebrew] (Ph.D. diss., Bar Ilan University, 1977), 357, 373–78.

20. Eliezer Don-Yehiya, "The National Yeshivot and Political Radicalism in Israel," in *A Hundred Years of Religious Zionism*, vol. 3 [Hebrew] (ed. Avi Sagi and Dov Schwartz; Ramat Gan: Bar Ilan University Press, 2003), 187–88, 192–93.

21. Salmon presents an interesting argument, regardless of the different approaches in religious Zionism, and claims that in comparison to other types of national movements, Zionism has many religious characteristics (Yosef Salmon, *Do Not Provoke Providence: Orthodoxy in the Grip of Nationalism* [Hebrew] [Jerusalem: Zalman Shazar Center, 2006], 12.)

22. Yishai Rosen-Zvi, "The Dispute in Yeshivat Merkaz HaRav," in *A Hundred Years of Religious Zionism*, vol. 3 [Hebrew] (ed. Avi Sagi and Dov Schwartz; Ramat Gan: Bar Ilan University Press, 2003), 425.

23. Some communities developed an alternative version of this prayer that presents their suspicious approach to the country. See Efrat Weiss, "A New Prayer" [Hebrew] *Ynet*, May 14, 2005, www.ynet.co.il/articles/0,7340,L-3084866,00.html, accessed August 16, 2019.

24. After the evacuation, a group of high school students published a letter they sent to the army in which they said that they refuse to serve because of the army's role in the evacuation. See Efart Weiss, "The Youth's Petition: We Will Not Serve in the Army because of the Evacuation" [Hebrew], *Ynet*, September 1, 2005, www.ynet.co.il/articles/0,7340,L-3136525,00.html, accessed August 16, 2019.

25. Moshe Hellinger and Isaac Hershkowitz, *Obedience and Civil Disobedience in Religious Zionism: From Gush Emunim to the Price Tag Attacks* [Hebrew] (Jerusalem: The Israel Democracy Institute, 2015), 119.

26. A similar argument can be found in ibid., 19–20.

27. Asher Cohen, "Religion and Patriotism," in *Patriotism: Homeland Love* [Hebrew] (ed. Avner Ben-Amos and Daniel Bar-Tal; Ra'anana: Hakibbutz Hameuchad, 2004), 468–69.

28. Ruth Linn, "Soldiers with Conscience Never Die, They Are Just Ignored by Society," *Journal of Military Ethics* 1(2): 59–60.

29. For instance, Yoni Kampinski, "If the Haredim Were in Gush Katif, the Evacuation Would Not Have Happened" [Hebrew], *INN* (July 25, 2017), www.inn.co.il/News /News.aspx/351653, accessed August 19, 2019.

30. Gideon Aran, "From Pioneering to Torah Studying," in *A Hundred Years of Religious Zionism: Ideological Concepts* [Hebrew] (ed. Avi Sagi and Dov Schwartz; Ramat Gan: Bar Ilan University Press, 2003), 45–46.

31. Cohen, "The Yarmulke and the Barret," 86.

32. Amir Oren, "IDF: One-Third of Soldiers Might Refuse to Evacuate Outposts," *Haaretz* (August 19, 2009), www.haaretz.com/1.5093722, accessed August 20, 2019.

33. Aaron Rabinowitz, "Court Upholds Acquittal of Rabbis Who Offered to Pay Soldiers Who Refused to Evacuate Settlements" [Hebrew], *Haaretz*, October 11, 2018, www.haaretz.com/israel-news/premium-court-upholds-acquittal-of-rabbis -who-offered-to-pay-soldiers-who-refused-to-evacuat-1.6550828, accessed August 20, 2019.

LEAVING THE FOLD

Dissent from Communal Authority in the Orthodox World?

MARK TRENCHER

INTRODUCTION

QUANTITATIVE RESEARCH HAS been lacking among those who have left the American Orthodox community. While there have been many memoirs written by some who have left Orthodoxy,[1] the anecdotes have not adequately shed light on the many varying themes and reasons why people are leaving.

The central question explored in this essay is the extent to which leaving the community has been a way for Orthodox individuals to express dissent from the community's authority, as imposed largely by its authority figures and normative behaviors.

While the departure of Jews from Orthodoxy has often been cited as a "crisis,"[2] there has been a dearth of solid, quantitative data to answer the question of why people leave. Some research has been done[3] but it has been limited in scope (i.e., the breadth of community segments studied), and the Orthodox community has been relying largely on memoirs, anecdotes, and punditry for an understanding of the reasons for departure.

Communal rabbis and other observers have pointed to all sorts of reasons—often simplistic in citing a few purportedly explanatory reasons. But there has been frustration with the relative lack of deep understanding, both within the broader Orthodox community as well as among those who have left.[4]

Further hampering deeper self-reflection, departure has often been blamed on character flaws among those who leave. They are often portrayed as troubled, promiscuous, lacking religious seriousness, and weak in moral character, and so their departure is often viewed as their fault and not due to anything that is occurring within the community.

OUTLINE OF THIS ESSAY

In an effort to better understand the Orthodox community, the nature of its authority, issues that might generate dissent from authority, and whether dissent-driven depar-ture is taking place, we will cover the following:

> *A profile of the U.S. Orthodox community*—The Orthodox and Haredi (ultra-Orthodox) world are not widely understood, and this background will help the reader to understand the particularities of this group as they relate to our hypotheses regarding departure as a form of dissent.
>
> *The nature of authority*—Authority in the Orthodox community is very differ-ent from what is found in secular society and the non-Orthodox Jewish world. Further, it varies substantially among the subsegments of Orthodoxy (Modern Orthodox and Haredi and their subgroups).
>
> *Possible causes of dissent*—We draw upon quantitative (and some anecdotal) data to develop hypotheses relating to factors that might be causing people to dissent and leave their community.
>
> *Testing the hypotheses*—Finally, we will draw upon primary quantitative data.

QUANTITATIVE RESEARCH CONDUCTED

To answer the question of the extent to which departure from Orthodoxy is a form of dissent against authority, we will draw largely on primary quantitative data, specifically an original field survey: The 2016 Nishma Research survey "Starting a Conversation: A Pioneering Survey of Those Who Have Left the Orthodox Community."[5]

This was the first broad quantitative study undertaken among those who have left Orthodoxy, and it covered a broader spectrum of the Orthodox community[6] that had not been adequately covered in prior research or memoirs.

The survey posed the following question: "Please think back to when you started moving away in belief or practice from the Orthodox community in which you were raised. What were the key things that caused your beliefs and practices to change?"

Respondents were not presented with a checklist of potentially triggering events or situations that might have caused them to leave. We were looking to not limit the responses in this manner, but to allow respondents to share their thoughts in some detail. The responses may thus be viewed as "top-of-mind awareness"—those things that were most often remembered, sometimes many years after the events. Thus, when we say that X percent left Orthodoxy because of Factor Y, what we are really saying is that Factor Y was important enough that X percent of respondents recalled it as a factor that had been important in their decision to leave Orthodoxy (perhaps many years later) and cited it.

This survey explored why respondents left Orthodoxy, focusing on (1) the extent to which they have been pulled or lured out by the outside world and, if so, by what aspect of the outside world; and (2) the extent to which their departure was precipitated by intolerable or objectionable communal authority figures or behaviors—that is, they were "pushed out." It is the latter reasons that will lend themselves to consideration as drivers of dissent.

Overall, the factors most often mentioned are shown in fig. 1.[7] We shall draw upon these data and explore some differences among the Orthodox subgroups as we test our hypotheses.

PROFILE OF THE JEWISH AND ORTHODOX COMMUNITIES

It is widely believed and inarguably true that the U.S. Orthodox population is disproportionately influential in American society,[8] despite its small size. In fact, while the Jewish population represents about 2 percent of the total U.S. population, the Orthodox community is a very small subset of Judaism, comprising about 12 percent of the total U.S. Jewish population and thus about a quarter of a percent of the U.S. population (see fig. 2).[9]

ORTHODOX SUBGROUPS AND THE VARYING NATURE OF AUTHORITY

The differences between the Orthodox subgroups as shown in fig. 3[10] (Modern Orthodox and Haredi, which in turn comprises various Chasidic sects and the Yeshivish group) are important, as their differing worldviews (in the area of insularity vs. engagement with secular society) and practices affect the reasons people might leave those groups.

Orthodox Judaism across all of its subgroups believes in adherence to and guidance by Jewish law (halachah). However, while a cornerstone of Modern Orthodoxy is its attempt to synthesize Jewish values and the observance of Jewish law with the secular, modern world,[11] Haredi Judaism is characterized by insularity and a rejection of modern secular culture.

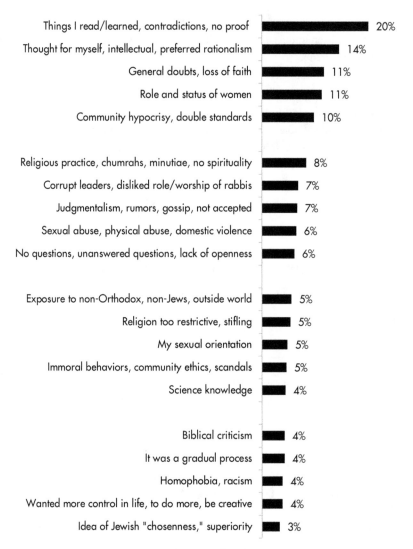

Fig. 1 Why people left Orthodoxy.

Modern Orthodoxy is itself quite heterogeneous. It covers a wide range of approaches, from very liberal to near-Haredi. Except for those on the extreme right of Modern Orthodoxy, adherence to halachah is less stringent than it is among the Haredi.[12] The authorities in the Modern Orthodox community are of course halachah (albeit with lower levels of normative adherence than among the Haredi): the local synagogue rabbis (as synagogue membership is virtually universal among the Modern Orthodox), the national Jewish organizations (e.g., Orthodox Union,

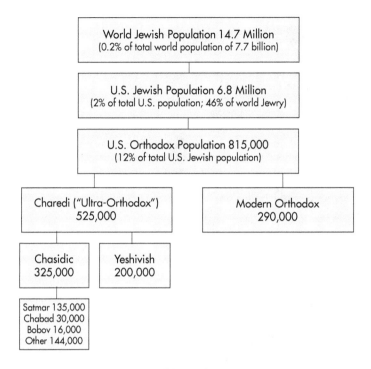

Fig. 2 Size of the Jewish community.

Yeshiva University), and the rabbinic leaders who guide those organizations, as well as prominent synagogue rabbis.

The Haredi world comprises the Chasidic and the Yeshivish. The Chasidic are known for their extreme insularity and their distinctive garb (e.g., long black coats, fur hats, and sidelocks among the men and very modest garb with head coverings for the women) and are ruled by an authoritarian charismatic leader (the "rebbe").

Probably the most widely known (although not the largest) of the Chasidic groups is the Chabad-Lubavitch, with authority emanating from the teaching of the late Lubavitcher Rebbe and Chabad customs. The Chabad have a mission of outreach to less religious (often secular) Jews and are therefore less insular than other Chasidic sects. In our research we looked at the Chabad and the other Chasidic groups separately, given their substantial differences—notably in their engagement with the outside world (secular as well as other Jewish groups).[13]

The Yeshivish (also known as Litvish/Lithuanian, Agudah, and Misnagdim) focus on advanced religious study and their authorities are halachah and the deans [Roshei Yeshiva] of advanced Torah schools. The Yeshivish tend to have a leery attitude toward secular society but are not as insular as the Chasidic groups. The youth have significantly

	Modern Orthodox	Chasidic	Chabad/ Lubavitch	Yeshivish
	• Orthodox Judaism believes in adherence to and guidance by Jewish law (halachah). • Modern Orthodoxy attempts to synthesize Jewish values and the observance of Jewish law with the secular, modern world. • Charedi Judaism (or ultra-Orthodox) is a broad spectrum of groups, all characterized by insularity and a rejection of modern secular culture.			
Summary, Insularity, Authority	Covers a wide range of approaches, from very liberal to near-Charedi. Adherence to halachah is less stringent than among Charedi. Synagogue and school rabbis are authoritative.	Ruled by authoritarian charismatic leader ("rebbe"). Very insular, with minimal exposure to secular society. Stringent religious practice; education generally limited to religious study.	Authority is the teaching of the late Lubavitcher Rebbe and Chabad customs. Less insular due to its mission of outreach to less religious (often secular) Jews.	Deans ("Roshei Yeshiva") of advanced Torah schools are communal authorities. Focus on Torah study and stringent adherence to halachah. Limited—but some—exposure to secular society.
	The community exerts great influence across all groups. "Being Orthodox involves not only a system of belief and religious observance but also a set of cultural practices. . . . Religious and cultural practice may take precedence over full acceptance of the underlying system of belief. . . . The centrality of the community persists in contemporary Judaism." (Sarah Bunin Benor, *Becoming Frum* [New Brunswick, NJ, Rutgers University Press, 2012], 2–3.)			

Fig. 3 The nature of authority in the Orthodox community.

stronger secular educations (although not as strong secularly as among the Modern Orthodox), and they interact more with the secular and other Jewish segments.

Finally, it should be noted that the community itself exerts great influence across all groups and acts as an authority figure of sorts. As one sociologist noted:

> Being Orthodox involves not only a system of belief and religious observance but also a set of cultural practices . . . religious and cultural practice may take precedence over full acceptance of the underlying system of belief. . . . The centrality of the community persists in contemporary Judaism.[14]

In summary, the authorities in the Orthodox community are halachah (Jewish law), rabbis (synagogue rabbis, Chasidic leaders, and yeshiva deans), cornerstone organizations, and communal normative behaviors.

In contrast, the Orthodox community views these as less authoritative: the non-Orthodox Jewish world, popular culture and societal norms, the secular government, and academia, especially when it conflicts with Orthodox beliefs or is viewed as irrelevant to one's living an Orthodox lifestyle.

POSSIBLE CAUSES OF DISSENT

In our quantitative research study of people who left Orthodoxy, respondents cited many reasons for their departure. As noted earlier, to explore the extent to which reasons may have been spurred by dissent, we divided the fifty-plus reasons cited into two broad categories: (1) factors whereby people were pulled or lured out by the external world; and (2) factors whereby departure was precipitated by intolerable or objectionable communal authority figures or behaviors (i.e., they were "pushed out").

The research showed that communal elements that pushed people out—that is, spurred dissent and gave them reason to leave—were cited far more often than outside world elements that lured people (see fig. 4).[15]

This supports the theory that there are reasons for dissent. But how much dissent is actually occurring? How many people are leaving Orthodoxy? A 2017 Nishma Research survey of the Modern Orthodox community found that about 10 percent of adults do not agree that their Orthodoxy is important to them,[16] and the study offered an opinion that this group is "at risk" of departure. In addition, an informal social media survey conducted in 2018 estimated that 25 to 30 percent of Modern Orthodox Jewish high school graduates were no longer observant an average of ten years after graduation.[17] So, while in fact the extent of communal departure is still largely a matter of speculation, it is a growing concern.[18]

Admittedly, however, there are no solid data on the extent to which people are leaving Orthodoxy. Thus, the following analysis is conducted in a relative sense—that is, considering which drivers of dissent/departure are more prevalent than others, without solid quantified data as to their prevalence. In other words, we may know that a particular driver of dissent is more impactful than other drivers but are unsure of its exact impact in terms of the percentage of the community affected.

TESTING THE HYPOTHESES

After reviewing the many reasons people gave for leaving their Orthodox community, both overall and among various community subgroups (i.e., Modern Orthodox and Haredi as well as differences by gender),[19] we hypothesize four possible manifestations of dissent that might be taking the form of communal departure: community

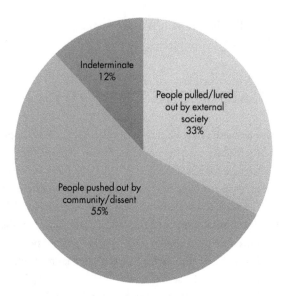

Fig. 4 Push versus pull factors influencing people to leave Orthodoxy.

insularity, poor secular education (in the Haredi community), the role and status of women, and communal inadequate addressing of abuse.

Community Insularity

The Haredi community is characterized by extreme restrictions on exposure to the outside world (e.g., Internet/technology, secular education, social interactions). Insularity is more severe in some of the Chasidic groups (i.e., Satmar, Skver) and less severe in others, particularly Chabad. Simply put, society is seen as increasingly base and dangerous to Orthodox Jews' spiritual health and continuity, and insularity preserves Jewish values.

Insularity is a minor factor, at best, in the Modern Orthodox community. It was found to be a far less significant driver of departure in that group than among the Haredi, where it is the most frequently cited factor in causing people to leave the community. Following are some recent newspaper headlines:

Rabbis Tell 60,000 in NY: Get Rid of the Internet if You Know What's Good for You[20]

Hasidic Leaders Sharply Limit Members' Web, Smartphone Use: "It's Like We're in North Korea"[21]

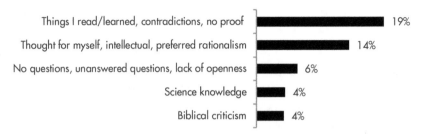

Fig. 5 Most-cited specific reasons for leaving Orthodoxy.

Ultra-Orthodox Rabbis Ban Women from Going to University in Case They Get "Dangerous" Secular Knowledge[22]

Insularity was found to be the top driver of dissension, more for men than for women, although few respondents specifically cite the Internet (which the Haredi community greatly fears) as having spurred their departure. Dissent is driven by gradual awareness of the external culture and its beliefs, and an inability to reconcile those with the religious beliefs, all of which are a result of the insularity. See fig. 5 for the percentages of respondents citing various aspects of insularity and its effects.[23]

Following are typical comments offered by those who left the community in explaining why they did so:

Access to books and other worldviews. Questions on the logic and validity of religion. Quest for truth.

The secular world seemed more free and breathable so I naturally gravitated towards that world.[24]

I just was questioning things. I was told I was bad for thinking and being me. I sometimes think, if I had someone who understood me or had a conversation with me, I might have stayed.[25]

Poor Secular Education (in the Haredi Community)

In the Haredi community, the focus of children's education is very much on their religious studies. Among boys, secular education virtually disappears after the eighth grade, at which point it is common for students to have only religious studies. The Haredi value Torah study as a core purpose of Jewish life, while secular studies have at most pragmatic value for employment.

As Shulem Deen (an advocate of sorts among Chasidic Jews who have left Orthodoxy) wrote:

> When I was in my 20s, already a father of three, I had no marketable skills, despite
> 18 years of schooling. I could rely only on an ill-paid position as a teacher of reli-
> gious studies at the local boys' yeshiva, which required no special training or certi-
> fication. . . . I remember feeling . . . anger at those responsible for educating me who
> had failed me so colossally. . . . Ten years ago, at age 33, I left the Hasidic commu-
> nity and sought to make my way in the secular world. At 35, I got my G.E.D., but I
> never made it to college, relying instead on self-study to fill in my educational gaps.
> I still live with my educational handicaps.[26]

However, in the survey of those who left Orthodoxy, fewer than 2 percent of respondents mentioned poor secular education as a reason why they left. While it has been
mentioned by some (often those who have left for other reasons), secular education is
unknown and generally not "missed."

The Role and Status of Women

Orthodoxy defines and limits gender roles, and there has been growing activism aimed
at women achieving more involvement (in synagogue, organizations, etc.), almost solely
among the Modern Orthodox.

While it is true that some Haredi women bridle at their destined role as largely
stay-at-home mothers of large families[27] (although some have jobs to make money,
allowing their husbands to pursue Torah studies), not many mentioned this. The role
and status of women were mentioned far more often in the Modern Orthodox community. It is relatively unusual for Haredi women to speak out on this issue.[28] On the other
hand, Modern Orthodox women do speak out about their role and status, and they
are not fearful of expressing dissatisfaction.[29]

Statistically, the role and status of women were found to be a notable driver of
people leaving Orthodoxy, especially among Modern Orthodox women. Overall, 11
percent of respondents cited this as a factor in their leaving their community, but it
was even higher among the Modern Orthodox—22 percent, compared to 6 percent of
the Haredi. It was higher yet among Modern Orthodox women, at 37 percent.[30] Many
respondents commented on this in the survey of those who have left Orthodoxy:[31]

> As I grew up it became very clear to me that despite teachings, men and women were
> certainly not considered or treated equally. Once I began questioning that, I ques-
> tioned everything else I had been told.

It started (with) my interaction with women's issues. . . . As a child the gender roles bothered me but only marginally. As I grew older these issues became much more intense. I started realizing that I was working so hard for a system that was rejecting me at every turn. I can not accept sexism as divine.

It seems clear from the data that the role and status of women are a strong driver of dissention among Modern Orthodox women—statistically the number one driver—and a lesser driver in the Haredi groups. Still, there are many women in Orthodoxy who are quite happy with their role and status.[32]

Communal Inadequate Addressing of Abuse

Recent years have seen an increase in reports on sexual and other forms of abuse in the Orthodox community. In studying whether this is a driver of dissent, we focus not so much on the incidence of abuse (it is unknown whether the levels in the Orthodox community are different from those in society at large) but on the view that it has been very far from adequately recognized and addressed.[33]

While the Modern Orthodox community has been increasingly active in addressing the problem,[34] there continues to be a view, especially in the Haredi community, that incidents of sexual abuse are too often kept hidden, with alleged perpetrators shielded and the victims and their families silenced:

Sexual abuse within the community is often not reported to police. Many feel that to report a Jew to non-Jewish authorities constitutes [a] religious crime. . . . Samuel Heilman, a professor of Jewish studies at Queens College, writes that one reason why cases or patterns of sexual abuse are rarely reported to law enforcement is because "they think that anyone who turns over anyone to the outside authorities is committing a transgression to the community at large."[35]

The survey of those who have left Orthodoxy found the community's inadequate addressing of this problem to be a moderately important driver of dissension. While 6 percent explicitly cited sexual abuse, physical abuse, or domestic violence as their reason for leaving the community, 10 percent cited "community hypocrisy," often relating this hypocrisy to the treatment of perpetrators by communal leaders. As two survey respondents commented:[36]

Seeing the rabbis constantly ignore abuse in the community. Plus the complete lack of checks and balances plus transparency amongst the hierarchy of the entire system. And so once I peeled away at the hierarchy, my entire belief system collapsed.

Even when people do leave and have been abused, it's not the abuse that causes dislike of the community. It's usually that the abuse causes them to question the community, and question what we have been told, to the point that we eventually cannot reconcile the answers.

Confirming this finding, a recent study by two Orthodox researchers found a widespread history of sexual abuse among the formerly Orthodox, noting:

This report supports the anecdotal evidence I've seen that indicates a close link between abuse in a religious context and the subsequent rejection of that community, its practices, values, and often everything it stands for.[37]

SUMMARY

The research suggests the following:

- Community insularity is relatively the strongest driver of dissent/departure among the Haredi population but is a minor factor (at best) in the Modern Orthodox community.
- Poor secular education in the Haredi community is not a significant driver of dissent among that population.
- The role and status of women are by far the strongest drivers of dissent/departure among Modern Orthodox women (albeit less of a driver among Modern Orthodox men and the Haredi).
- The Orthodox community's inadequate addressing of abuse is a moderate driver of dissent.

NOTES

1. See for example: Shulem Deen, *All Who Go Do Not Return* (Minneapolis: Graywolf Press, 2015), which won the National Jewish Book Award; Tova Mirvis, *The Book of Separation* (Boston: Houghton Mifflin Harcourt, 2017), about leaving Modern Orthodoxy, by a *New York Times* best-selling author; Faranak Margolese, *Off the Derech: How to Respond to the Challenge* (Scotts Valley: CreateSpace Independent Publishing Platform, 2005), based on research conducted among people who have left Orthodoxy; and the film *One of Us* (directed by Heidi Ewing and Rachel Grady; Los Gatos: Netflix, 2017).

2. There is much published on this topic. See, for example, Harry Maryles, "When Good Children Go OTD," *Emes Ve-Emunah — A Forum for Orthodox Jewish Thought on Halacha, Hashkafa, and the Social Issues of Our Time* (8 August 2013), http://haemtza .blogspot.com/2013/08/when-good-children-go-otd.html; and "The OTD Crisis: Observations," *The Yeshiva World* (27 January 2009), https://www.theyeshivaworld .com/coffeeroom/topic/the-otd-crisis-observations.

3. Margolese, *Off the Derech.*

4. Saul Sudin, "There Is No 'Off the Derech,'" *Hevria* (21 May 2015), https://hevria.com /saul/there-is-no-off-the-derech/.

5. Mark Trencher, *Starting a Conversation: A Pioneering Survey of Those Who Have Left the Orthodox Community — An Exploration of Journeys, Practices, Beliefs, Identity, Community and Relationships* (West Hartford: Nishma Research, 2016), http:// nishmaresearch.com/assets/pdf/Report_Survey_of_Those_Who_Left_Orthodoxy _Nishma_Research_June_2016.pdf.

6. The survey reported detailed findings obtained from 885 people who had left Orthodoxy: Chasidic excluding Chabad (216 respondents), Chabad (97 respondents), Yeshivish (221 respondents), and Modern Orthodox (230 respondents). Most of the previous research that had been conducted on this topic had focused on the Chasidic segment, and nearly all of the memoirs emanated from the Chasidic and Yeshivish groups. For a discussion of why Chabad was analyzed separately from the other Chasidic groups, see Mark Trencher, *Starting a Conversation*, 16.

7. Mark Trencher, *Starting a Conversation*, 24.

8. Much has been written on this topic, and "Jewish influence" is an oft cited trope in Antisemitic writings. For an analysis of Jewish influence, see J. J. Goldberg, *Jewish Power: Inside the American Jewish Establishment* (Boston: Addison-Wesley, 1996), ch. 1, downloadable at http://www.washingtonpost.com/wp-srv/style/longterm /books/chap1/jewishpower.htm?noredirect=on.

9. The following population data were assembled from various sources: World Jewish Population — Sergio Della Pergola, Hebrew University, *The Times of Israel* (8 September 2018); U.S. Jewish Population — Ira M. Sheskin and Arnold Dashefsky, *American Jewish Yearbook 2017* (Cham, Switzerland: Springer, 2018), 179; U.S. Denominations and Percentages Modern Orthodox/Haredi — Luis Lugo, Alan Cooperman, et al., *A Portrait of Jewish Americans: Findings from a Pew Research Center Survey of U.S. Jews* (Washington, DC: 1 October 2013), with projections to 2018 by Nishma Research; Chasidic Community Size and Distribution — Marcin Wodzinski, *Historical Atlas of Hasidism* (Princeton: Princeton University Press, 2018), 194.

10. For a detailed description of key differences between Orthodox subgroups, see Mark Trencher, *Starting a Conversation*, 16.

11. Norman Lamm, *Torah UMadda* (Jerusalem: Koren Publishers, 1996).

12. Mark Trencher, *The Nishma Research Profile of American Modern Orthodox Jews: Religious Beliefs and Practices, Views on the Importance of Orthodoxy as a Part of Life, Shul Life, Jewish Study, Women's Roles, Children's Education, Sexuality, Israel Connection and Advocacy, Overall Successes, Opportunities and Challenges* (West Hartford: Nishma Research, 28 September 2017), 16, http://nishmaresearch.com /assets/pdf/Report%20-%20Nishma%20Research%20Profile%20of%20American %20Modern%20Orthodox%20Jews%2009-27-17.pdf.

13. Tzvi Freeman and Menachem Posner, *Chabad.org*, "17 Facts Everyone Should Know About Hasidic Jews," https://www.chabad.org/library/article_cdo/aid/4079238 /jewish/17-Facts-Everyone-Should-Know-About-Hasidic-Jews.htm.

14. Sarah Bunin Benor, *Becoming Frum* (New Brunswick: Rutgers University Press, 2012), 2–3.

15. Mark Trencher, *Starting a Conversation*, 25.

16. Mark Trencher, *The Nishma Research Profile of American Modern Orthodox Jews*, 24. Respondents were asked to rate on a scale from 0 to 10 the importance of their Orthodox observance. This scale is often used in research (and widely used in creating a metric called Net Promoter Score), with those providing a rating of 6 or less being labeled as "detractors,"—that is, those with a weak connection to the entity being assessed. A similar methodology was used in the Nishma survey.

17. Mark Trencher, observed results of Facebook postings among approximately thirty participants, September 2017; an anecdotal and nonscientific finding, but one that we see as directionally noteworthy given the lack of harder statistics.

18. See, for example, Mark Trencher, "Survey Highlights Risk of Modern Orthodox 'Going Off the Derech' (Leaving Orthodoxy)," *The Times of Israel*, 20 December 2017, https://blogs.timesofisrael.com/survey-highlights-risk-of-modern-orthodox -going-off-the-derech-leaving-orthodoxy/; and Anshei Pferrer, "Opinion the Biggest Upheaval for the Jewish People This Century Is Starting Now, and We're Not Ready," *Haaretz*, 10 November 2017, https://www.haaretz.com/opinion/premium-the-biggest -upheaval-for-the-jewish-people-this-century-is-coming-1.5464307.

19. Mark Trencher, *Starting a Conversation*, 22–30.

20. David Shamah, "Rabbis Tell 60,000 in NY: Get Rid of the Internet if You Know What's Good for You," *The Times of Israel*, 21 May 2012, https://www.timesofisrael.com /rabbis-get-rid-of-the-internet-if-you-know-whats-good-for-you/.

21. Elizabeth Liorente, "Hasidic Leaders Sharply Limit Members' Web, Smartphone Use: 'It's Like We're in North Korea,'" *Fox News.com*, 12 June 2018, https://www.foxnews .com/us/hasidic-leaders-sharply-limit-members-web-smartphone-use-its-like-were -in-north-korea.

22. Siobhan Fenton and Dina Rickman, "Ultra-Orthodox Rabbis Ban Women from Going to University in Case They Get 'Dangerous' Secular Knowledge," *The Independent*, 22 August 2016, https://www.independent.co.uk/news/world/americas/ultra-orthodox

-rabbis-ban-women-from-going-to-university-in-case-they-get-dangerous-secular
-a7204171.html.

23. Mark Trencher, *Starting a Conversation*, 24.

24. Mark Trencher, *Starting a Conversation*, sample verbatim comments by respondents.

25. Melissa Weisz, "Off the Beaten Path," *Vogue*, 8 March 2018, https://www.vogue.com
/projects/13541582/american-woman-style-after-ultra-orthodox-life/.

26. Shulem Deen, "Why Is New York Condoning Illiteracy?," *New York Times*, 4 April 2018,
https://www.nytimes.com/2018/04/04/opinion/yeshivas-literacy-new-york.html.

27. See, for example, a widely read memoir that is being made into a film: Deborah Feldman,
Unorthodox: The Scandalous Rejection of My Hasidic Roots (New York: Simon &
Schuster, 2012).

28. See, for example, Ruth Eglash, "Two Ultra-Orthodox Feminists Challenge Israel's Political
Landscape," *Washington Post*, 23 July 2017, https://www.washingtonpost.com/world
/middle_east/two-ultra-orthodox-feminists-are-challenging-israels-political-land
scape/2017/07/23/4695134c-6b3e-11e7-abbc-a53480672286_story.html?source=post
_page--------------------------&utm_term=.c2140ff8a1b7.

29. Miriam Gedwiser, "Orthodox Women Are Dissatisfied and 'Checking Out.' Here's
Why," *Forward*, 9 October 2017, https://forward.com/opinion/384335/orthodox
-women-are-dissatisfied-and-checking-out-heres-why/.

30. Mark Trencher, *Starting a Conversation*, 26, 26–28.

31. Ibid., sample verbatim comments by respondents.

32. Arlene Becker Zarmi, "How Orthodox Judaism Elevates the Status of Women," *PJ
Media*, 24 October 2017, https://pjmedia.com/faith/2016/10/24/how-orthodox
-judaism-elevates-the-status-of-women/.

33. See, for example, Majorie Ingall, "Out of the Silence: A New Young-Adult Novel Tackles
Sexual Abuse in the Ultra-Orthodox World," *Tablet*, 8 November 2010, https://www
.tabletmag.com/jewish-life-and-religion/49697/out-of-the-silence.

34. Mark Dratch, "Here's How the Orthodox Deal with Sexual Assault," *Forward*, 24 October 2017, https://forward.com/opinion/letters/386012/heres-how-the-orthodox-deal
-with-sexual-assault/.

35. See for general background see "Sexual Abuse Cases in Brooklyn's Haredi Community,"
Prevalence and Underreporting, *Wikipedia*, last edited 4 May 2019, https://
en.wikipedia.org/wiki/Sexual_abuse_cases_in_Brooklyn%27s_Haredi_community
#Prevalence_and_underreporting.

36. Mark Trencher, *Starting a Conversation*, sample verbatim comments by respondents.

37. Manny Waks, founder of Tzedek, an Australian advocacy group for victims of sexual
abuse, as cited in Sam Sokol, "Study Finds Widespread History of Sexual Abuse
among Formerly Orthodox," *Jewish Telegraphic Agency*, 18 July 2018, https://www
.jta.org/2018/07/18/united-states/study-finds-widespread-history-sexual-abuse
-among-formerly-orthodox.

BRIT WITHOUT MILAH

Adapting and Remixing the Dominant Ritual System

LINDSEY JACKSON

O N MARCH 13, 2019, discreetly embedded in a conversation on Twitter, Democratic presidential candidate Andrew Yang declared his opposition against routine infant circumcision.[1] In a subsequent interview with *The Daily Beast*, Yang communicated his opposition even further by stating that he is indeed "aligned with the intactivists" and "history will prove them . . . correct."[2] Yang explained how he wanted to circumcise his own sons but was convinced not to by his wife.[3] For Yang, it is important to "inform parents that it is entirely up to them whether their infant gets circumcised, and that there are costs and benefits either way."[4] On March 19, 2019, Yang took to Twitter to clarify his stance on circumcision: "Just to clarify—I support the freedom of parents to adopt circumcision for any religious or cultural ritual as desired. I actually have attended a brit milah [covenant of circumcision] myself and felt privileged to be there. Thanks Mikael. Always up to parents [thumbs up emoji]."[5] Some intactivists expressed dismay over Yang's clarification because of what they perceived to be a reversal of his original statement.[6] His position has even been a topic of conversation on several episodes of the daytime talk show *The View*.[7]

Yang's initial "coming out" as "against the procedure" reflects the shifting perceptions about routine infant circumcision more broadly in the United States, where circumcision rates are slowly decreasing.[8] Despite this decrease, circumcision remains a controversial and difficult decision for many parents. A recent article in *HuffPost* claimed that "circumcision is one of today's most controversial parenting topics."[9] Within the context of increasing debates surrounding circumcision, it should come as no surprise that similar discussions are beginning to percolate in the Jewish community, and a small number of Jewish parents are choosing not to circumcise their sons.[10] Many of the parents who choose not to circumcise opt for non-cutting welcoming ceremonies in place of the traditional brit milah.[11]

This essay examines how problematic rituals are not abandoned in their entirety; instead, they are refashioned to suit the shifting values of contemporary practitioners. Adapting and creating new rituals, albeit sometimes controversial, is increasingly accessible in the current landscape of American religious praxis, where DIY (do-it-yourself) religion has become commonplace. Building on scholarly examinations of DIY religion, I contend that some families are utilizing the DIY ethos of American religious practice to calibrate the traditional brit milah into a covenantal ceremony that resonates with their views on circumcision. Non-circumcision Jews are actively reinterpreting and emphasizing certain elements of brit milah to craft a personalized, but identifiably Jewish, non-cutting welcoming ritual.[12] Differences between brit milah and non-cutting rituals are minimized in order establish a palatable equilibrium between tradition and innovation. These deliberate adjustments create a ritual enactment that appears familiar and recognizable, diminishing friction over this unconventional ritual choice. In this essay I examine these dynamics through an analysis of case studies from my field research. First, I analyze a brit shalom ritual I observed to highlight how the traditional brit milah was reinterpreted and adapted. Second, I examine how opting out of brit milah in favor of brit shalom elicits conflict in the family unit and how the ritual enactment itself reconciles the conflict. An analysis of these case studies highlights the delicate balance between tradition and innovation and showcases the consequences when one tips the scale in favor of innovation.[13]

DIY RELIGION AND RITUAL CHANGE

Studies demonstrate that millennials tend to be less religiously observant than previous generations and increasingly identify as unaffiliated to any tradition.[14] Changing attitudes toward religion and religious observance are not unique to millennials; scholars have noted a shift in the religious tenor of Americans since the middle of the twentieth century.[15] In addition to diverging attitudes toward religion, there has been a significant shift in the way people engage with and practice religion. Hyper-individualism, moralism, voluntarism, and universalism, values adopted and embraced by many Americans, are drastically impacting religious praxis in the United States.[16] Rejection of traditional religious authority, emphasis on individual choice, and prioritizing ethical and moral concerns enshrined by the values outlined above have given Americans license to adapt, innovate, and connect with their religion in a way that makes sense to them. Jack Wertheimer explains the implications of this ethos on American Jews: "What this has meant is that ever more Jews choose whether they wish to identify as Jewish and then define for themselves what such a decision means."[17]

Some scholars have used the term "DIY religion" to refer to the phenomenon of molding religious traditions to suit one's unique beliefs and worldviews. Michelle Shain and colleagues define DIY Judaism as initiatives that operate "outside the dominant structure of American Jewish life. The common thread linking DIY projects is that they empower participants, allowing them to define their own Jewish identities and create their own forms of Jewish expression."[18] Creating new initiatives and programs outside the Jewish establishment, reinterpreting the meaning of rituals or traditions, and creating entirely new rituals are examples of the ways in which Jews personalize and create their own forms of Jewish engagement. Rather than accepting religious authority and conforming to communal norms, American Jews are increasingly adapting and creating practices that are consistent with their personal values and belief systems. Jack Wertheimer nuances previous examinations of DIY Judaism by adding the trend of "remixing." Quoting video remixer Elisa Kreisinger, Wertheimer claims, "With remix, we can reedit tired narratives into more subversive ones or pay homage to the awesome narratives that do exist."[19] In other words, remixing provides an avenue through which practitioners can polish and fine-tune the tradition to their liking.

A poignant example of DIY and remixing Judaism is Ritualwell, a free website that allows Jews to create, browse, and share rituals.[20] The site provides the option for users to create a profile to connect with others and build an archive of personalized rituals. Users can also book a meeting with a rabbi for "personalized guidance."[21] Ritualwell explains its mission: "Contemporary life is rich in moments for which we have no traditional ritual or prayer. But we are certain that you can help us find ways to make the tradition speak—or sing—even in circumstances that our ancestors couldn't have imagined. We are delighted to work with you to craft and share Jewish rituals for the seasons of the year and the cycles of our lives."[22] Ritualwell captures the ethos of contemporary American religion and provides an avenue through which Jews can craft rituals that resonate with their individual experiences and worldviews. One category of rituals provided by the site are life cycle rituals. Although Jewish tradition provides a variety of life cycle rituals to celebrate pivotal milestones, not every Jew will follow this trajectory of life. As such, people may want to celebrate different milestones or commemorate hardships not accounted for in the typical Jewish life cycle. Ritualwell offers a plethora of such rituals and the tools to craft one's own, celebrating and commemorating a wide range of significant life moments.[23] With the help of Ritualwell, Jews no longer have to fit into the mold provided by traditional Jewish life cycle rituals; instead, Jews can find and create new rituals that celebrate their unique life course.

DIY religion also allows people with identities and views that conflict with the central tenets of a religious tradition to reconcile their incompatibility. Melissa M.

Wilcox examines how the "societal shift toward individualism" provided an avenue through which gay, lesbian, bisexual, and trans Christians could "create coherence between their religious and sexual or gender identities."[24] Wilcox examines the strategies LGBTQ Christians used to reconcile these conflicting identities, which include ignoring biblical passages that condemn homosexuality and reinterpreting Christian theology to affirm their queer identities. In this sense, "religion has become a resource, to be utilized when it is expedient and ignored or rewritten when it is not."[25] Following a similar path identified by Wilcox, Jews who disagree with circumcision are not rejecting Judaism.[26] In many cases, non-circumcision Jews have a strong sense of Jewish identity and are engaged in Jewish life. Non-circumcision Jews are harmonizing their views about the body and human rights with their Jewish identities and remixing brit milah into a covenantal ceremony that resonates with their views on circumcision.

I would like to turn to a model of ritual change to frame my analysis of brit without milah ceremonies. Irit Koren examines the ways in which religious Jewish brides reinterpret and adapt certain ritual actions in an Orthodox wedding ceremony they deem problematic or unnecessary. Koren divides the way the women approached adapting the ritual in two categories: strategies of interpretation and strategies of action. Strategies of interpretation include rendering a troubling action as merely symbolic or applying an alternative interpretation of the ritual act.[27] Strategies of action include incorporating a parallel act or avoiding a ritual action in its entirety.[28] Elements of the ceremony they find troubling are ignored, reinterpreted, or changed.[29] To counteract what they perceived to be their passive roles in the wedding ceremony, some women created rituals to parallel the ritual actions of the men before and during the ceremony, such as parallel versions of the *tisch* [signing the ketubah], *bedekhen* [veiling the bride], and *kiddushin* [betrothal]. Women's ritual invention rendered them active agents in a ceremony in which they felt tangential. Koren's analysis of ritual change proves helpful in my examination of a brit shalom ritual I attended in May 2019. I utilize Koren's model of "strategies of interpretation" to argue that the couple "impos[ed] a personal and invented meaning upon the ritual act" and incorporated a new act to account for their alternative interpretation.[30] In this particular case, strategies of interpretation were employed to personalize the meaning of the ritual and diminish its divergence from tradition.

EZRA AND LEAH'S BRIT SHALOM[31]

It was a crisp, sunny day in Berkeley, California, when I pulled up to Ezra and Leah's home. I checked the address written on my scrap piece of paper several times before leaving my car and walking up to the front door. I was greeted warmly by Ezra, whom I had not met in person until this moment. I spent forty-five minutes mingling with other guests, walking around their communal home, and watching their chickens in their coop before the ceremony began. Rabbi Nancy Stein arrived, and the thirty or so guests gathered in the living room. The ceremony commenced with a niggun; and the guests enthusiastically followed Ezra's lead and joined in the singing. "That was my mother's favorite niggun so I thought it would be nice to start with that," Ezra explained.[32] Prompted by Rabbi Stein, Ezra contextualized the purpose of this gathering to their guests:

> The main reason that we're here is to welcome Doren into our community, our Jewish community and our extended family and friends of any denomination or belief system. And also to welcome Asher in his own right because we didn't get a chance to do this when he was born. A lot of you know this but Asher was born shortly after my stepfather passed away. I'll save more about that when I talk about Asher's name but we wanted him to have this experience too, even though he just turned three. This is for Doren and for Asher. Even though we're not very observant religious Jews, we are involved in Jewish community, Jewish life, and Jewish culture. It's an extension of our own personal spiritual practice and what's so important to us about it is the community, the sharing of food, and music and song and a commitment to justice in the world. That's really what we're welcoming our sons into—this community that is committed to making the world a better place, as a team.[33]

Rabbi Stein subsequently interjected with an explanation of the meaning of the covenant:

> The word "brit" means covenant. I'll just say one thing about the covenant. It's like a promise between at least two parties, and it's an important promise. Unlike in a promise if one side falls down on their promise then the other side can say, "Well you fell down on the promise so I don't have to do my part of the promise." But in a covenant, we sometimes do fall down and we just have to get back on and nobody walks away. That's what the covenant of the Jewish people and between the Jewish people and the creator of life is. That's the covenant we are welcoming the boys into and it has justice at its center also.[34]

Ezra then provided the reason for their choosing brit shalom:

> We decided that we wanted to have a brit shalom. Traditionally a Jewish family would have a bris on the eighth day of the boy's life. A bris is a circumcision ceremony and in Jewish culture it usually takes place on the eighth day. We decided that we were going to take a new approach to that. We felt it was more in alignment with how we wanted to treat our sons to not put them through that experience.[35]

Rabbi Stein expanded on Ezra's point and rooted the ceremony as a covenantal ceremony. The symbols and actions may be different than that of a traditional bris, but the ceremony serves as an official welcoming of Ezra and Leah's sons into the covenant between God (or in this case, the creator of life) and the Jewish people:

> Let me just jump in and say that the tradition Ezra is talking about is called brit milah and milah is actually the circumcision. Brit means covenant, and bris is just another pronunciation of that. So same covenant, different symbols. The symbol of blood, which is a symbol of life, is part of a bris and this ceremony because Ezra decided to give blood sometime in the next month or so in honor of the boy's lives and that will be your way of acknowledging the covenant of that symbol of life.[36]

After this brief introduction, the ceremony proceeded with the reading of a poem to honor Ezra's deceased parents, singing a *hinei ma tov* [prayer based on first verse of Psalm 133], reciting blessings, wrapping Doren in a tallit, and revealing and explaining the significance of the boys' Hebrew names (the longest part of the ceremony). It concluded with kiddush and was followed by a celebratory meal. The ceremony was approximately forty minutes long, and its overarching structure bore resemblance to a traditional brit milah or *brit bat* [covenant for a daughter] ceremony. Despite the structural resemblance, deliberate adjustments were made and reinterpretations were provided to create a unique but recognizable welcoming ceremony.

Reinterpreting the Ritual

In his initial explanation of the purpose of this ritual enactment, Ezra reinterpreted the meaning of the covenant. Ezra and Leah were welcoming their sons into their Jewish and non-Jewish community of family and friends. Ezra specifically addressed their "extended family and friends of any denomination or belief system." This welcoming ceremony, therefore, was not only about the Jewish people; it extended to the communities, regardless of religious affiliation or observance, to which Ezra and Leah are connected. In addition, the purpose of officially welcoming their sons into their communities was "to mak[e] the world a better place, as a team." This deviates significantly from the original account of the covenant of circumcision in Genesis 17. In the biblical account, brit milah represents the covenant between God and Abraham, where God promised to make Abram the "father of a multitude of nations" and blessed Sarai (later Sarah) with a child and declared "she shall give rise to the nations; rulers of people shall arise from her."[37] This foundational text, which is referred to in most circumcision ceremonies, proved irrelevant for Ezra and Leah's interpretation of the ritual and was omitted as a result.[38] For Ezra and Leah, brit shalom represented welcoming their sons into their communities, with a commitment to justice as its foundation. This alternative reading of the ritual was affirmed by Rabbi Stein, who subsequently claimed the covenant "has justice at its center," without offering further explanation of how that is so. Ezra and Leah's reinterpretation was assumed to suffice.

Ezra and Leah also reinterpreted the significance of blood in the ritual. Extracting blood from a circumcised penis is a central component of brit milah.[39] So central is this element that blood is extracted from babies who are circumcised in the hospital in a ceremony called *hatafat dam* or *hatafat dam brit*.[40] Rather than discarding the extraction of blood from the ritual, Ezra decided to donate blood shortly after the ceremony to honor his sons' lives and acknowledge the covenant as a symbol for life. Retaining this element of the ceremony, albeit enacted in a different way, pays homage to the central role of blood in brit milah and maintains its presence in the ritual. Ezra and Leah reinterpreted the meaning of blood and incorporated their alternative reading by creating a different act that allowed for blood to remain part of the ritual enactment.

Emphasizing the Brit in Brit Shalom

Ezra very briefly explained that he and Leah opted for brit shalom instead of brit milah: "We felt it was more in alignment with how we wanted to treat our sons to not put them through that experience [circumcision]." Although he declared their ritual choice to the group, Ezra did not elaborate on the reasons for their choice. Announcing that he and Leah did not want to put their sons "through that experience" points to possible ethical concerns they have with circumcision. Ezra recognized their divergence from tradition but refrained from providing a lengthy justification of their ritual choice. Immediately following Ezra's explanation of their choice to opt for brit shalom, Rabbi Stein elaborated on the meaning of the word "brit." Through her elaboration, Rabbi Stein effectively disconnected brit from milah. Brit is a covenant, and a covenant can be established through "different symbols." Circumcision is one way, but not the only way. By honing in on the word "brit" and refraining from using the term "brit shalom," Rabbi Stein was positioning the ritual as a slight deviation from tradition rather than an entirely new ritual. The main component of the ritual, the brit, remains intact, with the only difference being the symbol of that brit. By doing this, Rabbi Stein established a palatable balance between tradition and innovation. Some changes are incorporated but the structure and purpose are no different than brit milah. Rabbi Stein created a ritual space that "appropriated some changes while maintaining a sense of cultural continuity."[41] In the words of Jack Wertheimer, this brit ceremony represents a remix of a traditional brit milah.

THE REPERCUSSIONS OF
REMIXING RITUAL

Departing from convention and engaging with a religious tradition differently from one's parents can elicit tension and conflict within the family unit. Ephraim Tabory and Shlomit Hazan-Stern examine the ways in which Orthodox parents cope with children who become nonobservant in their adult life. Parents adopt a variety of strategies to mitigate the conflict posed by their child becoming nonobservant, such as avoiding discussions of the issue and purposefully remaining ignorant of their child's lack of observance. Newly nonobservant children avoid flaunting their nonobservance, conceal their nonobservant behavior, and perform certain rituals in front of their parents in an effort to "avoid evoking conflict" and to "accommodat[e] their parents' feelings."[42] Paralleling the responses to children becoming nonobservant, it is the (grand)parents who take issue when their adult children choose not to circumcise. But unlike the families outlined in Tabory and Hazan-Stein's study, the strategy of avoidance is not utilized in families where someone is considering opting out of circumcision. Conflict over the decision is at the forefront, and family members will often do everything in their power to convince their relative to circumcise their son.

The decision to opt out of circumcision is very often an arduous process and requires considerable thought and research. The majority of my research subjects describe in detail the challenges they faced throughout their decision-making process. Couples put considerable thought into their decision and spend time doing research and reflecting on the consequences of this choice. The decision to opt out of circumcision is significantly more difficult when the family is unsupportive of the decision. Disdain from the family puts a lot of stress on the couple during an already stressful and overwhelming time. To highlight how opting out of circumcision can result in conflict and tension within the family, I turn to the story of Laura and her partner, Michael. Laura was raised in a Jewish household and continues to observe certain Jewish traditions, such as fasting on Yom Kippur, keeping Passover, and celebrating the holidays. Michael was raised Catholic and currently identifies as atheist. Prior to meeting Michael, Laura never questioned circumcision: "It was never a question. It was kind of like, this is the way that my family is. This is our tradition. It's what we do. It wasn't going to be questioned for me."[43] Laura started to look critically at circumcision only when the conversation arose with Michael in connection with extending their family. Michael made it clear that he was uncomfortable with circumcision, which prompted Laura to research and further explore this issue. Laura now describes herself as "not against [circumcision] per se, but I'm not for it either."[44] After doing research Laura felt her decision to opt out was supported by the lack of sufficient medical evidence for circumcision:

"I know the research isn't there. I know the science isn't there for actually cutting it. There's no health benefits to it. That I understand and I recognize."[45]

Although the research Laura gathered led her to deduce that circumcision was medically unnecessary, the decision to opt out remained a difficult one, primarily because of the reaction of her family. Laura comes from a rather traditional Jewish family, and she knew her parents and grandparents would not be happy with this decision. Opting out also presented an intense deviation from tradition for Laura, who lived a fairly strict Orthodox life throughout part of her adult life. Laura explains how she grappled with this decision: "It wasn't easy. Even after I gave birth, the few days in the hospital we were still kind of like, not fighting it out, but it wasn't easy still and while I was recovering from my C-section we were still discussing it. I even had my eighty-seven-year-old grandfather come by the hospital and he was like, 'I wouldn't feel I did my due diligence if I didn't come and try to convince you guys one more time.'"[46]

Laura had spoken with her parents about her concerns with circumcision prior to finalizing her decision. This resulted in a lot of yelling, crying, and her mother threatening "to pull support from our family."[47] Her mother made it very clear that if they did not circumcise their son, she would not be as readily available to their family as she previously had been. Laura recalls her father saying, "I recommend if you don't want your grandparents to keel over and die, just basically do it for them."[48] Upon telling her parents they were going to host a brit shalom ceremony, Laura's mother, Judith, made it very clear that they would not help out, financially or otherwise, with the planning of the ceremony. Judith also vowed not to invite any of her friends to the ceremony. Despite Judith's initial refusal to help out with the ceremony, she explains how that did not work out as planned:

> If it were a bris, we offered to do a big shebang for her. So when she decided to do brit shalom I said, "Okay, we're out. We're not doing anything." Then when she told me what she was serving I said, "Can you add a few more things? We'll pay for the difference." So that's what we did. We didn't wash our hands of the whole thing. Because I didn't want my family to come and have just a little continental breakfast. They're coming, you know, be something decent. We would never do anything different.[49]

When Judith became aware of how Laura and Michael were planning the brit shalom, she could not help but become involved with the planning of the ceremony. Her desire to plan a decent event for her family overpowered her disdain toward their ritual choice and resulted in Judith helping organize the event. Judith even attempted to locate a rabbi to officiate the brit shalom ceremony and became frustrated when this proved to be difficult. The brit shalom ritual itself also helped abate Judith's contempt for this choice, and she admitted there was no difference in feeling or significance between brit shalom and the brit milah that took place for her other grandson.[50] The trajectory of the conflict between Laura and her family highlights that the pressure exerted by the family and the disagreement that stems from the decision to opt out of brit milah eventually dissipate, especially after the ritual enactment. Brit shalom and brit milah serve the same purpose—to welcome a baby boy into the Jewish community and into the covenant between God and the Jewish people. The symbol of that welcoming is different, but the overall purpose of the ritual is the same. Once the resistant family members see this for themselves, their initial fear and anxiety over such a seemingly drastic change begin to fade away.[51]

Adapting the brit milah ritual, and the conflict that ensues as a result of this decision, bring to the forefront the issues of ritual change and invention, phenomena analyzed by ritual theorists Ronald Grimes, Ute Hüsken, and Frank Neubert. For Grimes, rituals are dynamic entities that change constantly.[52] Rituals have an overarching structure, but the details in the actions, objects, order, and actors vary for each ritual enactment. Hüsken echoes this sentiment and contends that "contrary to the widespread assumption that rituals are rather static and unchanging, most rituals do in fact undergo slight or even significant changes—be it in the course of time, as a result of their transfer to another cultural context, or simply because they are 'updated' to meet the requirements of changed circumstances."[53] The strong association between ritual and tradition, and the assumption that rituals are unchanging, can result in disputes when a seemingly drastic adaptation is made to a particular ritual. Inventing or adapting an existing ritual destabilizes the balance between stability and innovation, and tipping the scale too much in favor of innovation can result in a conflict-ridden negotiation process.

According to Hüsken and Neubert, negotiations refer to "any process of interaction during which differing positions are explicitly or implicitly debated and/or acted out."[54] Opting out of brit milah incorporates negotiation in several ways. First, opting out of circumcision is a process, and this process begins with the expectant couple. Couples come to the decision through a process of discussion and debate between themselves. Once the decision not to circumcise is made, the negotiation process is transferred to family members, who often express disappointment and disagreement over this ritual choice. For Laura's family, removing the milah component from a brit ceremony represented too drastic a diversion from tradition. The negotiation process started to fade away with Judith becoming involved with the planning of the ceremony and the ritual enactment itself. Active negotiation over this choice ended with the ritual enactment, but some family members remain in disagreement. Judith avoids seeing her grandson's uncircumcised penis and refuses to change his diaper. The negotiation process regarding the ritual choice may have settled, but remnants of the disagreement continue to linger.

CONCLUSION

The DIY ethos of American religious praxis provides an avenue through which practitioners can fine-tune religious traditions to suit their individual needs, values, and belief systems. Jewish couples who choose not to circumcise are not rejecting brit milah. Instead, they are utilizing this DIY ethos to calibrate this quintessential life cycle ritual into a ceremony that resonates with their beliefs about circumcision. As Ezra and Leah's brit shalom demonstrates, alternative rituals simultaneously reinterpret and pay homage to brit milah. Instead of forgoing brit milah in its entirety, families are adapting the traditional circumcision ritual into an identifiably Jewish non-cutting covenantal ceremony. In this sense, ritual is used as a means through which to negotiate seemingly paradoxical views and identities. By adapting and reinterpreting brit milah, non-circumcision Jews are participating in the trend of DIY religion and are actively finding ways to engage with, not reject, Jewish tradition.

ACKNOWLEDGMENTS

I would like to thank my supervisor, Dr. Naftali Cohn, for reading earlier drafts of this paper and for his relentless support, guidance, and feedback throughout this project. I would also like to thank Dr. Norma Joseph and Dr. Hillary Kaell for their invaluable insights and encouragement.

NOTES

This essay is based on my ongoing dissertation research. A large component of my dissertation examines Jews who are choosing not to circumcise their sons. Brit milah (the covenant of circumcision) refers to the ritual removal of an infant male's foreskin.

1. To access this Twitter thread, see https://twitter.com/AndrewYang/status/11059 16268971020289.
2. Intactivists, an amalgamation of the terms "intact" and "activist," are against routine infant circumcision. Will Sommer, "Andrew Yang, Upstart Democratic Presidential Candidate, Comes Out against Circumcision," *The Daily Beast*, 19 March 2019, https://www.thedailybeast.com/andrew-yang-the-upstart -democratic-presidential-candidate-comes-out-against-circumcision.
3. Ibid.
4. Ibid.

5. Andrew Yang, tweet on March 19, 2019, https://twitter.com/AndrewYang/status /1108146755311407105.

6. J. K. Trotter, "Anti-Circumcision Activists Are Angry with Democratic Presidential Candidate Andrew Yang over His Stance on the Procedure," *Insider*, 26 March 2019, https://www.insider.com/andrew-yang-infant-circumcision-2019-3.

7. *The View*, July 8 and 30, 2019. *The View* attracts a large audience, with an average 2.625 million viewers per episode in 2018. For more on this see "ABC's 'The View' Concludes Season 21 Posting Gains in Total Viewers Marking Its Most Watched Season in 4 Years," *Disney ABC Press*, 7 August 2018, https://www.wdtvpress.com/abc/pressrelease /abcs-the-view-concludes-season-21-posting-gains-in-total-viewers-marking -its-most-watched-season-in-4-years/.

8. The language of "coming out" against circumcision was used in the title of the article in *The Daily Beast* detailed in note 2. Andrew Yang, tweet on March 13, 2019, https:// twitter.com/AndrewYang/status/1105916268971020289. For statistics on circumcision rates in the United States, see Maria Owings et al., "Trends in Circumcision for Male Newborns in U.S. Hospitals: 1979–2010," *National Center for Health Statistics, Center for Disease Control and Prevention*, August 2013, https://www.cdc.gov/nchs /data/hestat/circumcision_2013/circumcision_2013.htm.

9. "The Circumcision Controversy: The Risks and Benefits of Circumcision for Babies," *HuffPost*, 7 December 2017, https://www.huffpost.com/entry/the-circumcision -controversy-the-risks-and-benefits-of-circumcision-for-babies_b_6950586.

10. Because my dissertation is an ethnographic study, I cannot share the percentage of Jews who have chosen not to circumcise. Based on my researching this small movement, the majority of Jews opt for brit milah.

11. The majority of my informants choose a non-cutting alternative to brit milah. Only a handful opted out of circumcision without replacing brit milah with another ritual.

12. There are different ways to refer to non-cutting ceremonies. *Brit shalom* [covenant of peace], *simchat ben* [celebration of the son], *brit ben* [covenant of the son], or simply naming or welcoming ceremony are the most common ways people refer to these types of ceremonies. Brit shalom was most often used by my research subjects. In this paper I use brit shalom and welcoming ceremonies interchangeably to refer to such rituals.

13. Adapting brit milah is not a novel phenomenon. Rather, the brit milah ritual has undergone considerable changes since the first century of the common era. For more on this, see Shaye J. D. Cohen, *Why Aren't Jewish Women Circumcised? Gender and Covenant in Judaism* (Berkeley: University of California Press, 2005); Leonard B. Glick, *Marked in Your Flesh: Circumcision from Ancient Judea to Modern America* (Oxford: Oxford University Press, 2005); and Eric Kline Silverman, *From Abraham to America: A History of Jewish Circumcision* (Oxford: Rowman and Littlefield, 2006).

For a more general history of circumcision in the United States, see David L. Gollaher, *Circumcision: A History of the World's Most Controversial Surgery* (New York: Basic Books, 2000).

14. I use the Pew Research Center's definition of millennials as people born between 1981 and 1996 (twenty-three to thirty-eight years of age). For more on these trends, see "U.S. Becoming Less Religious," *Pew Research Center*, 5 November 2013, https://www.pewforum.org/2015/11/03/u-s-public-becoming-less-religious/.

15. For example, see Wade Clark Roof, *Spiritual Marketplace: Baby Boomers and the Remaking of American Religion* (Princeton: Princeton University Press, 1999); and Robert Wuthnow, *After Heaven: Spirituality in America since the 1950s* (Berkeley: University of California Press, 1998). For more on millennials and religion, see Robert Wuthnow, *After the Baby Boomers: How Twenty and Thirty Somethings are Shaping the Future of American Religions* (Princeton: Princeton University Press, 2007).

16. Jack Wertheimer, *The New American Judaism: How Jews Practice Their Religion Today* (Princeton: Princeton University Press, 2019), 257.

17. Ibid., 258.

18. Michelle Shain et al., "'DIY' Judaism: How Contemporary Jewish Young Adults Express Their Jewish Identity," *Jewish Journal of Sociology* 55:1 and 2 (2013): 4.

19. Wertheimer, *The New American Judaism*, 255.

20. Ritualwell categorizes rituals under the following: life cycles, healing and hard times, everyday holiness, holidays, and Shabbat and daily life. See "Browse Rituals," *Ritualwell*, https://ritualwell.org/browse-rituals.

21. "Rabbi Connect: One-on-One Time with a Rabbi," *Ritualwell*, https://www.ritualwell.org/rabbi-connect. Meetings with rabbis are one hour long and cost $75.

22. "About Us," *Ritualwell*, https://www.ritualwell.org/aboutus.

23. In the section dedicated to life cycle rituals, for example, Ritualwell offers rituals for "starting a family," "sanctifying intimate relationships," "gender and sexual identity," and "ending a relationship." See "Life Cycles," *Ritualwell*, https://ritualwell.org/lifecycles.

24. Melissa M. Wilcox, "When Sheila's a Lesbian: Religious Individualism among Lesbian, Gay, Bisexual, and Transgender Christians," *Sociology of Religion* 63:4 (2002): 500.

25. Ibid., 501.

26. The following are the most common reasons my research subjects have shared to explain why they chose not to circumcise their sons: (1) circumcision is an unnecessary and harmful procedure, (2) circumcision is not necessary for one to be considered Jewish, (3) circumcision is a violation of human rights, and (4) circumcision is a form of genital mutilation. There is also variety in the degree to which Jews oppose circumcision. There are some Jews who chose not to circumcise their son(s) but are

not against circumcision per se, and there are Jews who are vehemently opposed to circumcision and want to see the practice abandoned in the Jewish community. The most extreme opponents of circumcision support its criminalization.

27. Irit Koren, "The Bride's Voice: Religious Women Challenge the Wedding Ritual," *Nashim: A Journal of Jewish Women's Studies and Gender Issues* 10 (2005): 32–33.

28. Ibid., 35.

29. Ibid., 34.

30. Ibid., 32.

31. All names are pseudonyms. The following excerpts are from the same brit shalom ceremony I attended in May 2019 in Berkeley, California. Ezra and Leah graciously allowed me to film the ritual.

32. Fieldnotes, May 23, 2019.

33. Ibid.

34. Ibid.

35. Ibid.

36. Ibid.

37. Genesis 17:4 and 17:16.

38. It is common to allude to the covenant between God and Abraham or include stories about Abraham and Sarah (not necessarily from Genesis 17) in brit shalom ceremonies. The absence of circumcision does not necessarily render biblical stories about the covenant between God and Abraham irrelevant.

39. In ancient times, suctioning blood from the wound was understood to aid in healing. For more on this and the rabbinic construction of brit milah, see Cohen, *Why Aren't Jewish Women Circumcised?*, especially 24–26.

40. Blood is also extracted from the penises of male converts who are circumcised. The extraction of blood renders the brit halachically complete.

41. Catherine Bell, *Ritual: Perspectives and Dimensions* (Oxford and New York: Oxford University Press, 1997), 251.

42. Ephraim Tabory and Shlomit Hazan-Stern, "Bonds of Silence: Parents and Children Cope with Dissonant Levels of Religiosity," *Contemporary Jewry* 33 (2013): 179 and 182.

43. Laura, personal interview, April 27, 2016.

44. Ibid.

45. Ibid.

46. Ibid.

47. Ibid.

48. Ibid.

49. Judith, personal interview, February 11, 2016.

50. Ibid.

51. The majority of the couples I have interviewed so far have not had a falling out with family members over their decision not to circumcise. There is one exception to this, but in general the family eventually comes to terms with and accepts the decision.

52. Ronald L. Grimes, *The Craft of Ritual Studies* (Oxford: Oxford University Press, 2005), 294.

53. Ute Hüsken, "Ritual Dynamics and Ritual Failure," in *When Rituals go Wrong: Mistakes, Failures, and the Dynamics of Ritual* (ed. U. Hüsken; Leiden: Brill, 2007), 338.

54. Ute Hüsken and Frank Neubert, "Introduction," in *Negotiating Rites* (ed. U Hüsken and F. Neubert; Oxford: Oxford University Press, 2012), 1 and 3.

CPSIA information can be obtained
at www.ICGtesting.com
Printed in the USA
LVHW050219011020
667593LV00008B/96